LETTERS TO EMMA

Early Oamaru through the eyes of the Sumpter family

Edited by
Fiona McPherson
(Emma's great granddaughter)

Wayz Press
Wellington, New Zealand

Published by Wayz Press, 31 Gloucester Street, Wellington, New Zealand.

ISBN 978-1-927166-09-3

Acknowledgments

The newspaper clippings shown in this book have all come from the National Library of New Zealand's wonderful resource of digitized old newspapers, "Papers Past", and I'd like to thank them for creating this resource and making it freely available.

I should also give due acknowledgment to W.H.S Roberts' wonderful "History of Oamaru and North Otago, New Zealand, From 1853 to the end of 1889". Mr Roberts provides an incredible wealth of detail, year by year, and I was very fortunate that my mother had managed to hold onto the family's copy of this 1890 book.

Top row, from left: Blanche, Millie, George Jnr, his wife Marian, Walter. Seated: Harriet, Walter's wife Eva
Second row, from left: Winnie, Susannah, George, Emma, Lottie. In front: Bertie

Contents

PREFACE 1

BEGINNINGS 3

OUR HERO ENTERS THE STORY 25

RICHARD THE LOVER 35

RICHARD THE BUSINESSMAN 41

RICHARD THE PINING LOVER 65

MARRIED AT LAST! 113

TOUGH TIMES FOR RICHARD & EMMA 141

THE FAMILY IN 1884-5 153

EPILOGUE 177

APPENDIX 187

REFERENCES 193

NAME INDEX 194

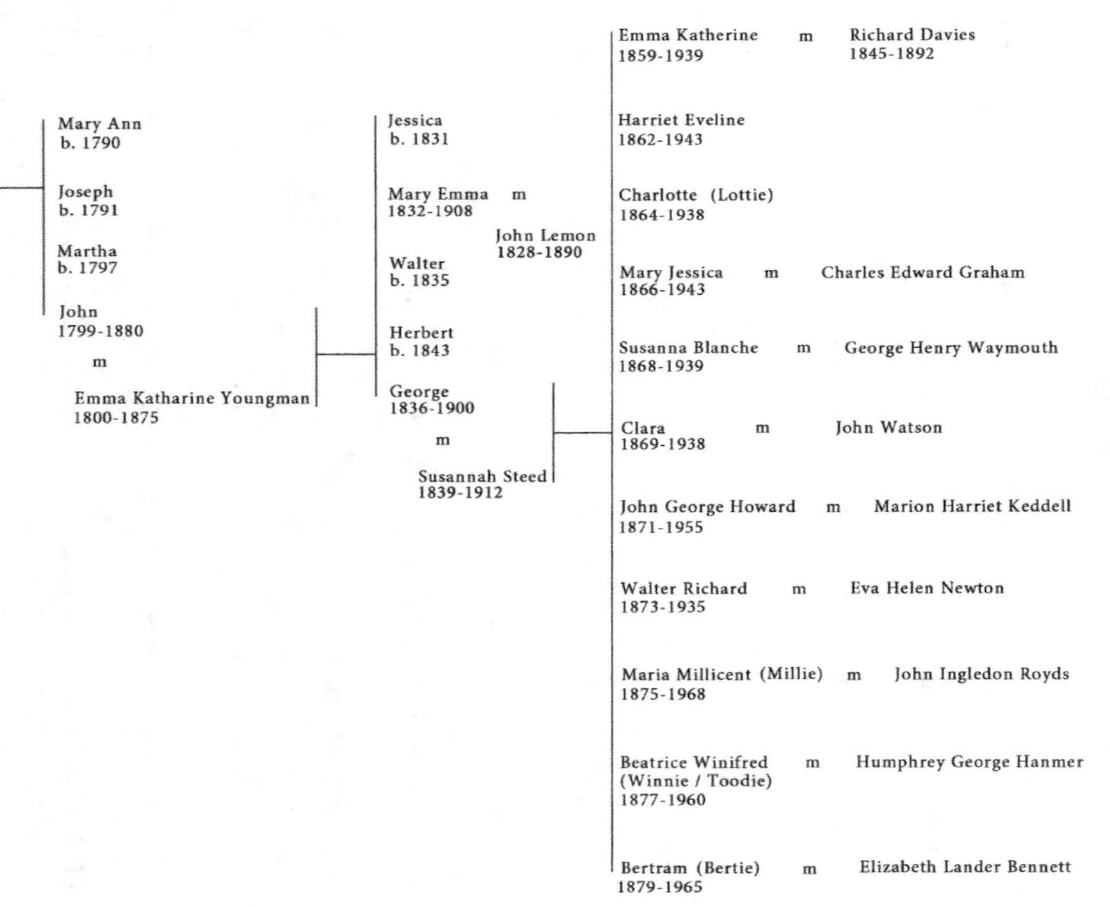

The Sumpter line

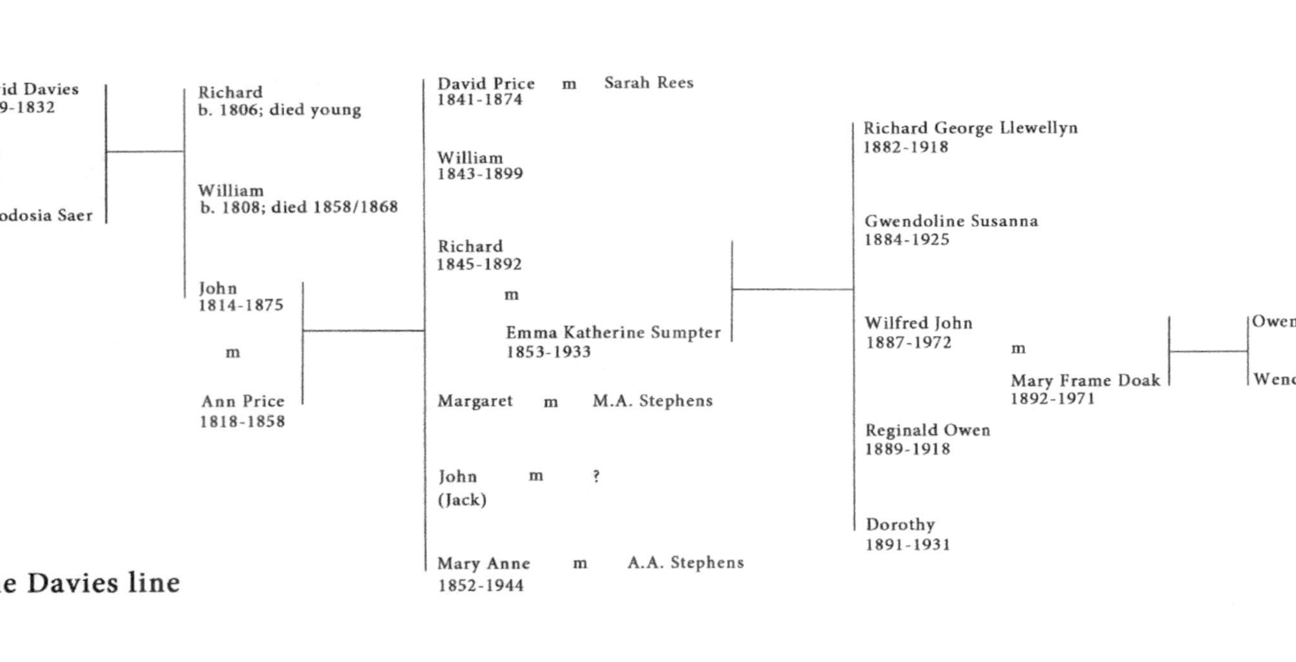

The Davies line

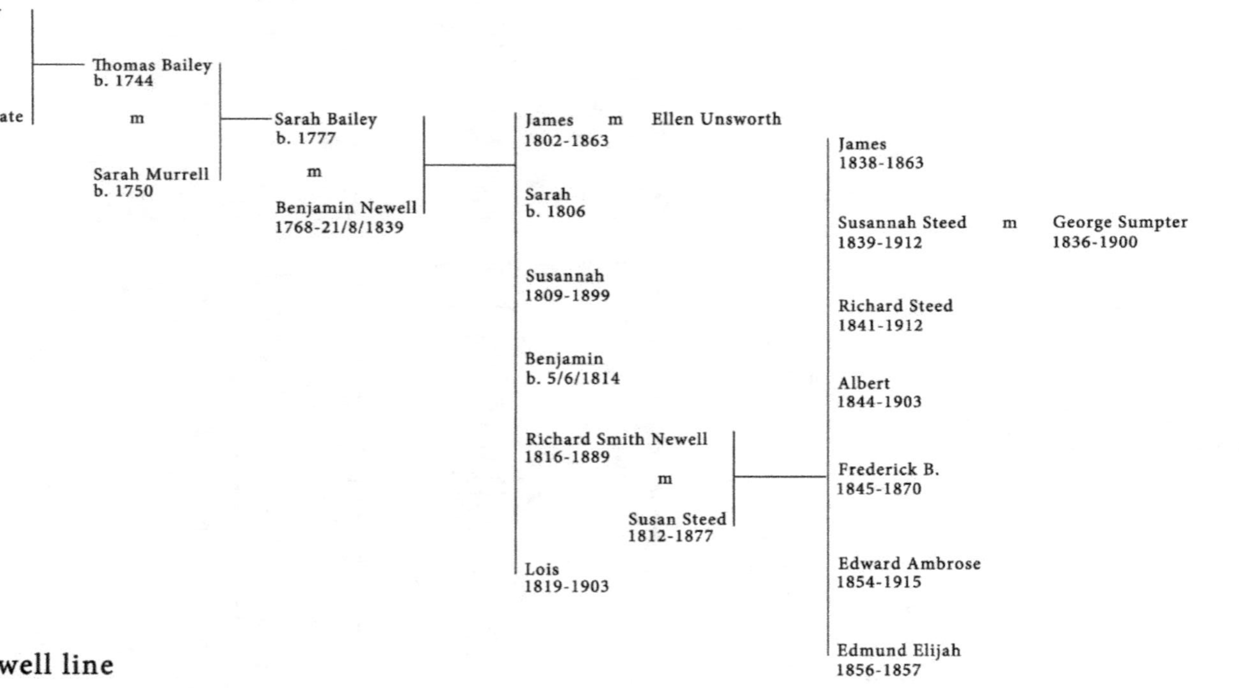

The Newell line

Preface

I have never liked New Zealand history, having been turned off it at a young age. (My primary school days taught me that New Zealand history was all Captain Cook and Vogel's public works, and deadly boring! I imagine it's different now.) But my mother inherited a quantity of old letters that had been written to her grandmother (the 'Emma' in this book's title), and when I was 16 or so I blithely said I'd type them up so that we could read them more easily. The typewriter I had was, I think, my grandfather's — keys went down with a solid clunk, requiring quite a bit of force. My typing skills, too, were very primitive. On top of which, I found the letters very hard to read. I gave up, but the promise haunted me for the next several decades.

Eventually personal computers made the job of production so much easier, and with much improved typing skills I revisited that old task. This time I could get in the practice needed so that my reading of the letters became much easier (although still something of a decoding task at times!). As I ploughed through the letters, these people became real to me; I discovered an interest in the early colonial days of my country that I had never felt before. Those who have been seduced by genealogical research will understand the thrill of reading in old newspapers about events and people described in these letters (how wonderful that the National Library has so many of these online now!).

My initial task was simply to transcribe the letters for the family, and for my mother in particular (in her 80s now and still patiently waiting!). But the project grew, as such things are wont to do, and with the resources of the old newspapers and Mr Roberts' unbelievably detailed history of the time, I wanted to flesh out the letters — provide some of the background that had helped me build the picture I now had of early Oamaru.

Oamaru was a town I was very familiar with, having spent a good part of my school holidays there all through primary school — we lived in Christchurch, but as my father was a lecturer at the teacher's college, we were able to go down regularly to stay with my mother's parents. I have, accordingly, very strong memories of Oamaru and of my grandfather, Wilfred Davies, Emma's youngest son.

Every now and then, as I've painstakingly transcribed these letters, I've reminded myself that this world — the world of colonial New Zealand, the world that seems so distant to us now — was the world into which my grandfather was born. My grandfather, who I can still see so clearly in my mind's eye, sitting by the kitchen stove in the low wicker chair, fastening his black boots (so Victorian in style at the time, although more familiar now perhaps), in his old-fashioned black suit, as he prepared to go down to Familton's hardware store on Thames St, where he kept an 'office' (I remember him perching on a high stool in a back cubby) for the accounting work he did for many small businesses.

So this book is not only for my mother, but in memory of my grandfather, a gentle, kindly man who served his community long and well, and of all those 'ordinary' people who made that hard journey from the other side of the world to build a new place in a very different land.

One of these (although he could not, I think, by any means be described as 'ordinary'!) was Emma's father, George Sumpter. George is the reason that these personal letters expanded into a reflection on old Oamaru. The North Otago Times, in his obituary, put it very well, when it referred to "the multifarious duties Mr Sumpter took upon himself as a citizen. These are closely interwoven with the history of Oamaru, and are recorded in nearly every institution in the town." George and Emma, two of our three principal characters, arrived in Oamaru in 1862, when the town was still very raw indeed. Their lives are, therefore, entwined with Oamaru's development.

Do note that I have preserved many of the vagaries of spelling and punctuation in the letters (especially in those from the children) — punctuation in particular seems to have been an optional and rather random extra! I have thrown in a number of extra full stops for clarity's sake, but have tried to keep such amendments to a minimum. Those attuned to such things may also note a certain 'Americanization' of some spellings — I assure you that these are (intriguingly) as originally written.

Remarks in square brackets, within the letters, are mine.

In a few cases I have transcribed newspaper cuttings, where the reproduction has been too poor.

I have put a number of images on the website associated with this book. You can find that at www.wayz.co.nz/wayzpress/history/emma.

Beginnings

The days of Victoria, the days of colonial New Zealand, seem very distant to us now. But it was in so many ways the birth of our own era, a backward echo of our own times. For the 19th century was a time of great change and excitement and opportunity.

Great opportunities breed great disasters, and the century was marked by both. Booms and busts were the order of the day.

In New Zealand, one such 'bust' occurred during the 'black 1880s'[1], during which some 10% of the adult white male population experienced bankruptcy. They were hard times for families, whether their breadwinner was a young man struggling to establish himself or an established and successful businessman trying to maintain what was his.

This is a story told through the personal correspondence of one family that contains both narratives. George Sumpter, the patriarch of the Sumpter family, was a prominent citizen of Oamaru, stalwart of the Harbour Board, sometime-Mayor, father of eleven, and general wheeler-dealer. His oldest child, Emma, fell in love with one of George's employees, a Welsh immigrant who, on proposing to Emma, was sent to Rakaia to prove his ability to support George's much-loved daughter.

It will not, I hope, be giving away too much to say that, despite the difficulties of proving himself in a time of great trial, Richard was eventually permitted to marry his Emma. It is our good fortune that Emma kept so many of the letters written to her, and passed them down to her last surviving son, who in turn passed them to his daughter, my mother.

Some of these letters concern the difficulties of business (from Richard to George), but most are purely personal (from Richard to Emma; from Emma's siblings), giving us a picture of colonial life in New Zealand, and most particularly in Oamaru and Rakaia.

That world — the early days of New Zealand European settlement — is 130 years in the past, and yet, when I hold these letters in my hand, I marvel every time that my mother — still alive at 88 — remembers Emma as her doting grandmother, and I myself well remember Emma's son Wilfred, my grandfather, who died when I was 12. The 130 years seem much shorter then.

But before we can enjoy the letters, let us meet our characters and establish our world. (Note that more exact details of the family tree can be found in the appendix.)

THE PATRIARCH

Roots of the family tree

George Sumpter's father, **John**, was born in Marylebone, Westminster, London, in 1799. He was christened at St Anne's, an Anglican church that still remains in what is now Soho.

England was then half-way through the reign of King George III (yes, the chap who talked to the trees), and under the leadership of the Tory Prime Minister Pitt the Younger. Britain had lost America and was in the middle of a long-running war with France. The first settlement in Australia had occurred eleven years earlier, and trading stations were being established in New Zealand, although it would be over 20 years before Britain would establish a proper settlement there.

In London, home to around a million people, coffee houses were popular, crime was rife and punished severely, and public hangings were popular entertainment.

Marylebone was in the heart of this immense city, within the City of Westminster, containing (among other well-known landmarks) Regents Park and Harley Street and Cavendish Square. In 1799, however, it was rather less respectable, containing, in addition to fine homes, the Marylebone Gardens, where raffish elements engaged in bear-baiting and prizefighting (by both men and women!).

This is the world into which John was born, the youngest of four children born to **Walter** & **Mary** Sumpter (née Galloway).

George is born

In 1829, aged 30, John Sumpter married **Emma Katharine Youngman** in Sunbury On Thames, London. By this time he was, presumably, a man of reasonable means, since he was noted in the census as a "Proprietor of Houses".

The couple had five children. Jessica, the first-born, never married and remained in her parents' household. Walter (also called Wallis in some records), third child and first-born son, was articled to a surgeon — perhaps through the influence of his uncle by marriage, for John Ringrose (who had married Emma's sister Louise), was a member of the Royal College of Surgeons. Herbert, the third son and last child, was born in 1843.

But the two who interest us are the colonists: Mary Emma, born in 1832, and George, born in 1836. Both of these were to migrate to New Zealand, and did so at a young age. George in particular must have been only around 15-16 when he arrived in Adelaide in 1851. Three years later, in November of 1854, his older sister Mary Emma arrived at Port Chalmers (Dunedin) on the barque Dolphin (see the charming letter that appeared in the newspaper, thanking the ship captain for the care he had taken of the passengers). She would have been 22.

Otago, New Zealand,
20th Nov. 1854.

To Captain JAMES TURNBULL,
Barque *Dolphin*.

DEAR SIR,—We, the passengers of the barque *Dolphin* from London to Otago, beg to express our sense of the very able and satisfactory manner in which you have discharged your duties as commander, and your kind attention and consideration of our comforts during the voyage.

Our united and sincere desire is that every good fortune and happiness may attend you in all your undertakings, and wishing you a safe and speedy passage to England,

We remain,
Dear Sir,
Your faithful and obliged friends,

Thomas Nimmo.	Robert Latter.
Charles Smith.	John Campbell Aikman.
Mrs. Charles Smith.	Henry N. Harrison.
Robina Rattray.	Awdry Badcock.
Mary Emma Sumpter.	Robert Christie.
Mary Stuart Maitland.	Jessie Christie.
Mary Milne.	Christopher M'Crae.
J. Barnes Borton.	Margaret M'Crae.

To the Passengers per *Dolphin* from London.

LADIES AND GENTLEMEN,—I feel grateful for the expressions of respect conveyed to me in your letter, and trust I shall continue to deserve them.

In return I can only wish you every happiness in this your adopted home, and should any of your friends come out from England under my care, I shall add the warmth of kindly and respectful remembrance to the regular discharge of my duties to them as a shipmaster. A hearty farewell from your humble servant,

JAMES TURNBULL.

Dunedin, 30th Nov. 1854.

Shortly after, on February 21 1855 (suggesting, surely, that the marriage was arranged before her arrival), Mary married **John Lemon**.

First beginnings in Oamaru — John Lemon's story

John Lemon was an early settler and a prominent citizen. Arriving in 1848, having been born twenty years earlier to the Jamaican Postmaster-General (also a sugar plantation owner), he was later to represent his district in the Provincial Council, and then, after moving to Oamaru in 1853, served on the Oamaru Town Board and the Harbour Board. His brother, **Dr Charles Lemon**, joined him in 1854, and for some years they were in business together in Oamaru as timber merchants and builders. Eventually Dr Lemon became Commissioner of Telegraphs.

John Lemon is our entrée to Oamaru, one of the very first settlers, buying land at Otepopo in 1853. From Mr Roberts' very detailed history of Oamaru and North Otago, published in 1890, we have the following remarks from another early settler, Mr F. Every:

> I have before me a letter, dated, Waitaki, Nov. 10. 1853, in which I

> wrote home an account of my arrival at Papakaio, Messrs. Filleul's station, which had then been started about three months. The party there then consisted of Mr. W. G. Filleul and his brother Richard, their man Jonathan Woonton and his two boys, Jim and George, James Saunders (known better as Jimmy the Needle, shearer, &c., and one of the old whalers, who lived about Moeraki before any settlers came into the country), and myself. Mr. Hugh Robison and his brother Harry took up the Oamaru Run at the same time, and lived in a small whare built mostly of cabbage-trees, raupo, and flax, which stood on the north bank of the creek, just about where the railway line now crosses it. Mr. John Lemon came up about a fortnight after I did, and was at Papakaio getting out the framing of a house for his station at Waikoura (now the residence of Mr. Peter Aitcheson), on the 26th. At this time our only habitation was burnt down, and with it all our bedding, clothes, food, and even our boots; for, being busy at shearing we were some of us wearing Maori pararas for comfort, and had left our boots in the hut. In consequence of that loss I had no boots to wear for nearly two months after, when we got fresh supplies from Dunedin, and Mr. J. S. Jeffreys, who came up with me, rode down to Dunedin with a pair of pararas lined with red blanket instead of boots ...

This account gives us an idea of the rough and ready conditions at the time!

At the time of John Lemon's marriage to George's sister, in February 1855, there were 15 electors (that is, adult male freeholders or householders, with property over a certain value) in the district. The Lemons' home was in Goodwood, an area containing 91 settlers, of whom 35 were female (all but one married), and 50 were under 21. At that, Goodwood contained the largest share of the district's settler population, which numbered 206 settlers in total, along with 334 Maori and 42 "half-castes".

In a letter to the newspaper, John Lemon himself offers a correction to Mr Roberts' history, advising that "Dr. Robert Williams' Station" was in fact owned by the firm of Williams and Lemon, and that Mr Teschemaker's mule was unfairly maligned:

> Mr. Teschemaker lent me the mule, and Mrs. Lemon as well as myself frequently rode it, and I never saw or wished to ride a quieter animal, nor did it ever while in my possession attempt any of the tricks attributed to it.

Mr Lemon also had another charming anecdote, which I think gives us a good flavour of the times:

> The journey from Dunedin to Oamaru in these early times occupied three days, the first stopping place being either Waikouaiti or Goodwood, the next Moeraki or the Kuri, and at these places were the usual accommodation houses. Settlers, of course, made their own bread, which was usually cooked in a camp oven. The sponge was, as a rule, put into a tin dish, and then placed in front of the fire to rise during the night. At one of the stopping places in question which shall be nameless, this method was pursued, but in addition to this, as soon as the old couple turned out of bed in the morning the tin dish containing the sponge was thrust in between the blankets to get the benefit of the animal heat, which no doubt tended to improve the lightness of the bread. Having witnessed the operation myself, it is needless to add that I carefully avoided their house for the future.

By 1860, the town of Oamaru was growing apace, and somewhat wild (a reputation that grew rather than diminished over the next two decades: in 1879, the Ashburton Mail referred to it as "that drunken metropolis", and certainly convictions for drunkenness were well above the national average). Charles and John Lemon, as two of several "master carpenters" in the district, won a tender to build a "lock-up" at Oamaru (said building to contain two cells and an apartment for the constable, although it was to lack a constable for several months after its completion in October).

A good picture of Oamaru in 1860 comes from the pen of another early settler, Mr W. Falconer (description expurgated):

> On reaching the shore the boat was driven as far as possible upon the beach, when the passengers, watching the chance of a receding wave, sprang ashore. .. The means of exit from the landing-place was by a rope dangling over the face of a steep bank, while a derrick had been erected for the purpose of hoisting the heavy goods to the top. On the left stood the Government shed for storage of wool and other goods—a frame building, boarded and roofed with Hobart Town palings. To the right were two sod whares, the quarters of Tom Hardy and his Maoris. Travelling northward, on the left of the track leading from the landing-place and fronting Tyne street, stood a small pisé hut, the residence of Mr Charles Trail, of Trail and Roxby, and at a short distance a nice verandah cottage, the abode of the other partner, Mr. E. W. Roxby. On the extreme left, also fronting Tyne street, was a small weather-boarded cottage owned by a Mr Miller. Material was being laid down to build the store for Dalgety, Rattray & Co. Further north along Tyne street, at its junction with Wansbeck street, stood the store of Messrs Trail and Roxby—a long, low building, well stocked with general merchandise. In the same street a large wool store was in course of erection for Mr. James Hassell. A little further on was Mr. John

> Hambleton's butcher's shop, and standing rather further back a small cottage inhabited by Mr. John Haggie. What is now (1889) Bee's corner, was a sort of wilderness garden, surrounded by a low sod wall. Fronting Itchen street, and occupying the present site of the Star and Garter Hotel, stood the old accommodation house, the property of H. C. Hertslet, at that time under the management of Fred. and Edwin Collie. At the corner of Tees and Itchen streets stood the stockyard of the accommodation house, and near the south end of it was an old whare built of cabbage trees and mud, which at one time had been the residence of Mr Traill. Descending the steep bank of the Oamaru creek, the crossing for foot passengers was opposite where Frank Robertson's blacksmith's shop now is, and was by two planks joined together, and chained to stakes driven into the bank on each side of the creek. On the south side of the creek, close to where the Crown Flour Mill now stands, was the private residence of Mr Hertslet. On the north side of the creek, further to the east and looking seaward, stood a pretty cottage surrounded by a well-fenced garden, the residence of Mr John Lemon. The cottage of Mr James Wate (pronounced Wait with the "a" soft), blacksmith, fronted Thames street, and adjoining it was his blacksmith's shop, in rear of which a stone building was in course of erection. To the left, a little north of the junction of the Glen and Oamaru creeks, on a knoll which had received the name of the "Barn's Head," ..; and near the site of the present old Court-house, stood what had been the residence of the owner of the Oamaru run. It was a sod erection, plastered with clay and thatched with raupo, a long reed that grew in great abundance in the lagoon at the mouth of the Oamaru creek. An addition to it had been built with posts and weatherboards, and that was also thatched with the same material, raupo, but a lean-to at the other end, and used as a bedroom, was of clay and roofed with iron. What might be called the principal part of the building was occupied by Mr Oscar Davis (now of Island Stream Farm), who there carried on his trade of shoemaker.

In addition to the town residence referred to here, John Lemon also had a rural property, on which he built a fine house in 1861.

Oamaru being declared a "port of entry" in August 1861 (one hopes that passengers no longer had to use a rope to clamber up the steep bank from the beach!), and the town and environs being rapidly surveyed and sold, it's no wonder if Mary sent word to her brother that this was a land of opportunity, where his entrepreneurial talents would not go unappreciated.

Especially with the Lemon brothers being such prominent members of the community. With as yet no representation on the Provincial Council, nor any local council, some of the residents decided to form a "vigilance committee", to "watch over the interests of the town." Charles Lemon was one of these.

Over the course of the next 20 years, Mary & John Lemon would have nine children (**Constance**, **Grace**, **Edith**, **Gertrude**, **Mildred**, **Amy**, **Mabel** and **Herbert**), including one son who died at 10 weeks. These are the Lemons so often referred to in the letters. (More details can be found in the appendix.)

George marries

By this time, George had been ten years in South Australia, and on 18 March 1858 had married another English immigrant: Susanna Steed Newell.

MARRIED

On the 18th inst., at Hindmarsh Island, by the Rev. John Watson, George, second son of John Sumpter, Esq., Whetstone, Middlesex, to Susanna Steed, only daughter of Richard Smith Newell, Goolwa.

Susanna had migrated to Adelaide with her family from Chichester, in Sussex. Her parents, **Richard Smith Newell** and **Susan Steed**, were both born in Chichester, and married in 1835 at a young age (Richard was 19 and Susan only 17) in St Peter The Great Sub-deanery of Chichester. They had five children before emigrating (**James, Susanna**, **Frederick**, **Albert**, and **Richard**) and another two in Adelaide (**Edward** and **Edmund**).

Susanna was 12 when the Newells came out on the *Gloucester* in 1852. Not a journey for the faint-hearted! There were 23 deaths on board during the voyage, as well as one birth.

Susanna's father, Richard Newell, was described as a carpenter on the ship's manifest, but was described more specifically in the census as a master of churn maker's turners. Richard later came to live with the Sumpters in Oamaru, sometime after his wife died in 1877. Richard died in 1889, and was in residence during much of the period covered by the letters.

Richard's brother **James**, together with his wife **Ellen Unsworth** and their two younger children, also emigrated to Australia. They came out on the *Taymouth Castle* in 1855. Like Richard, James was described with the catch-all "carpenter" in the ship's passenger list, but in the 1851 census he's described as a cabinet maker. His oldest son, Benjamin (married when the rest of his family migrated), was a pianoforte maker, adding credence to the view that James was more a furniture maker than someone who works on a building site. James died in 1863 in Sydney, and is buried at the old Camperdown Cemetery.

More details about this part of the family can be found in the appendix.

GEORGE, BUSINESSMAN & POLITICIAN

I found no mention of George in the Australian newspapers before his marriage, but after that time there are notices of him importing goods, as well as a notice of "Sumpter & Packer" of Port Elliot and Goolwa being granted a slaughtering licence. He also complains to the council about some lots of purchase land not being rated. Here we can see George in his familiar roles: entrepreneurial and civic! He is also seen participating in the local cricket team – again, a pursuit he would continue.

But George now had a wife and daughter to support (our heroine, Emma, was born in 1859), and, as I've suggested, perhaps his sister and brother-in-law convinced him that there would be more opportunities for success in the newly-established town of Oamaru. The family left Port Adelaide right after Christmas in 1861.

PORT WILLUNGA SHIPPING
SAILED.
FRIDAY, DECEMBER 27.

GOLDSEEKER, brigantine, J. Blanch, master, for Melbourne. Passengers—Mr. and Mrs. Sumpter and child, and S. Hart, in the cabin. Cargo—85 tons flour, 18 do. bran, 1 winnowing-machine, S. White.

They arrived at Port Chalmers nearly a month later, on the *Omeo*.

Jan. 20, s.s. Omeo, Captain McLachlan, with 40 cabin passengers and 109 steerage, and general cargo. Per Omeo.—Cabin: Mr. and Mrs. Smith and 2 children; Mrs. McCallum; Mr. and Mrs. And Miss Bronly; Mrs Marshal; Miss Binge; Mrs. Collie; Mr. Dickson; Mr. and Mrs. White; Mr. Wilson; Brown; Rupul; Mavering; Mrs. Mavering; Mrs. Brooke, infant and 2 children; Mrs. Martin and infant; Mrs. Bruce and infant; Mrs. Gregg; Mrs. Jenkins; Grace, Martha, and Selina Jenkins; Mrs. McDonald; Mr. and Mrs. Sumpter and infant; Mrs. Hart; Mrs. Blythe; Mrs. Daniel and 2 children.

Our local historian Mr Roberts takes note of George's arrival:

> On 24th January, 1862, George Sumpter landed in Oamaru from Australia. Ever since then he has been one of Oamaru's most pushing, energetic and useful public men.

One of George's first activities was to drive a wagon to the gold diggings in Central Otago, bringing stores to the workers there:

> In the middle of August [1862] the great rush to the Dunstan took place, which led to the discovery of gold at Cardrona, Kawarau, and Shotover, and as the most direct and easiest route to these places was by Oamaru, a large influx of waggoners with six and eight horse teams was the result. Goods for those diggings were brought in large quantities by steamer and sailing craft from Dunedin. The trade of the port greatly increased, and driving to the diggings at high freights was the order of the day. Farming, which had been making a little progress, was again neglected, the whole attention of the population being devoted to the goldfields. Among those who arrived overland from Dunedin with horse teams and waggons, and who have settled in the town or district might be mentioned: in the month of October, Thomas Shalders and the late James Thomas; a little later, Messrs Peter, Alexander, and George Aitcheson. George Sumpter, who arrived in Oamaru in the beginning of '62, also piloted a waggon to the diggings. The Elder brothers were also on the road; besides numbers of bullock teams and horse drays.

In July 1863, the newspaper records George's importation of "4 cases, stores" from Geelong, and in April of the following year, a case of coffee from Melbourne. All of this suggests that George was making his living as a general storesman.

That same April also sees the beginning of what would become a close and enduring involvement with the Harbour Board, marked by the eventual naming of the "Sumpter Wharf". George was one of the gentlemen appointed to serve on a committee to petition the Provincial Council for a Commission to "decide on the best means to be adopted for the improvement of the Harbor of Oamaru." (Those interested in such things may like to note that this spelling of harbor is indeed what appeared in the local newspaper.)

George is beginning to get his feet under him, and in August, we see his first steps in another role, that of financial agent:

MR GEORGE SUMPTER is authorised to receive Subscriptions and Accounts due to "The Oamaru Times and Waitaki Reporter."

F. PINKERTON & CO.

Oamaru, August 11, 1864.

This was closely followed by the announcement that George had commenced business as Estate, Commission and Shipping Agent.

A nice touch is the "Having business relations in London, orders home will be promptly attended to"!

The newspaper is now full of his ads as he occupies himself advertising houses and land in his capacity as 'Land Agent', and in October, we see him acting as 'pro tem' secretary in the setting up of a Land and Building Investment Society. In 1865, we see him buying a number of blocks of land being sold by the Government.

GEORGE SUMPTER begs respectfully to announce to the inhabitants of Oamaru and its vicinity that he has commenced business as

ESTATE, COMMISSION AND SHIPPING AGENT.

Having business relations in London, orders will be promptly attended to.

Up-country Settlers may rely on orders home being punctually executed per first opportunity.

My Waggon will still leave Oamaru, about every three weeks, for Alberton.

2, Thames-street, Oamaru,
September 19, 1864.

Busy bee that he is, we also see him chairing the Oamaru Cricket Club committee, serving on the Oamaru Education Board, secretary of the committee setting up the Oamaru Rifle Rangers, convener of the committee setting up a Branch Savings Bank in Oamaru, on the committee of the Mechanics Institute, and doing his bit for St Luke's Church as Treasurer for the Vestry.

SALE OF TOWN LANDS.

On the 15th instant, Mr Short, Government Auctioneer, offered for sale a number of Oamaru and Herbert town sections, in the Court-house here, at 12 o'clock. The following were the sales :—

OAMARU.

BLOCKS.	SECS.	PURCHASERS.	PRICE.
25	30	Charles Galbraith	£24 10
,,	23	Andrew Grey	17 10
,,	24	George Sumpter	13 10
,,	26	Do.	13 10
43	23	George Bruce	12 10
,,	24	George Quarrie	12 10
,,	25	Do.	12 10
,,	26	John Pringle	12 10
21	13	George Sumpter	12 10
22	13	Do.	12 10
,,	18	Do.	16 0
19	8	Do.	12 10
,,	22	Do.	12 10
44	13	John Mackay	12 10
,,	13	— Barclay	13 0
,,	15	Do.	12 10
,,	16	Do.	14 10
53	1	Daniel Roxburgh	12 10
,,	2	Do.	12 10
HERBERT.			
25	2	George Orr	12 10
4	12	R. Watson, Jun.	12 10

Oamaru is thriving, and Mackay's Almanac for 1865 says:

> No township in the Province has shown so steady and satisfactory an advance during the last three years as Oamaru.

In June 1865, 'telegraphic communication' between Dunedin, Oamaru and Christchurch was completed (initial fee of 1s 6d for a message not exceeding ten words; for every additional word above ten, one penny, either way.[2]).

The public debate concerning the setting up of a bank branch in Oamaru is interesting, in light of the recent excitements in the banking system. At this point in history, it was apparently felt necessary to argue for the advantages for having a savings bank in the town! (see next page)

£5 REWARD will be given to any one delivering to the undersigned one BAY MARE, branded JL, belonging to George Sumpter; or £3 Reward will be given for information that will lead to her recovery. The above Mare was lost near Messrs Miller and Gooch's Station, about two months since.

GEORGE SUMPTER.

Oamaru, June 27th, 1865.

We also see George offering a reward for the return of his horse.

Another interesting window into colonial life is shown when in 1866, George nominates Mr Ingram, long-time Editor of the Oamaru Times, to represent the Electoral District of Oamaru in the General Assembly. The vote (which Mr Ingram did not win) was based on a simple show of hands (Mr Campbell 49; Mr Ingram 34)!

BRANCH SAVINGS BANK FOR OAMARU.

PUBLIC MEETING.

A public meeting of the inhabitants took place in the Court-House, on the 2nd instant, for the purpose of considering the advisability of establishing a Branch Savings Bank in Oamaru. There was a pretty fair attendance on the occasion.

In the absence of T. W. Parker, Esq., R.M., James Ashcroft, Esq., was called upon to preside.

The Chairman then stated that he much regretted that our worthy Resident Magistrate was not present to take the chair on the occasion, as arranged; but he had no doubt that only business of a very urgent nature had occurred to necessitate his absence. He was sure, however, that the object of the meeting would commend itself to every one present, so that he required not to preface the proceedings of the meeting by any lengthy speech. He had before him the rules and regulations of the Dunedin Savings Bank, from which he might glean some interesting particulars of the working of the Savings Bank system elsewhere. For example, in 1833, the number of Savings Banks in England, Scotland, and Ireland was 78, and the deposits amounted to upwards of 15 millions of pounds; while in 1862, the number of such Banks had increased to such an extent that the total amount of balances due to depositors reached the large sum of 40½ millions sterling. In Melbourne, the first Savings bank was established in 1842, and during that year some 230 accounts were opened, the deposits amounting to the sum of L4227. In 1853, however, the deposits had amounted to L155,662, and the depositors to 2287, and since then they have gone on increasing. These results showed to what an extent the Savings Bank might be made useful to the working man; but not only was it useful in that respect, there was the double use, as it were, of the money thus saved being circulated advantageously amongst the community, &c. He thought this was a strong argument in favor of the establishment of Savings Banks. He eulogised the system of Post Office Savings Banks, which had worked so beautifully and successfully wherever established; but said that perhaps, as a country, we are too young to think of establishing them in New Zealand yet. Mr Ashcroft then gave a digest of the "Savings Bank Act, 1858," and concluded by saying that the present is peculiarly a time when Savings Banks were needed. Money now is neither so plentiful nor so easily made as it was some years ago, and it was necessary for working men to save all they can, for in these times it may be said that "happy is the man who has any money to save" (laughter). As a means of investing small sums of money, Savings Banks were most useful, and he hoped that the resolutions to be brought before the meeting would meet with their approbation.

The Rev Charles Connor then rose and said:—Mr Chairman and gentlemen,—The resolution that I have the honor of proposing to the meeting is to the effect that "in the opinion of this meeting it is considered advisable to establish a Branch Savings Bank in Oamaru." This resolution commends itself, and requires not a long speech to enforce it. I am sure that all the working men will agree that it is desirable to establish a Savings Bank in Oamaru. I sometimes say when I marry a couple that marriage induces habits of industry, sobriety, and economy. I may say the same of Savings Banks. (Hear, hear.) When a man has a few odd shillings in his pocket, he might, perhaps, be unable to find anything definite to do with the money; if he deposited it in a Savings Bank, it would save him from spending it in a way that would be neither advantageous to himself or family. I certainly regard Savings Banks as calculated to promote sobriety and temperance. I know how they work in Liverpool, in Glasgow, and in Edinburgh, and I know that whenever a missionary succeeded in his labors, he almost invariably noticed, as a sure sign of success, that the possession of Savings Bank pass books was the result. The institution of Savings Banks, however, should not only secure the approbation of the working men, but also that of the merchants. (Hear, hear.) If working men deposited their spare earnings in Savings Banks, there would be some hope of their accounts being paid. (Laughter.) Little children also should be taught thus to invest the money which they may have at command. I believe in "learn young, learn fair." If persons begin to lay past their money when young, their savings would soon amount to something which will be of service to them in after years. But in advocating the claims of such an institution as the Savings Bank, I cannot do better than fall back on the experience of other places. We know that they have worked wonderfully well in England, Melbourne, and even in Dunedin; and I am sure that the resolution, "That in the opinion of this meeting it is considered desirable to establish a Branch Savings Bank in Oamaru," will be accepted by every one in the room most cordially. I heartily wish all success for the movement, and am sure that a Savings Bank will be an element of prosperity to the district.

The resolution was seconded by Mr W. F. Ingram, and carried unanimously.

I find this example of democracy in action somewhat alarming, but we must remember that the first parliamentary election had only occurred twelve years earlier.

George, in his capacity as acting Town Clerk (a part-time position), was also put in charge of preparing the citizen's roll for the forthcoming Mayoral elections. These were consequent upon the 1865 Municipal Corporations Ordinance of Otago being brought into operation and the subsequent visit of the Provincial Secretary to Oamaru, recommending that the town should apply to be brought under the operation of the Act.

Interestingly, this was initially opposed, "because no additional advantages in the shape of funds were held out", but when the Amendment Ordinance was passed, providing for a Government subsidy of £2 for every £1 raised by the town, it was seen to be a very good idea indeed!

Oamaru, proclaimed a Municipality on April 3, 1866, was the third town in Otago to do so, Dunedin (of course) being the first, and Queenstown (less obviously) the second.

The first election was close (Mr Gilchrist 27; Mr Gibbs 24), and Mr Gibbs called for a "poll", in which votes were recorded by ballot (rather than a show of hands from an excited crowd). This produced a clearer result (and greater involvement by the citizenry): Gilchrist 100; Gibbs 82.

Once the Mayoralty and Council had been decided, the appointment of Town Clerk had to be decided — apparently by what amounted to a tender process! George's offer was under-cut by another. But this would return to bite the council.

Shortly thereafter, Mr Ingram withdrew from the Clerkship, citing the smallness of the salary, the obligation to find security for £200, and his "not feeling at present in very robust health". George graciously agreed to act as clerk "for one or two meetings", until a successor could be found. Something which would not happen, it turned out, for four years, until September 1870.

THE TOWN CLERKSHIP.

The appointment of a Clerk to the Council, which was the business for which the meeting was specially convened, was next considered.

There were only two applications which could be entertained; the others had not been sent in before the date specified by advertisement. The two applicants were Mr George Sumpter, who volunteered to perform the duties for L100 a-year, and included the use of his office, and Mr W. F. Ingram, who agreed to act at the salary voted by the Council, viz., L75 a-year.

The matter was discussed in Committee. As Mr Sumpter had declined to act at the salary fixed, it was the general opinion that Mr Ingram's application was the only one requiring consideration. Mr Ingram did not make any mention of an office in his application. After some conversation, it was resolved that Mr Ingram be asked to attend an adjourned meeting at three o'clock, to give some explanations as to the understanding of his application, i.e., as to the salary being fixed at L75 for the year, without prospect of an advance.

At three o'clock, Mr Ingram gave the required explanation, whereupon it was moved by Councillor Pinkerton, and seconded by Councillor Roxby, "That Mr Ingram be appointed Town Clerk, with a salary of L75 a-year." Carried unanimously.

It was resolved that the Town Clerk should find the requisite security for the due performance of his duties.

It was next unanimously and cordially agreed that the thanks of the Council be tendered to Mr Sumpter for his efficient services while acting as Interim Clerk, and for his courteous and obliging demeanour.

Interestingly, after this initial reluctance on the part of the new Council, George's salary was increased to £150 the following year, in addition to that other, intriguing, part of his remuneration: 5% commission on rates collected!

His role as "Collector" of rates fits in nicely with his general capacity of debt collector, endorser of 'bills', and money lender in the town.

Oamaru was growing at a cracking pace. By the end of 1867, it had 1376 residents, and received some £9452 in Customs revenue for the year, from 11 ships bringing imports to the value of £92,165. Wool to the value of £173,904 had been shipped out: "Homeward and coastwise".

DISSOLUTION OF PARTNERSHIP.— NOTICE IS HEREBY GIVEN that the partnership between the undersigned JOHN MATTHEWS and ROBERT REID, in the trade or business of Blacksmiths and Wheelwrights, at Oamaru, under the firm of "Matthews and Reid," was this day dissolved by mutual consent. The business will in future be carried on by the said John Matthews, on his separate account, and Mr George Sumpter, of Thames-street, Oamaru, is hereby authorised to receive and pay all debts due to or owing by the said partnership in the regular course of trade.

Witness our hands, this 24th day of January, 1865.

JOHN MATTHEWS.
ROBERT REID.

Witness to signatures—
J. O'MEAGHER,
Solciitor, Oamaru.

> No township in the Province had made so steady and satisfactory an advance during the previous six years, having even eclipsed Dunedin itself in the number and importance of the buildings erected.

However:

> The advance made was greater than was justified by the circumstances and Oamaru afterwards found that it had over-built itself.

Of course, New Zealand as a whole was growing fast. In 1858, the population was around 116,000, of whom a little over half were Europeans. Ten years later, the European population had increased from around 59,000 to over 217,000 (the Maori population had meanwhile fallen slightly). Of these, around 60,000 were in Otago[3] — the high proportion reflecting one of the main reasons for the dramatic increase in population: gold fever.

In Oamaru, the first two months of 1868 saw "unprecedented" rainfall, with the heaviest causing streams to rise so much "that several homesteads were washed away .... And nine persons were drowned". Moreover, the violent storm wrecked two ships, driving them onto Oamaru beach, at the loss of four lives, two of them small children.

In August,

> an extraordinary marine disturbance occurred all along the east coast of New Zealand, caused by the disastrous convulsions of nature on the western coast of Central America. At Oamaru the tide rose and fell 20 feet in a few minutes, first rushing to a great height against the cliffs, then receding rapidly to an unprecedented distance from the shore, so much so that at one time a surf boat moored 400 feet from low water mark was left aground.

These events were factors in the project to build a Breakwater, which would, it was hoped, render the harbor safe. It was a project that George would come to be closely involved in.

In January 1869, George and his brother-in-law John Lemon went into partnership in George's business (Land, Estate, Shipping & Commission Agents and Valuators), under the name "Sumpter and Lemon".

In September, the "The All Nations Water Race and Mining Company" was registered, to operate at the Marewenua gold field. One hundred £20 shares were offered, and all were quickly snapped up. The manager was John Evans, at the office of Sumpter and Lemon.

The interest in gold should perhaps be considered in the light of a "commercial depression", stemming from a fall in the price of wool, which had been the main export. Oamaru was also disappointed by the Legislative Council rejecting their request for a provincial loan to build a dock — vitally needed since the loss of the jetty in a severe gale — and a bridge over the Waitaki River. This depression, which began in 1868 and was accompanied by numerous insolvencies, worsened in 1870.

Perhaps reflecting the hard times, Sumpter & Lemon were the victims of a "dastardly trick" of vandalism in January 1871:

WANTON MISCHIEF.—On Sunday night, 1st instant, senseless and malicious tricks which, unfortunately, we have from time to time to record, were perpetrated, part of the sign at the Swan Hotel being cut away, and all the windows of Messrs Sumpter and Lemon's offices smashed. The latter, which were of plate glass, will cost L20 to replace. We hope the perpetrators of these dastardly tricks will be discovered, and made an example of.

We can also see the hard times in the fall in customs revenue: 1871 saw customs revenue of £6531, with imports valuing only £15,070, and exports of £23,696.

On the positive side, 1871 saw George appointed as a Justice of the Peace and a Trustee of the Municipal Sinking Fund (despite its odd name, this has to do with the management of municipal bonds). He also stood for Mayor but did poorly, getting only 46 votes, compared to the incumbent's (James Udall) 107 votes and S. E. Shrimski's 90. However, he could console himself with his new position as Representative for Waitaki on the Provincial Council, a position he continued to hold until the abolition of the provinces in 1876.

Whether because of the commercial difficulties of the times, or because there was a falling out (or perhaps simply reflecting the rather marked ebb and flow of partnerships in these times!), the firm of Sumpter and Lemon was liquidated in October 1872.

The following year, however, saw a return to more prosperous times for the town. It did, after all, have so many advantages:

> Looking at it from a commercial, agricultural, or mineral point of view everyone admitted that the district was a highly favoured one; with its large area of agricultural land, which is only to be equalled for richness by the Taieri; its quarries, the stone from which is admired all over the colonies, and its auriferous district of Marewenua, and the golden sands of Moeraki, Oamaru appeared to have a bright future before it. The improvements made in the town were many and varied. Handsome stone edifices gradually replaced many of the old wooden ones, and the buildings extended towards the north. The first sod of the Moeraki-Waitaki Railway was cut by the mayor, John Stubbs Wait, on 10th March 1873, amid great rejoicings.

Work was also proceeding on the much-needed Breakwater (there were five wrecks in 1873 alone—admittedly, a particularly bad year).

And George was promoted to Captain of the No. 1 Company of the local Volunteers. Interestingly, this came about through an election of eligible men (see cutting).

The Volunteer movement in New Zealand, in which George was closely involved for so many years, had its roots in the New Zealand wars of the 1860s. Although the activity of these local militias had periods of decline, they continued until replaced by the Territorial Force in 1910. Certainly, in the 1870s and 1880s in Oamaru, they were a significant part of the social landscape, with inspections, drills, and rifle competitions regularly reported on the newspaper. These activities were not simply parochial, but helped connect more distant communities. Thus, for example, in February of 1872, the Oamaru Rifle Rangers competed against the Karori Rifles from Wellington, each 20-man team on their own range, and each man's individual score being reported in the newspaper (I am pleased to report that Oamaru won, 594 vs 505, with George achieving a very creditable 35).

THE VOLUNTEERS.—The adjourned annual general meeting of No. 1 Company was held on the 3rd inst. at the Northern Hotel. The minutes of the previous general meeting having been confirmed, Lieut Locke read the balance-sheet showing a credit balance of L11, against which however there are certain out-tain outstanding accounts. The balance sheet as read was adopted. The election of officers then took place. It was stated that the following gentlemen nominated at last meeting for the captaincy declined to stand, viz , Messrs J. Allan, Christie, O'Meagher, and Mowat. Lieut. Locke and Sub-lieut. Sumpter were then proposed, and Major Steward having taken the chair those gentlemen withdrew and the election proceeded by ballot, the Company's choice falling upon Sub-lieut. Sumpter. The officers being re called the Chairman announced the result of the ballot, and vacated the chair in favor of the Captain-elect. The election of sub-lieutenant then took place, the choice of the Company falling upon Sergt. Hay-Mackenzie. Sergt. Henderson, who was also nominated, declining to accept office. To fill the vacancy caused in Committee three names were proposed, the result being the election of Sergt. King. This completed the business, and the health of the newly-elected officers and of Major Steward having been drunk, the meeting terminated.

In 1873, George also became Superintendant of the St Lukes' Sunday School: 85 pupils and 11 teachers.

But let us not forget amongst all this earnest activity, that George is also a family man.

GEORGE THE FAMILY MAN

By 1870, George was the proud father of six children: Emma (11), Harriet (8), Lottie (6), Mary (4), Blanche (2), and Clara (1).

Two and one part letters from George to his parents back in England have been found. Because of the quality of the paper they are difficult to read, and the dates have also had to be guessed. (Note that George tends to use dashes to end his sentences, and this quirk has been preserved.)

The household back in England included in 1861 Emma Katharine's older maiden sister Harriet Youngman (that is, George's aunt) and was situated in Finchley. By 1871, according to the census, the family had moved to Whetstone, Middlesex, and the household had shrunk to just John and Emma, and their maiden daughter Jessica. Their 9 year old granddaughter, Katherine, is also recorded in the census, but she was probably just visiting. She was the oldest child of George's brother Walter and his wife Esther, who are recorded as living in Cley Next the Sea, Norfolk.

[Part letter, tentatively dated to 1870, based on the report of heavy floods, and reference to the ship *England's Glory*, which arrived at Port Chalmers on September 22 1870.]

The children are all growing up healthy & strong & are getting on well. We have been most fortunate in getting a young lady teacher who comes three times a week who certainly has a most excellent method of imparting knowledge as the little ones are all fond of her and are making rapid progress. Emma plays very well for her age on the Piano which has now got its tone & keeps well in tune a most important matter in this country where tuners are not to be got every day – You do not know how much obliged I always feel for that present as I do not know when I should have bought one myself and it is a constant source of pleasure to many of us – The "Englands Glory" is in and we are anxiously looking forward to its arrival which I fear will not be for some time as we always have to wait sometime before we get them after their arrival in Dunedin unless they should happen to be at the top of the cargo – You will be pleased to hear that I managed to buy at an auction sale a very light & comfortable buggy & a quiet horse so that my dear wife can at last get out a little and take some of the chicks with her as she can manage to drive very well & I can quite trust the horse as he is exceedingly quiet – I was most fortunate in getting him – Mr Lemon has just returned from Melbourne he went there to sell a cargo of grain we sent over.

Dear Mary is very well she came down the other evening to hear me read at an evenings entertainment got up pro. bono. publico "sixpenny readings" – I am pretty old to make a commencement however I was very well received & the people seemed much pleased. How much I have to thank you for the pains you took to give me a good education – whenever successful I trust I do not forget who I have to thank for the loving care they bestowed on me in my young days–

We have had shocking floods here this year but they seem to have exhausted themselves and we are now having quite hot weather –

I don't know that I have anything more to write about just now except to give you all my very best love in which Susie joins and little ones send many kisses – Some of them will write you

Your affectionate Son George Sumpter

1874 saw George try again for the mayoralty, a better attempt this time, but still a disappointment (Shrimski received 246 votes, to George's 161). He writes of it to his parents:

Aug[t] 28th [1874]
My very dear Parents

I cannot allow the mail to leave without writing a few lines to you, and I hope that you may receive one or two more from some of us this time as so long a period has been allowed to elapse.

The mails have been so irregular of late that it has been rather a matter of difficulty to know when to write – it is a long time also since I had a letter from home – I hardly know what to write to you about as nothing of any great moment has occurred since my last letter – Oamaru is still steadily progressing although I do not think business matters are quite as brisk as they were a while ago –

We have all of us been more or less troubled with sore throats I was laid up for over a week with a severe attack of quinsy but am thankful to say I am now nearly well again although I was very weak as I was unable to take any solid food for about five days – Lottie is still complaining but the rest are pretty well. We are daily in fear of some disease being brought amongst us by the immigrants who are coming out just now in great numbers and some of the vessels have [unreadable] on board.

You will have heard by the Oamaru paper which I hope you get regularly that I am asked to stand for the office of the Mayor which I agreed to do & was unsuccessful although I must say I anticipated a different result - & excepting that a cry was got up about the appointment I cannot even now account for the defeat – Perhaps it is just as well for me that I was not elected although of course it is not pleasant to be beaten.

And now about the little ones – I certainly could not apply that cognomen to Emma for she has grown into quite a tall young lady – She is a very great assistance to us doing her utmost both to assist in the house & to go on with her studies. Had it not been for her efforts during my sickness to keep the house quiet and my dear wifes constant & watchful care my late illness was of so serious a matter that the result might have been very different to what it was – Harriet is getting on very well with her studies & has a great passion for dressmaking in the shape of ornamenting dolls etc & you would be quite surprised if you could happen to see her at her employment – Lottie is a neat tidy little body but just now complaining not being quite well. Mary is a sturdy little thing & is continually trying what she can do on the piano which to her delight she is just commencing to learn. Blanche and Clara are both strong romping girls although the latter is rather small – The former is making fast progress with her lessons being able both to read and write although about six – George although rather light and delicate looking is tolerably strong and very observant and makes some very sensible remarks – but the other boy Walter is a complete "ruffian" I call him being very vigorous healthy & noisy and always wanting to romp – He is having very good times of it at his mothers expense as he is not yet even weaned – He has so many little winning ways that his mother is always finding some excuse for putting off the to him first lessons of self denial –

I was pleased to receive and read Walters jotting re Dr Livingston & I intend to read it at one of the Amateur Entertainments to see whether it will please a Oamaru audience – I am very sorry he cannot open time to write to me occasionally – He will have told you perhaps that I saw Capt Fox who is master of the Scimitar & comes from Cley –

I trust dear Auntie is as well and comfortable as she can be at her advanced age – And now my dear Parents I must close this letter although having made a commencement I could go on about ad infinitum.

Begging you all to accept our fondest love,
I am your ever loving son,
George Sumpter

Though he failed at the mayoralty, he did find a place for his civic energies in the newly formed Harbour Board, and the Mechanic's Institute, of which he was President.

Mechanic's Institutes were another interesting invention of the nineteenth century — organizations for adult education that combined a subscription library with a newspaper/journal reading room, as well as a place to hold public lectures and classes. In Oamaru, the Mechanic's Institute, later renamed the Athenaeum and Mechanic's Institute, was housed in a fine Oamaru stone building on Thames Street. As with many of these establishments, it eventually morphed into a public library, which lasted until 1975, when a new library was built. Today the building houses the North Otago Museum.

His Honour the Mayor!

Third time lucky! In 1875, George was finally successful in achieving the mayoralty. The election was quite exciting (see next page).

Shrimski sounds rather a poor loser. Apparently he also took offense at the newspaper's reporting of the event, and tried to horsewhip a member of the editorial staff! Passionate times indeed.

THE MAYORALTY.

The poll for the election of a Mayor for Oamaru took place yesterday, and an unusual amount of interest was excited by the event—in fact more than we ever saw before in Oamaru. At an early hour the town had been placarded with the usual invitations to "vote for Shrimski," and "vote for Sumpter," and the betting, which had begun at 2 to 1 on Shrimski, gradually fell till 5 to 1 was offered on Sumpter, finding few takers. Cabs, buggies, expresses, and even a break-van, were pressed into the service, placarded in favor of some one, and some the other of the candidates, and at all events made a show of working hard. Of the 603 citizens on the roll 450 voted, showing of itself the interest felt in the election. At about four o'clock a crowd commenced to gather in front of the Council Chambers, till fully 1000 persons were assembled. At about five o'clock Cr. Falconer announced that the state of the poll was

Sumpter	267
Shrimski	183

He, therefore, declared Mr George Sumpter duly elected Mayor of Oamaru for the year 1875 6.

The announcement was received with loud and prolonged cheering.

Mr Sumpter then stood forward and said he thanked the citizens for the high honor they had done him in electing him Mayor. He had been beaten last year, and he had endeavored to bear his defeat well. He could only hope, now, that he would be able to bear his success equally well. He desired to record his earnest thanks to those gentlemen who had worked hard and well to place him in his present position. He had not expected to find himself elected by so large a majority, and he need not say how gratified he felt. The term "gentleman" had been freely used during the contest, and some inuendoes as to the contracted meaning he was said to apply to the word, had, he believed, caused him to be beaten last year, and had also operated to his detriment in the present contest. He did not consider the term applied merely to black-coated men, as a laborer in his working dress could be a true gentlemen, and many were so. It simply depended upon conduct. With regard to the reserves, a good deal had been said, but those who had lived in Oamaru so long as he had, knew that he had always striven to have them placed in the hands of the Corporation, for the purposes for which they had been set aside. Something had been said about the Rifle Range. Well. It was given to the Volunteers, and they had spent money on it, and had a right to it. He would not object to its being in the hands of the Corporation, if it was stipulated that the Volunteers should have it so long as there were any of that body in Oamaru. Regarding the tramway, it was a pity that Mr Dunlop had not published the reply given by the Council, as well as the application. He could only say that personaliy the matter did not much interest him, but he believed it would be for the benefit of the town. He trusted that the citizens would, now that he was elected, give him their cordial support. He would be happy to receive, and give attention to any suggestions which any citizen might make regarding municipal matters, and he hoped that at the conclusion of his term of office they would have the same confidence in him that they had then. (Cheers).

Mr Shrimski said he heartily thanked those electors who had voted for him. The position of himself and Mr Sumpter were the reverse of what they were last year. There he had given him a disgraceful beating. (Cries of Oh! and "No disgrace.") Well, what he meant to say was that he had beaten Mr Sumpter last year by one more than he (Mr Shrimski) was beaten this. He had served the town honestly during his term of office, without fear or favor to any. Regarding the tramway, since the reply sent by the Council to the projectors a letter had been received from the Minister for Public Works, stating that the General Government would not interfere in the matter. He might remind the Citizens that it was a serious offence to cut up and damage the streets. He intended to contest the election for Councillor for one or all the Wards, and if returned he would continue to look diligently after the affairs of the town.

A vote of thanks to the returning officer concluded the proceedings.

The following shows the voting in each Ward :—

	Sumpter	Shrimski
Jetty Ward	61	46
Thames Ward ...	58	44
Severn Ward... ...	90	68
High Ward	58	25

1875 should have been a good year for George, but a fire in Thames street on the very first day of his mayoralty caused an injury that must have had worse consequences than seemed at the time, for he did not stand again the following year, by reason of ill health. The cause of the accident was simple enough: he was apparently "running round from the street to the back of the premises [on fire], and when passing through the yard of Messrs Jack and Co's premises he stumbled and fell over a corn screen. He received a wound over the left temple and a deep cut above the right eye." Nevertheless, he attended the first meeting of the Council just a few days later.

Not coincidently, the fire was closely followed by the forming of a committee to look into establishing a Volunteer Fire Brigade. George was (of course) a member.

But although the accident didn't seem to hold George back from fulfilling his civic duties, it's clear that it must have taken a very serious toll. Indeed, in a speech two years later, George refers to the accident as "nearly cost[ing] him his life", and "necessitated his retirement, at the close of his term of office, from Municipal duties."

So, a hard year perhaps, which also finished sadly, with the death of his mother.

Still, notwithstanding his poor health, George managed to keep busy, submitting a lengthy report to the Superintendent of Otago in June 1876, detailing all the fine work done by the Harbour Board. The Breakwater was now 630 feet long; the Macandrew Wharf was now in operation (having been officially opened by no less a personage than the Governor of New Zealand, the Marquis of Normanby); a railway ran from the town to the Breakwater; a number of storage and office buildings had been built on the land set aside for that purpose. (This part of the town has been well preserved, in the "Historic Precinct", and I have put several photographs on the website — including the one still showing the name "Sumpter".)

DEATH

At Whetstone, Middlesex, England, on 24th December, 1875, Emma Katharine, aged 75 years, the beloved wife of John Sumpter, Esq., and dearly loved mother of George Sumpter and Mrs Lemon, of Oamaru.

All of this had substantially increased the activity at the Port. For example, in the year work began (1869-70) 408 vessels had visited the port, while six years later, there were 762 vessels. The money spent on the Harbour was, George averred, entirely justified:

> Presuming that the country from the Waimate southward finds its natural outlet at Oamaru, which reason and analogy would lead one to pre-suppose would be the case, Oamaru will be the commercial centre for a tract of country comprising nearly four millions of acres, more than one-third of the area being pre-eminently adapted for agricultural purposes. Possessing a soil and climate unrivalled for the production of cereals, backed by an extensive block of stock-raising country, possessed of immense deposits of the now famous Oamaru stone and

> slate quarries (producing a quality of this material equal to the best productions of Wales), famed throughout the colony for the excellence of its manufactured breadstuffs, as well as the superior quality of the raw materials, it is not too much to say that the expenditure on Harbour works is fully warranted by the necessities of the case. Abundant supplies of lignite can be obtained in the district, which has proved an important item in limiting the import of coal, and although not dependent on gold discovery for its progress in any way, the district possesses goldfields which only require capital and enterprise to make it an important industry.

Business was once again booming in Oamaru, despite the "very considerable alarm to the community" in February 1876 from repeated earthquakes. For George, too, despite his health, business was presumably flourishing, because in 1877, the family homestead that George named Oakleigh enters the scene.

Oakleigh Road was a major thoroughfare in Finchley, where George's parents lived, and I presume this is the source of the name George gave the house. It may be, given that George's father had been recorded as a "Proprietor of Houses", that the property in Finchley had been in the family's possession when George had been growing up. Or perhaps George merely wanted to make a connection between his home and his father's.

I have dated the following letter from George to his father at March 1877, on the basis of the events described. Note that a corner of the letter was torn, leading to several small gaps in the narrative.

> My very dear Papa
>
> I have not heard from home for several months & I am beginning to get anxious – I do trust that you are all pretty well and that dear Jessie is better than by last accounts oh how thankful I should be to hear that she had quite recovered.
>
> You will be pleased to hear that I have now pretty good health & have very nearly lost entirely the pain in my side – In fact as I told Walter in my last letter I have been well enough to play in several cricket matches – You will also be glad to hear that we have had no new shocks of earthquakes. Latterly the weather has been lovely although about two months ago we had very heavy floods which did an immense amount of damage to the crops & in consequence there is very little really sound grain in the Province – Strange to say although it is tolerably far advanced in Autumn owing to the dry weather previous to the rain the growth of fruit trees was pretty well delayed. Lately the trees have been in blossom as well as strawberries but I do not suppose they will produce any fruits – You will notice that I am writing this letter on my birthday & doubtless I am right in thinking you are remembering me on this day. My thoughts are

constantly travelling towards [missing] hoped that the mail would have arrived before [missing] this time & that I should have letters to reply to but I have been disappointed & do not like waiting any longer – My children are all well & are in a state of no small excitement as to a quiet dancing party that I have promised to give them next Wednesday the 4th April for my dear daughter Emma's eighteenth birthday – It hardly seems credible that she should be that age – I have been greatly blessed in her for she is a most good & affectionate girl & I may say next to her dear mother the mainstay of the house – Owing to the grain season Oamaru is very busy as regards railway traffic in particular travel coming in with sometimes nearly twenty trucks of produce & as Oamaru is the terminus of three lines there is plenty of bustle – Although business matters are tolerably brisk just now I fear that we shall have very dull times in the winter – in consequence of all the public works being stopped. We are now pretty well settled in our new house etc. The shrubs & trees are beginning to show themselves. It is a most hardy place & the view from the hill on which our house is is really magnificent – We can see the breakwater & shipping – the wide expanse of ocean in front & a beautiful plain with homesteads sprinkled all over — its divided nearly in the centre with the railway line on two sides & back with hilly country & farther back mountains usually topped with snows oh how I wish you could [look at it?]. I will try to get a photograph taken [missing] you may have more idea of the place – The only drawback is [missing] little too far from the town which we feel on a Sunday but I ought [missing] to be thankful that I have made splendid friends & hope I may before very long to be able to pay off the money I had to borrow to pay for building the house. I shall now close this letter asking you to give my best love to dear Auntie & all my dear relatives

I am Your loving son
George Sumpter

So here we are: it is 1877; Oamaru has new gas-lights, greatly improved streets, new "public pleasure gardens", extensive buildings of the famed white Oamaru stone, two banks, a new Masonic Hall, Steam Saw-mills, a smart new Brewery "with every modern improvement", two banks, two Building Societies (George was, of course, secretary of one of these), the establishment of the "Oamaru and Dunedin Steam Company" (George was a director), daily mail to Dunedin, public telegraph offices, a railway now running all the way from Moeraki Port to Christchurch, a steamer trudging regularly between the town and Dunedin, a new bridge over the Waitaki. This is a town on the rise, and George is one of its prominent citizens, his fingers in so many pies.

Emma, too, is coming into her maturity. She is 18 years old. We need, surely, a love interest. And here he comes, on his cue, our hero.

Our hero enters the story

WE INTRODUCE OUR HERO

Richard Davies was born in Carmarthen in South Wales in 1848, the third son in a family of six children. His mother died when he was 10. (See the appendix for more details of Richard's family.)

Richard was one of those many young men who found insufficient scope for their talents in the confines of Victorian Britain, and ventured out into Empire where opportunity abounded.

But to take advantage of those opportunities, you perhaps needed more energy and dedication than Richard could muster. In his own words: "my friends or rather acquaintances (they could not have been 'friends') continually impressed on my mind that I should never have occasion to work very hard as my father had plenty of money."

As a consequence, Richard found it hard to settle. He tried the sea (nine months), but, alas, found this was too much like "hard work". He tried working in a draper's (four months), but found this too "confining". (But we should bear in mind that he was only 16 when he embarked on these adventures!). He then tried shipbroking, first as an apprentice (six months), and then in partnership with another (2 ½ years!).

But then, poor Richard, although the firm "came to grief", he would nevertheless have "got along capitally" except that his Father (who has presumably been stoically providing all these opportunities) "thought that mixing so much in the societies of sea-captains was not good for me" (one suspects this is not the complete story!).

He then spent eight months in the coal business, again in partnership, and again the business collapsed ("I was glad to clear out with the loss of £450").

After six months of doing nothing, followed by his father losing significant money because of bank failures, Richard decided on something completely different. He got a job as a clerk for the Eastern Cable Company in Alexandria.

Although this didn't last long ("my fellow clerks were the greatest cads I ever met"), he eventually got in with John Matheson & Co, and started to prosper.

He was in Egypt five years, a respectable length of time, returning home on the death of his father. After spending some six months "recovering his health" after the hard work and climate in Egypt, he then proceeded to lose most of the money he'd amassed on the stock exchange. When he was down to his last £200, he decided there was nothing for it but to "try the colonies".

He must have been about 27 by this time. Quite when and where he arrived in New Zealand we don't know, but it would seem from this account that he left Britain sometime in 1876, and by early 1878 he is sufficiently settled to be writing a lengthy letter of explanation to George, presumably to help him make his case for being allowed to court George's daughter. The first 'love letters' we have begin in August.

Falling in love with the eldest child of such a prominent member of the community could surely only be good for our struggling hero, but the future wasn't as rosy as you might think. For George was clearly not convinced of Richard's worthiness (with some justification, we might think!).

Sent, one assumes, by George (or at least strongly encouraged), Richard went to Rakaia, a small township in North Canterbury. A road and rail bridge had been built in 1873, and the town's position at the main crossing of the Rakaia River, close to both railway and river, in the heart of the Canterbury Plains, surely suggested that an energetic young man could thrive there as an auctioneer. Canterbury had become rich through sheep and wheat – in 1885 the province held more than 3 million sheep (over a fifth of the national flock) and had more than half the total area of wheat land.

All the conditions seemed promising. Alas, the time was wrong.

RICHARD MAKES HIS CASE

But let Richard himself tell the story! Here he is, commending himself to his future father-in-law.

April 3rd 1878
Geo Sumpter Esq
Oamaru

Dear Sir,

Referring to our conversation on the evening of the first inst, I now beg to give you a brief sketch of my life since I left school at 16 years of age up to the present time. In the first place I may state that my friends or rather acquaintances (they could not have been 'friends') continually impressed on my mind that I should never have occasion to work very hard as my father had plenty of money. This will perhaps partly account for my roving propensities during the early part of my career. I had a brother a midshipman in the Black Ball Line and nothing would do but I must have brass buttons and gold band round my hat. My Father sent me a trial trip to South America in a small brig that he was interested in, the hard work of all soon made me forget the gold band and I was pleased to get home after a nine months voyage. I remained at home three months undecided what to do next, after a good deal of persuasion my sisters prevailed upon me to try the cashier's desk in a large drapery store at Newport. Mon. [Monmouthshire] I got tired of the confinement in about four months and then prevailed upon my Father to apprentice me to a shipbroker. I remained with him for about six mons: and then left to join his chief clerk who was just going in to business on his own account. My Father invested £300 for me which was to be increased when I became 21. In 2 ½ years the firm came to grief. I then went into the largest firm in the place and should have got along capitally but my Father thought that mixing so much in the societies of sea-captains was not good for me and just as I was offered charge of a department in the office he took me up to London and put me into a coal business with a young fellow who was highly connected and who was said to be doing a paying business, in 8 months I was glad to clear out with the loss of £450. I remained in London about 6 months doing nothing not earning a penny. Just at this time my Father lost several thousands in two or three banks and I then decided on going abroad and seeing that the Eastern Cable Company was in want of clerks I applied and got appointed as learner in the station in Alexandria. I got so disgusted with my fellow clerks who were the greatest cads I ever met with that I was glad to go as bookkeeper in a stationers store where I soon got acquainted with the English residents and after a few months I got into the firm of John Matheson & Co at a salary of £180, in 12 months I had £250 and the procuration of the firm and when I left them after about 4 years I had about £360. I left Egypt for two reasons – I found the climate too trying and I had to go home and settle some family affairs on the death of my Father. I remained in

Wales about 6 months recovering my health after 5 years hard work in Egypt. I then went to London where I remained about 6 months specialising in the stock exchange and after reducing my capital to about £200 I thought it advisable to try the colonies as I could not find suitable employment at home.

Rather a wasted life is it not? Until I came to Oamaru I never thought it as such but I can safely say I have nothing to regret only the years wasted. How many more of recent arrivals of my own age can say the same?

I may add that in giving you the foregoing information I have done what I would not do for any other man living.

I have written to my relative in Auckland and if my letter reaches him you will probably get a letter from him in about three weeks.

You will find this rather a disjointed epistle but as I am busy balancing the books for last month perhaps you will excuse this hurried scrawl.

I am yours truly, Richard Davies

If there is any further information you wish to have I will be pleased to furnish you with it.

The following lengthy account was also found among the family papers. There is no information about when it was written or who it was meant for, but it provides an interesting description of Richard's life in Egypt and his impressions of it.

On the 23rd May 1870 I left Southampton by the Peninsular & Oriental S.S. "Delta" bound for Alexandria. As the shore of dear old England receded from view I felt the tears rising into my eyes altho' I try my best to suppress them. After a pleasant passage of 5 days we reached Gibraltar the key of the Mediteranean with its steel sides bristling with guns. I went ashore for a few hours & rather enjoyed the novelty of mixing with the sallow faced Spaniards swarthy Moors & neatly dressed British troops who constitute the population of this almost impregnable fortification. After a stay of 4 hours we sailed for Malta, I cannot conceive anything more pleasant than sailing along the Mediterranean in a fine ship with a lot of passengers & a sea something like a millpond. On the evening of the fourth day after leaving Gibraltar we reached Malta, this is another strongly fortified place, I don't think there is much chance of any foreign nation obtaining possession of the island as long as it is held by the British. I had another run ashore here & can quite sympathise with Lord Byron in what he says about the streets, the numberless flight of steps are most trying especially for those who have a tendency to embonpoint. The steamer remained here 12 hours coaling then off again to our destination, in five days we reached Alexandria after a most delightful passage of 14 days. As the shores of Egypt came into view I thought it a most barren looking place, it seemed to be nothing better than a desert. As soon as we cast anchor in the harbor, the ship seemed to swarm with Arabs who crowded up on all sides offering their services to take us ashore for almost anything we liked to offer them.

On the passage from the steamer to the wharf I was much struck with the number of mosques & minarets which seem to stud the city. As I landed at the Custom House I fully expected to have my coat torn from my back by the crowd of donkey boys, who, seeing a new chum knew from experience that they could get at least treble the usual fare for taking me into the centre of the city. The streets near the shore are very narrow and dirty & crowded with Arabs & Greeks but in the European quarter the streets are wide and well paved & the houses are rather imposing some of them 5 & 6 stories high.

I shall never forget my first night in Egypt, on retiring to rest I thought I could dispense with the mosquito net which hung over my bed, I was not very long in finding out my mistake, my candle had not been extinguished over a couple of minutes before I was glad to tumble out again when I soon had the net hanging in its proper position, but to my dismay I found that a number of mosquitos had got underneath & there was no getting rid of them. I don't think I had 5 minutes sleep during the whole night & I was glad to rise at break of day & have a cold bath one of the greatest luxuries in a warm climate.

For the first few months I felt very miserable. I found the heat very trying & I did not take kindly to macaroni, salads, rissoles & stewed frogs (for all I know) which seem to be the principal dishes. I longed for the roast beef of old England, also felt the want of a few friends but I soon managed to become acquainted with some nice families, some people have a happy knack of making friends wherever they may be located & I am vain enough to think that I am one of them!!!!

In about six months I had got fairly reconciled to the country & could drink coffee & smoke cigarettes with as much felicity as any Arab. During the winter months Egypt is anything but a disagreeable place to live in, I have frequently been to Cairo where during the winter months being Dec Jan & Feb: the climate is simply perfect. This can be seen from the crowds of consumptive people who flock there during this season of the year.

On my first visit to Cairo I was told that the proper thing to do was to visit the pyramids before going anywhere else. I therefore persuaded 3 acquaintances to join me & lost no time in paying my respects to the mighty pyramids. On our drive we encountered a miniature sandstorm which brought our buggy to a standstill. We put our heads under the cushions hoping to escape without much discomfort but we found that the sand managed to find its way into our ears, nostrils and hair in spite of all our precautions. On our arrival at the base we found the Sheik or Chief of Bedouin Arabs & about 5 of his followers ready to receive us. We paid the old Sheik some money for the hire of 16 of his tribe to assist us in the ascent, although I had 4 Bedouins to assist me I was very glad to rest 2 or 3 times before reaching the top. One of my friends got very giddy & only went halfway. The others persevered & were amply repaid for their trouble in reaching the summit. I regret that I cannot find words to convey the beauty of the scene, on one side nothing but a desert as far as the eye could reach & on the other the land of Gosehen [Goshen; familiar as the land given to the Hebrews by the pharaoh, from whence they later left Egypt] & the fertile valley of the Nile. I could not help thinking that if the pyramids could speak what a wonderful story they would have to relate.

During the winter riding parties are very common & as donkeys are generally used the fun is immense more especially when some of us had to record a spill or two before our return. As bachelors' balls were not in vogue we used to substitute picnic parties, 2 or 3 of us would hunt up 20 or 30 good donkeys according to the number of visitors & send them to Ramlek [Ramleh] about 5 miles out of Alexandria. The visitors would go out by train & meet them, then we had a glorious ride of 10 miles on the hard sand which brought us to Aboukir the battle field of the Nile [Aboukir Bay was the scene of a famous battle between the British, under the command of Horatio Nelson, and the French, during the Napoleonic Wars; it is often called the Battle of the Nile]. Here we would dismount & under a group of palm trees never fail to do justice to the luncheon which was invariably sent in advance. I remember once going for a long ride with a friend when neither of us thought of providing for the inner man until we had reached our destination. As we did not care about starting our return without a lunch of some sort, we sent our donkey boys to reconnoiter. After some little delay we found an Arab hut where we obtained some black bread & a plateful of beans soaked in oil. We made an excellent report or rather, informed our host that we had done so, I don't think we could have told him exactly the truth as I do not remember ever having another meal in an Arab hut.

After one has residence in Egypt a year or two & has seen all the sights the life becomes very monotonous more especially in the summer months when the weather remains the same for at least six months. If I mention here how I managed to get thru one day it will perhaps give you an idea of how I spent most of my time. I used to rise at 7 am & have a cold bath then breakfast, office at 9 until noon, then to the Exchange & sometimes speculate a little in Egyptian Bonds, lunch at one o'clock after which a siesta of about 2 hours duration, office again until 5 pm, then a stroll round the principal streets until dinner time, in the evening wend my way to one of the numerous cafes which are mostly built on the beach in order that visitors may get the benefit of the sea breeze which generally springs up after sundown, remain here for 2 or 3 hours smoking cigarettes drinking coffee & listening to the not over melodious strains of a German string band, not a very intellectual way of spending my leisure hours, but really one gets into such a languid state in this most enervating climate that doing anything else is almost out of the question.

I will now endeavour to show how the country is governed, the present ruler of Egypt is Ismail Pacha or as he is more generally called the Khedive of Egypt. Some people seem to think that he is simply a vassal of the Sultan of Turkey. I don't think this is correct. As far as I could learn he is entirely his own master excepting that he pays the Sultan an annual tribute of I think £250.000 which does not trouble the Khedive very much considering that the poor oppressed natives have to pay it.

The government is a despotic monarchy, the Khedive makes all laws, levies taxes etc at his own discretion, he certainly has a kind of parliament consisting of the Ministers of Finance, Justice, Public Works, Foreign Affairs, & a few others, but I do not think any of them would like to thwart him in any of his projects. I remember one instance where the Commissioner of Police had made himself too officious, he was ordered to one of the Govt: offices to explain his conduct, on entering he was requested to partake of a cup of coffee (invariably offered to visitors) & in a few hours he was found dead in his own house, poisoned so it was said by order of the Government.

I think Egypt can lay claim to being one of the most corrupt Governments in the World, I once had an interview with Ismail Pacha, Mafeltink [?] (the highest officer in the Khedives Service) one of the most unmitigated rogues I ever had to do business with. He must have made tens of thousands of pounds during the few hours [he surely meant years!] he was in power. If the Khedive wanted a loan of £20,000 he would tell the Minister of Finance to get it from one of the Banks, this estimable old gentleman would go to one Bank & obtain their terms perhaps 20% & £1000 for himself, another Bank would quote 25% & £1500 gratuity, he would return to the Viceroy & say Your Highness I cannot obtain the money under 25% interest but forget to add that he made £1500 out of the transaction. Then again a wealthy Arab would interview the Minister & say Excellence, I have £1000 which I shall be glad if you will invest for me, or, if he spoke the truth, here is a present of £1000 then add, I shall esteem it a great favor if you will make me Commissioner of Customs. The Minister would reply, I will see what I can do. Knowing at the same time that the Arab would repay himself in a few months. The Arab would probably obtain the appointment if he managed to ingratiate himself with the Minister & in a month or two find himself superseded by another having some spare cash to invest in the same way. Who would not be Egyptian Minister of Finance?

Again a ship Captain coming to Alexandria for the first time with a cargo of coal for the Government would be accosted by one of the Govt: weighers as follows "Well Capt: how many tons of coal have you? 500 tons would be the reply, I will make the ship turn out 520 tons if you will give me £20, presuming that Captain to be an honest man, the reply would be I will do nothing of the kind, as I know that my ship has 500 tons on board as stated in my Bill of Lading, when the ship is discharged the Govt: weigher makes out the cargo to be 480 tons & the Captain is paid accordingly.

It is the same all thro' Egypt & I maintain that it is impossible for a Merchant doing business with the Government to deal honestly with them. If he does he is bound to come to grief sooner or later. Supposing the Public Works Dept: call for tenders for the erection of a Bridge. One firm quotes say £5000 & another firm quotes £5500 & promises the chief clerks in the Dept £300 provided they secure the contract, the tender of the latter firm would in 7 cases out of 10 be accepted.

I think the foregoing will suffice to show to what extent corruption is practiced, the Khedive sometimes makes an example of some of his officers, but this does not seem to deter their successors from doing the same thing, the only way I can account for such wholesale robbery is that most of the Government employees are paid such miserable salaries that they are almost compelled to be dishonest in order to enable them to live respectably, not to mention keeping a carriage & a number of servants as some of them do. I don't think they are altogether to blame when you take into consideration the bad example they have in their Ruler who is considered to be one of the most extravagant of Monarchs, he has at least ½ doz palaces each with its retinue of servants, Studs of horses etc etc also a magnificent steam yacht the "Mahroussah" with a complement of 400 men besides 2 or 3 smaller yachts. Then again he has an European Opera Comp^{y} for three months every season which costs him £60000 a year. Whenever he attempts to float a loan in the European Market the prospectus states in most glowing terms that the money is required to open up the fertile valley of the Nile & to build railways to the Sugar & Cotton growing districts of the Soudan etc etc whereas perhaps one third of it goes to Public Works the remaining two thirds to pay interest on existing loans & to gratify his extravagances.

You are probably aware that Egyptian Securities are now lower than they have ever been & I predict that in a few years this country will be unable to pay the interest on its debt, or, in other words become bankrupt like its sister state Turkey.

I have often talked with the natives respecting the Government of the country, if they were not the most submissive people in the world they would long ere this have risen in rebellion. I have frequently been asked why the English lady, as they call the Queen, does not rescue them from this thralldom, they would gladly hail the day when they could call themselves British Subjects.

If England should take possession of Egypt it would be the making the country, the fertility of the soil cannot be surpassed anywhere & under a good Govt: the resources of the country would soon be doubled, not to mention the opening up of a large extent of country in Upper Egypt & the Soudan.

Richard seems to have worked for George as a book-keeper in his auction business, and was also involved with him in the Oamaru

Athenaeum & Mechanics Institute, acting as the Secretary of the Committee. I feel sure there's a deep sub-text to this role, as his name first appears as "Hon. Sec." in February of 1878, after a special meeting in January, which followed on from much acrimony in the papers. This outcry concerned a proposal that a Mr Robertson be granted a lease for a small piece of land on the Institute's land on Thames St, for the purpose of erecting a smithy.

Two days after the "hole-and-corner meeting" in which the lease was granted, an irate member of the Institute wrote (anonymously) at great length to the Editor of the North Otago Times, saying

> "Did any one ever hear of such a monstrous affair? All Oamaru was indignant, and justly so, ... Better a thousand times, that the remainder (that from the Institute to the Post Office) should remain vacant than that such buildings as the Committee of the Institute are sanctioning being erected should be permitted in the centre of the town.
>
> And how do you think Sir this little scheme was worked? On Saturday evening last, the 22nd inst., the Librarian was instructed to call a special meeting of the Committee "on Important business," for Monday evening, the 24th, this being Christmas Eve; the conveners well knowing that some members of the Committee, being engaged in banks, could not attend, and that others, being business people, could not attend either; ...
>
> We have heard a good deal of late of parliamentary jobs—the Piako Swamp and such like. I am almost inclined to say that we need not go far from our own doors for jobbery."

(In 1873, the Government was persuaded by former Minister of Defense Thomas Russell to sell the enormous Piako Swamp to a syndicate of which he was the leading member. He also received a number of "lucrative government commissions" and came close to being indicted for fraud[4].)

Little wonder if a certain re-organization of the Committee might occur in the wake of such strong feelings!

(To the Editor of the NORTH OTAGO TIMES.)

SIR,—I have frequently of late with pleasure seen articles in your journal giving descriptions of the various new and handsome buildings which have been lately erected in Oamaru, and which buildings not only in a great measure help to render it one of the handsomest towns in Otago, but prove unmistakably the vast strides the Oamaruites are making in population, commerce, enterprize, and wealth.

It is, therefore, with no little regret, and I had almost said indignation, that I notice a movement of a retrograde nature showing itself in our midst; one which if not nipped in the bud we know not where it may stop. And whence comes it? From a body who of all others one would think had next at heart the well-being and respectability of our town, the beauty of our streets, and splendour of the architectural designs of the buildings erected in them. I allude to the Committee of the Oamaru Mechanics' Institute, a body composed of well-known citizens—the President being a gentleman of high social standing, refined intellect, extensive learning, and urbane, gentle manners; another of its most influential members being an architect of no mean pretensions. The movement I allude to is supposed to emanate from the Oamaru Mechanics' Institute Committee, at least that body get the blame of it, but I believe it is only the action of a certain party in that body. And what, it may be asked, is all this about? This Committee, or, rather, a certain party of them, want to have a horse-shoer's forge and smithy erected on the ground belonging to the Mechanics' Institute, which is situate in the principal and most conspicuous part of Thames street—an old iron building which is to be removed from beside the Bank of New Zealand in Tyne street, where it has been for many years an eyesore to those having business places in the neighborhood, the frequenters of the Bank, and, though last, not least, those having offices on the opposite side of the street. And this monstrocity is to be erected on the ground of the Institute in Thames street facing the new street leading to the Volunteer Hall, at the other corner of which street and Thames street, I am informed, a magnificent pile of buildings is about to be erected which will, it is said, be superior in architectural design to any yet erected in Oamaru, the plans of which are being prepared by one of our leading architects (not he belonging to the Institute, however). Did any one ever hear of such a monstrous affair?

All Oamaru was indignant, and justly so, as the Hon. Mathew Holmes for preventing that part of Thames street between the Courthouse and Severn street being built upon. Better, a thousand times, that the remainder (that from the Institute to the Post Office) should remain vacant than that such buildings as the Committee of the Institute are sanctioning being erected should be permitted in the centre of the town. And how do you think Sir this little scheme was worked? On Saturday evening last, the 22nd inst., the Librarian was instructed to call a special meeting of the Committee "on important business," for Monday evening, the 24th, this being Christmas Eve; the conveners well knowing that some members of the Committee, being engaged in banks, could not attend, and that others, being business people, could not attend either; but they hoped, and it proved correctly, to get a quorum. Well, the meeting was held, the quorum got, and, without any previous notice or intimation to the other members of the Committee or of the Institute of the business to be transacted, this meeting let the premises—the property *not* of themselves but of the Institute—for the purpose of having this unsightly iron smithy erected upon it. Surely, if those forming that Committee meeting had the interest of the Institute or of the town at heart they would not act thus surreptitiously and hurry through a matter of such importance. One would think they might have let the Christmas week pass—when many of the Committee were unable to attend—and thus give them an opportunity of opposing the matter, if so inclined. But no; the matter had to be done, and done it was. And mark this: I am informed a draft lease or agreement, leasing the ground for the purpose of a smithy, was actually cut and dry, and leasing it too for a period of seven years at a rental of L1 per foot; while, I venture to say, if the section were put up to auction it would realise much more. And this lease or agreement was sanctioned by this hole-and-corner meeting of Committee.

We have heard a good deal of late of parliamentary jobs—the Piako Swamp and such like. I am almost inclined to say that we need not go far from our own doors for jobbery.

I would suggest, Mr Editor, that a special meeting of the members of the Institute should be called to protest against this act of a party or portion of the Committee.

I also think that the Mayor should take action in the matter, as chief Magistrate of the town, and one who is known for many years to have the interests of the town and district at heart. I would suggest that he should be called upon to convene a public meeting of the citizens to protest against the proposed unsightly defacement of our principal street under the authority of a section or party of the Committee of the Institute, acting in the name and on behalf of the Oamaru Mechanics' Institute.—I am, &c.,

A MEMBER OF THE INSTITUTE.

Oamaru, 26th Dec., 1877.

Richard the lover

But let us temporarily forego business and politics, and enjoy the pleasures and pains of courtship!

Oamaru
Aug 12th 1878

My own darling pet

Where in the wide world did you get to from Headlands [an Oamaru family] this evening? I went up to the library window to watch for you coming out. I remained there about 3 minutes then roamed about Thames St for over half an hour but no signs of my darling, you must have gone out just as I was going up the steps of the Institute. I could have cried with vexation at having missed you. I hope you did not avoid me on purpose, did you Emma?

If your papa does not come down to the Office tomorrow evening I think I shall find my way to Oakleigh. As my fellow Auditor is going to a dance I shall be at liberty.

I wish you would write me a line Emma darling. I have nothing of yours in my possession, I long for something even if it is only a few lines.

Until you get tired of me
I am yours very sincerely

Dick Davies

[added in postscript] 13.8.78

Will you please try & come down town alone between 4.30 & 5 o'clock some other evening this week? If I do see you I will take particular care that you do not escape me a 2nd time. I don't quite know how to send you this. Shall I ask your papa to take it?

Dick Quite So Davies

We can only speculate how the courtship progressed, for we hear nothing more for seven months. But whatever travails may have occurred during that time, matters seem to have become more settled, from the tone of the letters, and their regularity.

Oamaru
March 12 1879

My own darling Em,

You must have thought me very selfish on Monday evening when I told you that I did not care about going to Mrs Lemon's until 8 o'clock. After I left it occurred to me that you would have preferred my going to tea, at least, I know if I was invited anywhere with you I should not be happy until you arrived.

If I can find that you have decided on going tomorrow I shall be there about 6pm.

Please forgive my thoughtlessness and believe me

Yours very sincerely
Dick Davies

What am I to do with myself this (my) evening?

Oamaru
Mar 18/79

My own darling Em

My sister's letter states "I enclose a note for Miss Sumpter which I will leave open & if you are not pleased with it tell me & I will write another one". As it has not been left open I have no knowledge of the contents. I am very anxious to know what she has to say about me. In another part of her letter she says "I have felt a little awkwardness in writing but hope it will be a proof to her of my interest in this matter".

I have a great mind to keep the note until tomorrow night so that I might see you read it & learn from your sweet face what you thought of it.

Fondest love daily
from Dick

Presumably, if Richard's sister is writing to Emma, the two are now betrothed. This seems to be confirmed by Richard's remark in the next letter, and is certainly confirmed by his salutation in the following one!

Oamaru
Mar 20th 1879

My own darling little Em

As I am not very busy I don't think I can be better employed than I am just now in writing to you.

I cannot say that I enjoyed myself very much last evening, is it to be always the same as long as Miss Barleycorn remains? If so, I tell you candidly that I shall not look forward to my Wednesday evenings the same as I have hitherto done. Why would you not come and sit near me in the drawingroom? You could not have got farther away if you had tried.

I have to thank Miss B for one thing and that is I wish more than ever now to take you to a home of our own.

I beg your pardon for knocking those views out of your hand.

Bless you darling
Yours Ever
Dick

Ask Harriet how the turkey is.

Oamaru
April 4th 1879

My own darling little Em

I wish you many happy returns of the day and do hope that your next birthday will be a happier one than this.

I have read your nice little letter to my sister over and over again. It will do very nicely I think.

I suppose you have received an invitation to Mrs Otterson's dance. I have not been honoured with one; quite right too. They must draw the line somewhere. As there is no cricket tomorrow I don't think I can venture up in the afternoon. I must therefore hope to see you on Sunday morning.

God bless my little darling and enable me to offer her a house ere long.

Goodbye wifie!
I am Ever Yours
Dick

Oamaru
May 2nd 1879

My own darling Em

You will see by the mail tonight that a reward is offered re the baths. I did not do it notwithstanding that I told you something about it. One of the few regular bathers asked me to subscribe to the reward. I promised altho' I know who did it. Shall I betray my friend & win the £10? I think not, I am much obliged to him for having done it as the water wanted changing. I hope you will not be grieved to find that I associate with such mischievous people.

Late on the night of Thursday, or early the following morning, some mischievous person obtained access to the Baths enclosure and turned off the water. A reward of £10 is offered for the conviction of the offender.

I think I must go to Oakleigh sometime on Saturday as I may not have many more opportunities of seeing you, at least, for a time.

Goodbye wifie darling,
Yours devotedly,
Dick
In haste

The baths were salt-water ones opened on the Esplanade as a public swimming pool in 1878.

Oamaru
July 25th 1879

My darling Em

I hear that your Aunt intends giving a party next Tuesday, how am I to know if you are going unless I see you on Sunday?

I am invited in the meantime I think I shall refer them to you.

Now confess darling that you were disappointed with what I told you on Wednesday about my pecuniary affairs, I should only have been too glad to have told you long long ago had it been worth talking about, but such a paltry account was not a pleasant subject by any means & I was too much ashamed to broach the subject, however, I am glad that you did so.

Next time we meet I don't suppose I shall find any difference in you, still something tells me that you are bitterly disappointed about it.

I won't write any more now
With fondest love still
I am
Yours Sincerely
Dick

THE LOVERS ARE PARTED!

Unfortunately, we don't hear any more about the disappointment Emma may have felt on hearing about Richard's financial status. When we meet our lovers again, they've been parted. Richard is now in Rakaia, about 120 miles north of Oamaru (and 36 miles south of the city of Christchurch).

But don't feel too badly — although that might seem a very great distance in those pre-automobile days, Rakaia and Oamaru were connected by what appears to be a thriving railway. This marvel raced daily from Oamaru to Christchurch in under 7 hours (on a good day)!

1880 begins sadly for the Sumpter family, with the death of George's father.

DEATH

On the 23rd January, at his residence, Whetstone, Middlesex, England, John Sumpter, aged 81, the beloved father of George Sumpter and Mrs John Lemon, of Oamaru.

The year began sadly for the town as well, with a large fire in Thames street completely destroying the Queen's hotel, Humphrey and Bailie's, D. Murray's, and McBride's shops, among others. This was said, at the time, to be "the most destructive which has yet taken place in Oamaru", and the wooden Queen's Hotel was consumed utterly: "So quickly did the fire extend itself that several of the inmates of the hotel had to make their escape by means of ladders placed to the windows of the upper apartments"[5]. Indeed, it was later found that one resident had lost his life in it (tragically, Mr William King, seeing the hotel on fire, rushed inside to rescue his property, which included his valuable carpenter's tools, and so perished).

Perhaps in response to this fire, although it took until the end of the year to happen, a fire-bell was erected at the fire-house (behind the Council Chambers). Signals were arranged to indicate where the fire was happening: Thames Ward, a peal and one toll; Severn Ward, a peal and two tolls; High Ward, a peal and three tolls; Jetty Ward, a peal and four tolls.

Fire was, indeed, a major peril of colonial life — not only in New Zealand, but in all "boom towns" of Australia, Canada and the United States. The explosive growth, hasty constructions, and dominance of wood led to many disasters. In North America between 1815 and 1915, for example, it's estimated that 290 major urban fires occurred[6]. Little wonder that Oamaru took advantage of its natural resources to build in stone!

To add to the town's woes, the harvest of 1879 had not been a good one, and along with the rest of New Zealand, Oamaru was experiencing a general depression in trade.

Nevertheless, building was continuing. George is recorded as building two shops and premises in Coquet street. The Northern Hotel (corner of Wansbeck and Tyne) was also completed, and an even more grandiose hotel to replace the destroyed Queen's Hotel started construction: billiard-room, three bars, two bar-parlours, two grand staircases, 10 sitting-rooms, 26 bedrooms, 2 bathrooms, a lavatory, passages 7 feet wide!

Additionally, the discovery that the bay had a less rocky bottom than thought encouraged the Board, under George's chairmanship, to order a dredge, which would allow bigger ships to enter the harbour. As usual, money was borrowed for this purpose.

Like the Harbour Board, the Borough was also heavily in debt — at March 1880, it owed £150,000, and was paying £10,500 a year in interest. Most of this was for Oamaru's other big project, the Waterworks, which were officially opened on September 2, 1880 (although not quite completed — for this a further £10,000 had to be borrowed, to add to the previous loans totalling £110,000).

But the go-getters of Oamaru were not, at the moment, concerned with such trifles. Oamaru was going to be big, they were sure.

The same year saw George promoted to Major of the 3rd Battalion Otago Rifle Volunteers.

In Rakaia, however, Richard is concentrating on his need to show George that he can support a wife, and finding it not so easy.

Richard the businessman

Richard is an interesting contrast to George. Where George is clearly a go-ahead sort, who will make the best of any opportunities that come his way, and indeed make opportunities if they don't, Richard is a ditherer. "Should I or shouldn't I?" "What do *you* think?" "Do you really think so?" He seems to ask everyone's opinion, yet remains undecided.

The letters also throw light on setting up a business in those free-wheeling times. Richard is in Rakaia with the intention of acting as a Commission Agent and Auctioneer. When he arrives, McLean & Winter are the Auctioneers for the area, but they are in the process of breaking the partnership — I surmise that George's sources (probably Mann) told him as much, and this is why he sent Richard there. There is talk of Richard joining up with Winter once he has disentangled himself from McLean, but, again, this is a decision Richard frets over.

While he is inclined to ask anyone, Richard seems to have a particular respect for Mann's opinion, and I surmise that Mann was George's contact in the town, as he seems to act as some sort of patron to Richard. Newspapers show John Mann as active in the establishment of the railway branch from Rakaia to Ashburton Forks, in the building of a Town Hall, chairman of the local school committee, presenting the departing Bank of New Zealand agent with a "purse of 32 sovereigns as a token of the esteem in which he is held by the residents of the Rakaia", and so on — a man after George's heart.

Rakaia
Feb 5/80

Dear Mr Sumpter,

I have to confirm my letter of y'day's date.

I learn from Mr Mann that McLean & Winter will not have anything to divide when they come to settle up for reasons which I will explain to you when I have the pleasure of seeing you. Mr Mann will advance Winter the necessary capital to start again when he gets clear of McLean. Both Messrs Mann & Winter advise me to start as Comm: Agent etc without loss of time so that I may make myself known to the settlers in the district. It will take the present firm of Auctioneers abt: 2 months to settle their affairs so that we have lots of time to learn whether it will be advisable for Winter & I to enter into partnership. I rode out to Darrochs this afternoon, & asked him his opinion, he seems to think that it would be very much to my advantage if I could make arrangements to join Winter.

I am staying at Mr Mann's house as he would not hear of my going to an Hotel, he wants me to go with the ballast train on Monday to Methven which is the terminus of the Rakaia & Ashburton Forks Railway. I have been introduced to Mssrs Patton & Clelland, two farmers in the vicinity of Methven both of whom have invited me to their farms. I don't expect to get back until Tuesday evening & on Wednesday I hope to leave for Oamaru. I cannot bear the idea of being away two Wednesdays at least not just yet. [I assume this is a reference to his apparently regular Wednesday evening visits — perhaps the family had set aside Wednesday evening as a regular social event.]

Tomorrow I intend going on a 30 mile ride towards the beach.

Have you any demand for Wood's reapers? I can obtain six @ £50 ea!

Yours very truly
R Davies

Rakaia
Feb 7th 1880

Dear Mr Sumpter,

The barley has been sold @ 3/5 Ch:Ch: Statn. I did not offer more than 3/4 fob* as you do not particularly care about it.

I fear that I shall not be able to get anything definite from Mr Winter before my return as his partner may not be back for another week or so; still, that need not hinder my returning almost immediately & with your kind assistance making a start at once.

I think I have got sufficient information to enable you to decide as to whether it will be advisable for me to join Mr W or start as G Sumpter & Co.

I hope to have the pleasure of telling you all about it on Wednesday. Meanwhile,

I remain
Yours very truly
R Davies

* fob is a trade term signifying the price offered "Free on Board", that is, for delivery on board a ship

Rakaia
Feb 25th 1880

Dear Mr Sumpter

I regret to state that Taylor is engaged by Mr Mann, I don't know in what capacity. I think it must be as storeman.

I saw Winter for a minute, I am to see him tomorrow. I shall ask Mr Mann if he can keep me going until Winter settles with his partner, I do hope that I shall get something to do as life here without plenty to do must be anything but pleasant.

I don't suppose Taylors engagement will hurt me, still, I wish he were employed somewhere else.

I will write fully tomorrow. Mr M says that Winter wants pushing as he is inclined to be dilatory.

With kind love to all at Oakleigh

I am
Yours truly
R Davies

Rakaia
Mar 2/80

Dear Mr Sumpter,

I have your favour of this date & regret to find that you gather from my letters that business prospects at Rakaia do not seem very bright, it was not my intention to give you that idea. Much as I regret leaving Oamaru I trust you will credit me for giving you an unbiased account of the place.

I have today had a long conversation with Mr Hardy (Manager for Orr & Co General Storekeepers & Successors to R McKerrow & Co) he said that he would start at Rakaia in preference to any township in Canterbury & advised me to join Winter as he is so well known & liked.

Hartnell the local butcher & baker a £10.000 man has just asked me as to when I intended starting Auctioneering as he would have about 1500 sheep to sell in two or 3 weeks. I told Mann of this & also that I might lose several sales if I waited 2 or 3 months for Winter, he replied "don't do anything in a hurry but wait & see how M & W get along".

Do you know Royse Stead & Co or P Cunningham & Co? I have had several farmers asking me if I am a buyer of grain, if I had an introduction to either of the above firms. I might send them samples & perhaps be able to make a little Comm: in that way.

I have not yet seen Mr Laurie as he has not returned from his brothers farm.

I hear that there is a lot to be done in Reid & Grays' drays etc, but McLean & Winter who are the Agents do not seem to push it.

Geo: Taylor must feel quite at home, whiskey drinking seems to be a recognized institution here, those that object to public houses have an unfailing supply at their own houses.

I hope to have a few hours tomorrow in reply to mine of y'day's date as I must get the balance of my clothes up if I am going to remain here

With kind regards to all at Oakleigh

I am
Yours very truly
Richard Davies

Rakaia
Mar 4th 1880

Dear Mr Sumpter,

In reply to your favor of this date I have to state that Mann McKerrow Hardy & a few others state that there is a good opening for a Comm: Agent here, as far as the township is concerned. I must state that I cannot see that there is any business to be done, however they must know best.

If I start I don't think it would be advisable to take out an Auctioneers license as I understand that a first one would have to be taken out in June. I have just told Mann that I must do something at once as I cannot live here 2 or 3 months doing nothing waiting for Winter, he replied wait another week as I think M & W will have to decide on something by that time, he does not seem to want me to start until Winter is free.

I don't know of any place that I could lease, perhaps I might be able to get a room that would do for an office in the meantime.

Mr Hardy tells me that the Springfield Coal Co want to open an agency here & that it was offered to him, he says that he could get it for me if I like to take it.

Mr Mann may be going to Mataura in a few days. I should so like you to see him as I do not like deciding without your approval.

I shall feel obliged if you will pay Mr Lemon on my a/c the £16 I mentioned to you.

I must try & put up with a flannel shirt & horrid paper collars until next week & by that time I sincerely hope something will be settled.

Please tell Emma Harriet & Blanche that I will write them tomorrow.

Yours very truly
Richd Davies

Richard then remarks to Emma:

I wish I could correspond like your papa. I fear that he cannot find my letters very explicit. I do hope that he credits me with saying the best I can of Rakaia, you must know darling that I wish to succeed so that I may call you my own as soon as possible.

Rakaia
Mar 8th 1880

Dear Mr Sumpter,

I had a long conversation with Mr Mann on Saturday evening, he now says that if Auctioneers licenses are not renewable until August that perhaps I had better get one as he knows of a sale of land & stock which will probably come off in a few weeks which he may be able to place in my hands. I will ascertain from Winter today as to when the New Year commences. I think that June is the time in Canterbury, if such is the case it would hardly do to get a license for so short a time, perhaps I could arrange with Winter to cry the sales during that time provided McLean had no objection.

McKerrow & Co have just bought M & W's store from the Bank, it seems that M & W are trustees & are also interested in an estate that cannot be realized until the crop is disposed of.

Mr Taylor returns to Oamaru in a day or two. Mr Mann tells me that he cannot do anything with him. Mr T may tell you that there is no opening here but I don't suppose you will attach much weight to what he says. I don't agree with him notwithstanding the gloomy tenor of some of my letters.

Yours very truly
R Davies

I have to say, if I were George, I would be thoroughly confused by these mixed messages from Richard!

Rakaia
Mar 11th 1880
George Sumpter Esq
Oamaru

Dear Mr Sumpter,

I have to confirm my letter of the 9th int: the last two days I have been driving round the district with Mr McKerrow & have seen the farm which will have to be sold after harvest, it contains about 250 acres, the stock may be withheld as the Cockatoo intends to keep it if the farm realizes enough to clear off his liabilities. The crop is stacked & will be in the market in 2 or 3 weeks provided a thrashing machine is to be obtained at once.

Mr Mann has given me to understand that I am to have this sale as it is not likely to be sold privately.

I think I had better write Medlicott to see if he will advance £200 against the mortgage of the Wesleyan Church, as I must have some credit here before I start.

Yours very truly,
R Davies

PS

Please send me per return a few tables etc of the Australian Mutual Provident Society, I don't know whether I can get any proposals but I mean to try, perhaps you can get me the appointment of agent for this district

To Emma, Richard says:

I have my doubts as to the future of this township still; I want to give it a time as I am so afraid your papa may think that the idea of living apart from you would make me speak more disparagingly of the place than I otherwise would do.

But George has his own troubles. Yet another fire has broken out in Thames street, and this time the properties are all George's. No wonder that George has started building new shops in Oamaru stone!

FIRE AT OAMARU.

[UNITED PRESS ASSOCIATION.]

OAMARU. 12th March.

A fire broke out in Thames-street this morning, and destroyed several wooden buildings, a boardinghouse, Roughton and Pocklington's wholesale boot manufacturers' premises, Feyer's furniture shop, and an unoccupied shop, all the property of George Sumpter. Roughton and Pocklington's, and Feyer's stocks are entirely destroyed. The greater part of the furniture of the boarding-house is burned, as also part of the furniture in the store adjoining, which was gutted. Total insurance—New Zealand, £1100; South British, £650; Liverpool, London, and Globe, £400.

Richard, meanwhile, is feeling (perhaps) a little more optimistic, telling Emma:

I am quite sure that I shall get in provided I can get a little capital to start with, without it I cannot do anything.

Rakaia
Mar 23/80
George Sumpter Esq
Oamaru

Dear Mr Sumpter

I hope my letter of y'day was sufficiently explicit re obtaining an advance on the deed. I want to obtain £200 — deposit the deed as security.

Mr Mann intends going south on Thursday.

I hope you will be able to meet him, he told me this evening that he does not want to push M & W as they have to settle with him for some sections at Methven, he also said that if they could carry on he would put all his business in my hands & discount bids for me & that he did not think I was losing anything by waiting a little longer.

I have heard of one or two more including Mr Mangham who have decided on leaving the local store.

Yours very truly
R Davies

A few days later, Richard writes Emma that

Your dear papa came thro' about 9 pm I only saw him for 2 minutes. … I think I will go to ChCh tomorrow & return the same evening as I want to see your papa very much. I am so sorry that he did not see Johnny Mann

And the next day:

Excuse my writing so often but I must tell you that I went to ChCh this morning as I wanted to see your papa. I had the pleasure of being in his company about 2 hours. Someone came & asked your papa to go with him, he replied you must excuse me as I have not seen Mr Davies for 3 or 4 months. He must have thought that I have been away all that time.

Rakaia
Apl 7/80
George Sumpter Esq

Dear Sir,

I hope I shall hear from you tomorrow as Mr Mann is not interested in the sheep which I have for sale on Friday. I don't want him to finance that if it can possibly be avoided.

I am now sending a long advt: to the North Otago Times at Mr Mann's request. I don't suppose anything will come of it as the vendor will want abt £8 per acre.

I think I can get a capital office with room attached for £1 per week, if you can manage the £200 I think I shall take it for 3 months as it is a capital site.

I may write you tomorrow as I am in rather a fix not having a bank a/c.

Yours very truly
R Davies

Please tell Emma that I shall not reply to her letter until after the sale on Friday.

Rakaia
Apl 12th 1880

Dear Mr Sumpter,

I have this evening sent an advt: to the Mail which will appear twice a week until date of sale.

The Otago Times has sent me an a/c for £5/12/6 for 6 insertions of the Tiverton Estate. This seems to me to be an exorbitant price. I expect Mr Dicken will grumble about it.

I don't think it will sell as the land is very poor, it adjoins yours on the other side of the Rakaia.

I shall have a sale of stock implements etc in about 3 weeks. Amount up to £1000. I hope to make £25 by it.

I have just dis^{d}: a bill @2 mons: per £20 @ 10% & 2½% Comm:.

Robert Darroch told me on Saturday that if he could not sell his farm privately I was to have the selling of it.

I hope you are doing your best to get me the £200 without delay.

I was chased by a constable today to serve on an inquest on a poor fellow who was killed on the railway a couple of days ago.

I trust that my dear friends at Oakleigh were not frightened on Saturday morning. [Two "tolerably heavy" earthquakes were felt]

11 p.m. I have £160 in my pocket just now which will go to the bank tomorrow to be paid out the following day.

Yours very truly
R Davies

INQUEST.—An inquest was held at the Rakaia Hotel on Monday, to inquire into the cause of death of the man who fell out of the express train on Saturday. From the evidence of Henry Giffins it appeared that deceased sat down on the platform of the railway carriage, directly over the buffer and couplings, where he had not been sitting above two minutes when some one called out "He's gone!" Charles Heaton, the guard of the train, said that he felt the train pass over some obstruction. He looked out and saw a man lying on the line. Had not seen the man before to the best of his knowledge. He did not even know that he had been a passenger in the train. Sergeant Carlyon, of the police force, stationed at Temuka, identified the body as that of James Clark, a tailor, living at Temuka, whither he had come from Invercargill. Deceased had told him that he formerly belonged to the 75th Regiment, of which he was staff-sergeant and tailor. He identified deceased by a bullet wound which he had in his left cheek and by his features. After hearing a good deal of evidence the jury returned a verdict of "Accidental death," with a rider to the effect that there is not sufficient protection for passengers on the platforms of the carriages.

Rakaia
Apl 14/80

Dear Mr Sumpter

I am sorry to put you to so much trouble re funds. I don't want any just now, still, I don't know the moment when £50 or £100 may be of service to me if you will be good enough to send me say 2 or 3 crossed cheques for £30 each I shall be obliged. I promise you that I shall not bank them unless I can make something by it.

I have postponed Tiverton sale for a fortnight as I have not been able to arrange with Matsons yet, it did not occur to me when I wrote out the advt: that they would wish their name inserted or I should have done so.

I should be particularly thankful if you would see him & say a good word for me also let me know when to meet him in his return, he is a fine fellow I have been given to understand.

Duncan Darroch told me last evening that my name is to appear in the advt: (if it goes in) in conjunction with the auctioneers.

Try & see Tiverton, the reserve is £8 for good land not shingle, £1600 cash would buy it, balance partly 5% & 8% interest. I thought of sending Jones an advt: but I don't see how I can do it after the local on Monday, it would look too much like gratitude.

Can you do anything with my leasehold section behind John McCombe's Reed St? I have paid £19 already & 6 mons: rent falls due today. Perhaps Collis would take it back!!

I have been asked to get the Agency of one of the Ch:Ch: building lots: as there are several here who would like to put cottages on their sections.

P & D Duncan of Ch:Ch: will allow co/d or their goods but they want my Bill @ 3 months.

H. MATSON AND CO. (in conjunction with R. Davies and Co., and Messrs R. M'Kerrow and Co.) have been favored with instructions from E. B. Dicken, Esq., who is leaving the district, to sell by public auction, at Messrs H. Matson and Co.'s Canterbury Wool Stores, Cashel street, Christchurch, on

THURSDAY, 29TH APRIL,

That well-known PROPERTY, called Tiverton, adjoining Messrs J. and D. M'Ilwraith, and situated on the Chertsey and Barr Hill Road, about two and a half miles from Mitcham Station, on the Rakaia and Ashburton Forks Railway.

The farm consists of 1045 acres of splendid land, viz.—

500 acres broken up very early
200 acres in stubble one year
300 acres wheat stubble
25 acres oat stubble
20 acres English grass

The property is ring fenced, and subdivided into four large and two small paddocks with good gorse fences. There is a good five-roomed house, 12-stalled stable, chaffhouse, 15,000-gallon tank, and other improvements.

The stock, implements, etc, will be sold on a future day.

This is an excellent opportunity for a highly profitable investment.

The books came duly to hand, rest assured that I shall do my best to fill them quickly.

I don't think I can tell Mann about the Comm: he owes you as he is such a queer stick.

I saw Harry Thompson this evening on his way to Napier.

If you should see Matson I hope you will let me know as to when he intends returning, it is most important that I should see him.

Yours sincerely
R Davies

Richard's opinion of Mann seems to have undergone a sea-change!

Rakaia
Apl 15th 1880

Dear Mr Sumpter,

I went to Ch:Ch this morning with D Darroch at his request & arranged with Matsons & Miles Hassel & Co re advt of the sale. Mann went up also, he hardly spoke to Darroch who wants to get clear of the old humbug as he calls him. I see that it will take me all my time to get along with him. I must do it for a time as it is to my interest to do so.

Darroch has a reserve of only £3/15/- per acre, it surely ought to sell at this figure. I wish you could dispose of one of the properties in the "Times" which I send you by this post. You will see another farm.

I hope you are keeping the mortgage before you, Lane & Co have hardly a month to pay the £600 & 6 mons: Int: viz £24.

Yours very truly
R Davies

To put all these costs in context, it's worth noting that in 1878 tradesmen earned about 12 shillings a day, labourers 8 or 9 shillings, male shop assistants about £2 10s a week (for 70 hours or more a week!), domestic servants £30-£36 a year plus board. House rents were £25-£50 a year; board and lodging for a single man £1 a week[7].

This could only have got worse by 1880, when the price of wool had slipped below a shilling a pound and there were said to be men in Oamaru willing to work for no more than food and lodgings.

But wheat was becoming the answer to wool's despair (the price of wool kept falling until it bottomed out at 8p in 1886), and here, surely, Richard was well-placed. The Canterbury Plains' involvement in wheat grew from 28,000 hectares in 1874 to more than 100,000 hectares ten years later[8].

But Richard is not so sanguine! On the same day, he is telling Emma:

I did feel nervous when I made my little speech, do you really think it would pay to get a licence now & another in June besides I fear that I should never make a good auctioneer. You must not pay much attention to the advts: they may come to nothing & do not be too sanguine wifie.

I went with Mr Darroch to Ch:Ch: today to arrange with an auctioneer about his place.

I wish Jones had not put in that local about me, respected citizen indeed. I suppose he wants an advt: I don't think he will get one just now.

When I say don't be too sanguine, you must not misunderstand me wifie, altho' you may be told that I am doing well, you must not credit that as it will be some time yet before I can say that, perhaps the end of the year unless I do better than I anticipate now, if I had my way you would be my wifie tomorrow but it cannot be helped; we must endure the delay.

So your papa told you that I seemed in good spirits, I am pleased to find that I can hide my feelings so well.

Rakaia
Apl 20th 1880

Dear Mr Sumpter,

You will see from the enclosed that I am mixing in good company at least as far as advertising is concerned.

Darroch's farm has only a reserve of £3/15/ per acre, it ought to sell. Mr Mann saw Mr Embling (Bank of NZ) today who made fun of McLean & W & asked about me. Mann now seems to think that it would not do for me to join Winter. I don't know what to think of it as I am not sure that I am cut out for an auctioneer.

Mr Bluett says that the Belmont Sale will take two days. I hope Mann will assist me as the sale cannot be all for cash. I must get an office as people do not all know where to look for me & it would be better for many other reasons.

I hope you will be able to send me some cheques in a day or two.

I am very much obliged to you for seeing Mr Matson, I saw him on his return journey.

People in ChCh want to know who the new firm are, if all the places were to sell.

I should so like to pay Oamaru a visit, but I fear the chances are very small indeed unless you can sell them down south.

Yours truly,
R Davies

I omitted to mention that Mann told Embling that I came here with introduction from you.

Two days later, he is telling Emma:

So you think I am going to make more than the price of the licence in two months, how do you arrive at it?

I hope I may but I do not quite see it just now besides do you think I should make a good auctioneer? I fear darling that I am not suited for it, I am too sensitive & cannot make myself agreeable to every one.

I hope you will not think that I am taking a morbid view of things.

I shall have to make a good many £5 before I consider that I have made a fair start. I cannot explain all I could tell you if I could see your sweet face, oh! that I could see it if only for an hour.

I expect I shall have to go to ChCh both on Thursday & Saturday next week & neither of the farms are likely to sell.

A few days after that, it's:

When is your papa coming up? He distinctly gave me to understand that he would be up this week, if he does not come I shall be very much annoyed & shall not fail to let him know it.

The following day, he writes to George:

Rakaia
Apl 29/80

Dear Mr Sumpter

Of course Tiverton did not sell, it may be sold privately.

I fear you cannot give me an offer for the barley I sent you or I should have heard ere this.

Did I tell you that there is not much demand for V D L parts. £4/10/- is the latest quotation.

Is there a disc: on the flour? Of course a Bill would be accepted.

Mann saw Craig today & mentioned my name, the latter spoke highly of Winter but did not decide anything.

The office etc that was offered me at £1 p wk could be purchased for £250, I am trying to get Mann to take it. Can you find a purchaser?

Yours very truly
R Davies

To Emma, on the same day, he says:

As I anticipated, Tiverton did not sell today, it may be sold privately but I am not sure yet.

If people ask you how I am getting on I think you may say that I am doing well. I have not done much yet but I have every hope of doing so.

But increasingly, people were turning away from farming.

Rakaia
May 3rd 1880

Dear Mr Sumpter,

I am sorry to find that you are likely to lose money by your shipments of barley. Tonight Stephenson & Co tried to place the samples I sent them but failed to succeed.

£3- was the best offer for D & R Darrochs' property, Mr Walton of Matson & Co told me that he expected to see the papers flooded with farms during the next two months as the Loan Companies will not be farmers any longer. This is not a living prospect & as you state I must be very cautious.

Belmont Sale realized about £1000. Mr Mann will take the bills & also the bank disct at 2½% which buyers will have to pay in lieu of cash. I wish I could have discounted the Bills as they are all good.

After all I think Mr Mann wants me to join Winter. I don't see how I can get out of it if he insists on it as I could not get on in opposition to him, at least, not for a year or two.

I have the Seafield Farm at Ashburton on the 5th. I don't for a moment expect that it will sell, still, I must hope that it may go off.

Yours truly
R Davies

Rakaia
May 6th 1880

Dear Mr Sumpter

I regret to state that there wasn't a bid for the farm at Seafield y'day, I don't know what things are coming to.

M & W will be in the Gazette this week or next at latest. Mr Mann seems rather downhearted just now, he has bought a lot of wheat @ 4/- fob & fears that he will not see his money returned to him, not to mention any profit.

The 14th will soon be here & if Lane & Co will not come to any decision re the mortgage I should like it placed in a lawyers hands.

Altho' the sale at Belmont grossed £1000 a lot of things were passed in & I must be thankful to get £20 by it.

I hear that a Mr Irving, who has a property adjoining the 1000 acres in which you are interested, expects to get your section at his own price, from what the Darrochs & Peter Drummond tell me I would advise you parting with it even at cost price. Mr Irving wants it because it would complete his block.

I don't know what to do about an office. I ought to have one if I am to do any good here.

I have now to charge Tiverton, Darrochs, Dannihy, & McDonald with a/cs for advts ranging from £15 @ £40. I don't suppose they will like it when they get their a/cs.

What about the flour? Is there any comm.: in it @ £10 will a bill @ 3 mons do?

Yours faithfully
R Davies

I wonder if your friend Mr C W Turner of ChCh would let me sell coal for him here on Comm: I see that he imports very largely.

Mournfully, he tells Emma:

There will not be much difficulty in keeping an account of what I make by auction sales in April & May, the first one was £6- & the one on Monday about £20. The land sales were not a success as farms cannot be sold just now. Not very encouraging is it wifie? Still I hope & pray for the best. I think you do the same.

Oh that I had come here 2 yrs ago when business was prosperous. I seem to have started at a bad time but I don't despair although it does seem cruel to try your patience so much.

Rakaia
May 11th 1880

Dear Mr Sumpter

As I shall have from £60 @ £70 to pay for advertising at the end of this month I hope you will have arranged with Lane before that time. I don't think I shall be able to get immediate payment from the advertisers.

Messrs Murray & Embling of the Bk of NZ were down here on Saturday looking over the different a/cs. I suppose they are satisfied with the place as they intend building a new bank.

I enclose advt: of another property, which, of course, will not sell.

I hear today that Bluett's cheques have been returned, he bought a horse at Belmont, fortunately his ½ comm.: comes to more than the price of the horse.

I think Mr Mann will be going south on Friday next.

Perhaps it would be advisable for me to wait until the new bank is built, the present one would make a capital office & dwelling.

If you are sufficiently intimate with Turner to advise him to open an agency here I hope you will do so, as I believe there is a good opening.

With kind regards to all
I am
Yours truly
R Davies

To Emma, he says:

If I had come here 2 years ago I should have made about £500 thro' McK & Co's sales alone, now farms are simply unsaleable, if all the farms I advertised had sold I should have made about £200.

I don't think £20 in 2 months is very encouraging.

I have to go to ChCh on Saturday. I don't expect to make anything by it, I regret to say.

The sale I had on the 3rd was on a/c of a Mr Cleland a nice gentlemanly fellow who was on the point of returning to Tasmania to get married. He has today written a long letter to his lady love stating that he is not in a position to marry & that he is compelled to set her free. So you see that we are not the only unfortunate ones if that is any consolation

Rakaia
May 26/80

Dear Mr Sumpter

As more than one kind of wheat is asked for in this district I write you to that effect. The samples are to hand but I cannot do anything with them until I get your prices. I hope you will not forget to state whether the prices cover comm: or not.

M & W have called a meeting of their creditors, I don't think it would do for me to write Wilkin & Co & NZ Insu Co until after the meeting.

I will send you Drummond's a/c against Buchanan by next post & trust you will Serve a Summons on him, I will go down if necessary.

Yours truly
R Davies

Rakaia
May 28th 1880

Dear Mr Sumpter

I have just received three samples marked Velvet, Red Chaff & Red Straw & hope to get prices for same by next post also for the pearl & Tuscan sent previously.

M & W have assigned their estate to the Bank Agent here, I went with Winter today to Methven to undertake the financial part of a small sale, it was hardly worth going for as my half Comm: only came to 30/- nett.

Mr Mann tells me that they will have to sell up two or three small farmers in a week or two.

I see from the N.O. Times that Maude has a number of sales thro' you, I wish I had them.

Yours truly,
R Davies

I may have to wire you tomorrow for prices as I promised one or two that I would be able to quote not later than Saturday

He complains to Emma:

I have telegraphed to your papa twice & written twice for prices of seed wheat, I suppose he has too much on his mind to be bothered with my little affair.

And so he's a little snippy when he writes to his future father-in-law:

Rakaia
May 29th 1880

Dear Mr Sumpter

Your letter of the 27th posted on the 28th too late for the express came to hand this evening. Mr McKerrow went to town this morning & I could have got him to bid for the Dunsandel property if your letter had reached me last night.

I fear your samples are too dear for me to do anything with them, the cheapest would be 4/6 deld here. Mr Mann intends going to Oamaru next week & will bring samples back, he says I shall have to give credit until next harvest, if such is the case I cannot expect to do much.

The Bank Agent has just displeased him in some way, I think he will go to ChCh on Monday simply to report him & will not rest until he gets him removed, he is a most vindictive old fellow

I see that the Evans' of Cloon Eavin have filed [for bankruptcy one assumes]. I hope you will not lose anything by them.

Your letter was open when it came to hand, it does not appear to have been closed at all

I believe that your Velvet & our pearl is the same wheat, the same as red chaff & Hunters white.

I hope you are doing your best to get John Reid in, & should not like to see either of the Radical candidates representing you.

Yours truly
R Davies

OAMARU, TUESDAY.
Mr Duncan Sutherland has retired from the Waitaki contest in favor of Mr J. Reid. Mr J. Jones announces himself as a candidate. There are now two Liberals in the field. Mr Reid has not given any indication of his political views, but is supposed to be a supporter of the present Government.

In Britain, "Radicals" had joined forces with the Whigs to form the Liberal Party some twenty years earlier. Here in New Zealand, a faction of the Liberal Party were becoming interested in forming a breakaway "Radical Party", though it never came to anything. However, certain politicians tended to be referred to as "Radical" in the press.

Political parties were very much in their infancy in New Zealand at this time. Only those with private means could afford to stand for Parliament, and these were all what we would call "independent". The main issue in the early days was "centrism" vs "provincialism".

It was not until 1891 that the first political party came to power (the Liberal Party), and another 18 years before any organized opposition party was established[9].

John Reid is the owner of Elderslie, referred to earlier. But we should be wary of making such simple distinctions as 'landowners' vs 'workers' — in 1881, the Oamaru Mail advised that Mr Reid had "received a requisition from 65 persons, principally labouring men, to stand for Waitaki." I'm not quite sure about the "Radical" nature of the other candidates — one was George Jones, editor of the Mail, and the other our local historian (and borough councillor) W.H.S. Roberts.

Rakaia
June 3rd 1880
George Sumpter Esq
Oamaru

Dear Sir,

I hope you have been able to get some money from Lane, I want to pay some £50 @ £60 for advertising in the course of the next week. [Richard appears to use @ as a "to"; perhaps this was an accounting use at the time.]

I enclose advt: of another sale which, I hope, will bring me about £5.

If M & W's creditors accept the deed of Assignment on the 15th inst: I fear W will start on his own a/c. If such is the case it will hurt me considerably, there may be a living for one, even in these bad times, but I am quite sure there is no room for two.

Your samples of wheat are much liked but I cannot get from 6@9 over current rates here

Yours truly
R Davies

Rakaia
June 7th 1880

Dear Mr Sumpter

I have your letter & samples but no cheque. I could get plenty of buyers for the seed @ 4/- to 4/3 but not at your price. Mr Mann says that he would not give 10/- for the land and strongly advises you not to touch it.

Buchanan, I take it on myself to accept his offer, in fact, I have authority to do as I like to secure the amount.

I have taken orders for about £100 in station stores for McK & Co's clients, they endorse the bill so I run no risk.

Yours truly,
R Davies

P.S. Robert must have taken your letter before it was finished as it does not bear your signature.

I hope you will be able to let me have my sister's Int before the mail leaves. [Later correspondence supports the idea that Richard's sister had deposited some money with George, presumably to support Richard's hopes.]

To Emma, he complains:

I shall not be able to get a licence until next month. I think I cleared about £8 by yesterday's sale.

Winter still seems to think that we are going to join when he gets clean of his partner but I don't think so

Rakaia
16.6.80

Dear Mr Sumpter

I have sent you another letter on business matters.

The Banker has just told me that Winter is only waiting the return of Mann to have a talk about going in with me.

I know that he can influence him if he chooses.

If Mann will not have left ere this comes to hand I hope you will tell him that it will be very unfair of him now to advise me to join Winter, of course, advise with him means insist & if I refuse get thrown overboard.

Winter was tipsy for 3 nights running a fortnight ago, he has now signed the pledge for 3 months, but there is no knowing what he may do at the end of that time.

I am confident there is not room for both & I don't know how to act.

I see that you have not yet commenced double entry. [A not-so-veiled insult there?!]

2pm I have now a 12 miles ride before

In haste

Yours truly
R Davies

I sent you two books y'day. Emma will know what they are.

But the next day he manages to be a little more positive for Emma:

I have just made out a balance sheet of my transactions from the 9th April the date of my first sale & it seems that the gross profits are at the rate of about £300 p auc: not very bad is it?

If Winter were to leave I should not mind, when he finds that I do not care about joining him I fear he will prevail upon Mann to assist him, then I should either have to join him or work in opposition which would not pay if he got all Mann's business.

But a week later, he's complaining again:

I cannot keep misunderstanding you, how can your papa admire my going down to ask his advise if I had made up my mind prior to going down? As a matter of fact I had not made up my mind as I had told both Winter & Mann that I could not decide definitely for a couple of days.

Rakaia
25.6.80

Dear Mr Sumpter

I enclose advt: of the sale I mentioned in my last, from all I can learn the farm is likely to sell. At the monthly sale we shall have a most miscellaneous collection of goods, the houses sections & furniture belong to McLean & Winters Estates.

I hope you will not forget to write to Mr Lowe of the A.M.P. Soc: re agency.

Per sample post I send you a sample of 700 bus [bushel, I assume] Danish Oats, if you are shipping to Melbourne perhaps you can make me an offer for them fob at Lyttelton.

Yours truly
R Davies

It's a difficult business, working with your future father-in-law! On July 7th, he writes to Emma:

Your papa told me that I had authorized him to advertise Darrochs' farm in the "Mail". I cannot see how this can be for the following reasons.

1st I should have sent the advt: direct as I did to the N.O. Times.

2nd I remember being very surprised at seeing the Advt: in the Mail.

3rd The Advt: did not appear until after the obnoxious local about me have appeared in the paper, if you refer to my letters you will find that I said "I could not send him (The Mail) an Advt: after what had occurred as it would look too much like gratitude" or words to that effect.

Rakaia
July 9th 1880
George Sumpter Esq
Oamaru

Dear Sir,

I fear I must have offended you in my last, I am always glad to have your advice, altho' I don't always act up to it.

I have not spoken to Winter re' both partners signing cheques & the more I think of it, the less I like the idea of it.

Harrison Bus Sale came off y'day, the Senior brother bought the farm @ £3 p acre & the stock realized about £560, we now fixed that the brothers have arranged to work together again & that they do not consider we should charge any comm.: on the sale of the farm. Winter says that we must not give in on any account as the sale was a bona fide one as far as we are concerned, such being the case the comm.: will be £80!

I don't know whether I told you that we intend having a monthly sale at Methven, the terminus of the Rakaia & Ashburton Forks Railway? This raily: has brought down 116,000 sacks of grain this season.

I see that George wants to see all the correspondence re H Houghton's appointment! [Henry Houghton was appointed chief Government Insurance Agent for Otago in June; there was some understandable questions about this, since he had been declared bankrupt the previous month. George Jones, editor of the Oamaru Mail, was the new member for Waitaki.]

Yours truly
R Davies

Oh dear, has he put his foot in it again? Two days later, he writes to Emma:

I am afraid your papa must be very much offended with what I said about both partners signing the same cheque as neither he nor you have mentioned it. Please let me know in your next

And a few days after that:

About the cheques, how can I propose to another what I would not have if it was proposed to me? Ronayne & Cotterill [Stationers & Fancy Goods Importers] must stand almost alone I think.

Rakaia
July 12th 1880
George Sumpter Esq
Oamaru

Dear Sir

Please let me know whether the mortgage on Aitken's property is for 2 or 3 years also dates on which Int. is payable.

I enclose copy of circulars we are now sending out, if the sales pay Expenses for the first few months I shall be very thankful.

I hope you have written to Mr Lowe for the Agency of the Australian Mutual P Soc as we intend getting some a/c forms printed & I want to insert the A.M.P.S.

Yours truly
R Davies

Notice the "we"! After all his unflattering comments, it seems he is now in partnership with Winters! He tells Emma mournfully:

DAVIES & WINTER.
AUCTIONEERS,
AND
COMMISSION AGENTS.

[July 14th]

I fear that we shall not make more than £30 after all on Harrisons sale, as the sale did not come up to their expectations. They have decided to work the farm together again, such being the case it will be better to forego the profit on the land rather than be called a hard firm just at the start – is it not annoying?

[July 15th]

I see by the paper that Mr Evans has started in Oamaru, I wish I could say that we had enough to do, I fear that things will not improve until next harvest. However, if we can average £250 p ann: each from now to Xmas I shall ask you to join me about that time. I said that I averaged £300 before I joined Winter, now we shall have to make double that to get me the same amount.

[July 22nd]

I don't think Johnnie Mann has frightened us about Harrisons Sale, we have done nothing in the matter yet, but I certainly think it would not be wise too [sic] charge the full comm.: as the farm is still in the hands of the two brothers, now if you were hear [sic] we could argue the matter pro and con.

We intend holding a weekly sale shortly & selling potatoes onions chaff chick wheat oats & I hope it will answer.

Rakaia
July 30th 1880
George Sumpter Esq

Dear Sir,

I have yours of the 29th int: & regret to find that 9/10 is the nett price as I thought that my letter of the 22nd inst was quite clear on this point, I also stated that the 100 tons had nothing to do with the order for a truck p month. When I got your telegram today I was afraid that the affair would fall thro' as the order was for Meeks flour, however, I have arranged with Hartnell to take 50 tons Andersons flour immediate delivery @ 9/10/ cash or equal & shall try to get a comm: out of it after a bit.

I hope to dispose of the remaining 50 tons tomorrow @ 10/-/- to be delivered in equal lots up to Dec: this would leave us £25/-/- as you have 100 tons Andersons flour under offer @ 9/10/-

Mann told me in the presence of Hartnell that he would not have Andersons flour at any price! H says it must be guaranteed as first class, the other brands he will not look at, I may state that he is one of the safest marks on the Rakaia. I will buy & get Hardy to take 2 trucks from Forrest, whoever he may be.

I don't think I am to blame for the comm: lost on the 50 Tons already sold.

Yours truly
R Davies

Rakaia
Nov 12th 1880
George Sumpter Esq
Oamaru

Dear Sir,

If you have any cheap feed oats please forward sample as we have had one or two enquiries for small lots.

I shall be glad to have the Deed of the £300 loan so that I may be able to send home the Bank receipt for same.

I hear that McKerrow & Co & another firm have a shipload of cornsacks coming to their order.

I hope that McCombe will soon take over the Section in Reed St:

Yours truly
R Davies

Lieutenant-Colonel George Sumpter

Richard the pining lover

We take up the story between our lovers some seven months after we last saw their correspondence and soon after Richard's move to Rakaia. As indication of their new intimacy, perhaps, Richard has now taken to calling Emma "Nannie", a name sometimes used by her siblings – perhaps it derives from the care she gave them, as eldest daughter. Given that her mother had given birth to her last child only a few months ago, she must have been almost a second mother to the younger children.

Richard's up-&-down nature, his touchiness (what he himself calls his "sensitivity"), and his jealousy, are all on display in these letters. But we should bear in mind that his financial stress is great, the pair have now been engaged for at least a year and their future is uncertain. He can be forgiven, perhaps, for his frets!

The openness with which he expresses his feelings is also in stark contrast to the image most of us have of our stoic, practical-minded forebears. It certainly surprised me!

Rakaia
Feb 17th 1880

My darling Nannie

I have had a 30 mile drive today with a Dr McKenzie who I think is a candidate for the appointment advertised. I hope he will come here as he appears to be a nice gentlemanly man.

Mary did not worry me at all so please do not think any more about it.

I did not see Miss Gleeson on Saturday, as you say they have made enough fuss about her leaving. The young fellow from Dunedin is very different to Pearson, he intends coming to teach at the Sunday School.

Please give my kind love to your Mama, I wish her very many happy returns of the day and hope she will have less anxiety with any future sons in law than she has had with me.

So you have got new blinds, what fun, you must be getting quite proud.

I have just written to your papa & left out the last part, if it does not do you must take some of the blame. [Unfortunately we don't have that letter]

Goodbye wifie, I do hope it will be right this time
With fondest love
I am Yours fondly
Dick

I am tired & sleepy

Rakaia
Feb 26 1880

My very own darling,

What a great cry-baby you must have thought me on Tuesday evening saying good-bye, crying like a small school girl while you were as firm as a rock. I could not help it wifie so please do not think any the less of me.

I feel very downhearted but perhaps that will go off if I can arrange with Winter.

It will be your turn to go to church on Sunday evening, try & think of me when you are walking home whoever you may have with you.

Rest assured darling that I shall do my very best to get along here.

I cannot help feeling ashamed at having to leave you in Oamaru unable to give any enquiring friends a satisfactory account of me

God bless you little darling.
Kindest love to all
I am Yours until you get tired of me
Dick Davies

Rakaia
Mar 1st 1880

My darling little Em

I used to consider a cool Sunday in Oamaru rather depressing but I shall never think so after yesterday. You will, I hope, have written me ere this reaches you in reply to my scrawl a few days ago.

Oh Nannie darling it seems an age since I left you, I do hope I may be able to offer you a home very soon.

Don't forget to write me & tell me everything
With fondest love
I am Your devoted
Dick Davies

Rakaia
Mar 5/80

My own darling Em,

Thank you very much for your two nice letters, I am glad to find that you did not think me a baby on Tuesday evening & that you do miss me a little bit.

I am very pleased to find that you looked "just right" (as Harriet said) on Sunday evening altho' you were nearly crying aloud. I know that the tears came into my eyes when I read your letters.

I should like to say a few words to A Bristed, I told your papa about him, he said that he had been cautioned before.

On Wednesday evening I went & sat down on some tussocks for a long time thinking of my darling & also how selfish my love has been, if all goes well darling I will try & make your future life happier than the last two years have been for you.

Please do not tell me again that you are the cause of my banishment as such is not the case.

Whatever I said I would do with birthday cards does not apply when they come from Oakleigh, thank you very much for yours.

If I am not to send kind love to your sisters, what can I send that does not belong to you?

I wish I could correspond like your papa. I fear that he cannot find my letters very explicit. I do hope that he credits me with saying the best I can of Rakaia, you must know darling that I wish to succeed so that I may call you my own as soon as possible.

Thank you very much for promising to keep a kind of diary, it is just what I should have asked of you if I had not already got more then I desire.

God bless my little wifie
Such is the plagues of
Dick Davies

I wonder if you were unkind enough last Sunday to keep A Bristed from walking with you next Sunday!

This is not the last we hear of poor A. Bristed! He and Richard have quite the falling out. One wonders what ungentlemanly behaviour Mr Bristed was guilty of! The following letter suggests it may have been nothing more than the crime of walking her home.

Rakaia
Mar 12/80

My own darling Em,

Thank you very much for posting your letter in time to reach me on Wednesday evening, I want you to write just as you feel & not to think of my crying over your letters, I think a good cry now & again does me good.

Last Sunday I went to church twice; as it was blowing a "nor-wester" in the afternoon Mr McKerrow & I went & reclined on some corn sacks in the store from 2 to 6 pm, it was such a long afternoon. Tell me what to do on Sunday evening after church. I cannot sit in the public sitting room of the hotel & 8 o'clock is a little too early for bed. If I was going to be an old bachelor I should do my best to get a home of my own here, so you may imagine how much more I long for one when I think of the dear little woman who has promised to share my lot.

What impudence of Geo Ferens to walk even part of the way home with you. I expect he will make a point of doing it now. Ah well I suppose it is part of my punishment.

I have my doubts as to the future of this township still; I want to give it a time as I am so afraid your papa may think that the idea of living apart from you would make me speak more disparagingly of the place than I otherwise would do.

There is such excitement here this afternoon; the Bank Agent has just received a piano & a number of the residents are looking on seeing it unpacked, I hear that he is a good hand at hair cutting I must ask him to trim my gray locks shortly.

Please tell Harriet that I will reply to her kind letter next week

With best love to all,
I am, dearest Nannie
Your own
Poor Dick

Rakaia
22/3/80

My own Nannie

I cannot resist the temptation of replying to your letter by return mail, I am so glad to find that I misunderstood you, don't say that you cannot write nice letters because if it were not for them I should collapse entirely; you must not think that your letters weary me if they were a thousand times as long I should never get tired of them so you cannot offer that excuse again. I do not consider that I have got you yet as you are not my own dear wifie, if you were here then this would be paradise for me.

I am quite sure that I shall get on provided I can get a little capital to start with, without it I cannot do anything.

Please thank your dear Mama for the kind consideration, if Mary had written me on black edged paper I should have been terribly frightened.

Mr Elton preached such a nice sermon last night, I felt quite cheered by it.

Please thank dear Mary for her letter I will reply in due course.

You want to see my dear face, you would not call it that if you could see the bristles on my chin.

I hope you will enjoy the Easter holidays better than I shall

Goodbye wifie, write me more about yourself

Your own
Dick

PS

Yesterday afternoon Mr Mann's little girl played hymn 341, I could not help it but the tears ran down my cheeks like rain. Was it not foolish of me?

I can't say which hymn Richard is referring to, since there are several different numbering systems, but this one did seem as if it might have spoken to Richard, in his contrition at his jealousy:

O JESUS, let thy dying cry
Pierce to the bottom of my heart,
Its evils cure, its wants supply,
And bid my unbelief depart.

Slay the dire root and seed of sin;
Prepare for thee the holiest place;
Then, O essential Love, come in!
And fill thy house with endless praise.

Let me, according to thy word,
A tender, contrite heart receive,
Which grieves at having grieved its Lord,
And never can itself forgive;

A heart thy joys and griefs to feel,
A heart that cannot faithless prove,
A heart where Christ alone may dwell,
All praise, all meekness, and all love.

Rakaia
Mar 26/80

My own dear Nannie

I am very much obliged for the photo, it is better than any of the previous ones, still, it is not half as handsome as my darling. I went to church this morning & dozed in an armchair all the afternoon. I am so glad Nannie wifie that you did not allow Mr Bull to stop you on Sunday. I drove thro' Leeston district y'day (abt: 15 miles away) what will you say when I tell you that it is far prettier than the Oamaru district. Splendid plantations & orchards & smiling homesteads as the novelists say.

Reid & Gray's agent was here while I was at Leeston. I hope to get their agency which is of some value.

I did not know that Dr T: was married.

Your dear papa came thro' about 9 pm I only saw him for 2 minutes. I have to thank someone for the fruit & Lottie for her letter

I think I will go to ChCh tomorrow & return the same evening as I want to see your papa very much.

I am so sorry that he did not see Johnny Mann

In haste as I have to be up at 6am

I am, my own wifie
Yours devotedly
Dick Davies

PS

Please tell your dear Mama that I am so sorry to find that she is unwell. I do hope that she will soon regain her usual health

I will write Lottie & Mary next week.

Rakaia
Mar 27/80

My darling Nannie

Excuse my writing so often but I must tell you that I went to ChCh this morning as I wanted to see your papa. I had the pleasure of being in his company about 2 hours. Someone came & asked your papa to go with him, he replied you must excuse me as I have not seen Mr Davies for 3 or 4 months. He must have thought that I have been away all that time.

Mr Bull came & shook hands with your papa. He simply said how do you do to me & asked me how I liked Rakaia. I suppose he meant to pay me out for what you did to him.

Of course I saw lots of the Oamaru people.

As the 31st is not a holiday how will the bank clerks manage to get to your picnic? Ah! that I could be there.

I am glad you do not care to be introduced to Atkins, am I not selfish?

I hope I shall have a long letter from you on Wednesday & also to hear that your dear Mama is quite well again.

I do miss you so much wifie if I could only asked [sic] you to come to me now then I think my troubles would be over.

In haste,
With fondest love
I am
Yours devotedly
Dick

Whether George's confusion was forgetfulness, a sign that George himself was frequently on the move, or due to Richard avoiding George on his visits to Oamaru, we can only speculate.

Rakaia
Apl 1st 1880

My darling Em

What a dear little girl you are to write me such a long & interesting letter. Your papa must have been hurt at my not having met the train, on his return. I don't care about asking any favour from the hotel people or I would have been at the statn.

He asked McKerrow as to when I intended paying Oamaru a visit. I wish he had asked me that question. As your birthday will have passed before you receive another letter from me, I must not wish you many happy returns of the day or rather hope that your next birthday will be spent in my company, rest assured wifie that I will do my very best to call you mine before the next one comes round. Bother Mr Bull, who cares for him?

I am indeed sorry to hear that Mr West visits Oakleigh so often. Harriet must be giving him some encouragement, notwithstanding what she told me about him. I do hope that nothing comes of it as he is not half good enough for her, it is quite enough for one to have made a mistake without having another in the same family doing the same.

We had a harvest thanksgiving service today also a tea fight & bazaar. I went to the latter. Mr Winter who was auctioneer, sold me a babys frock without my permission, McKerrow had to take a lot of dolls etc. They are now having a dance at the town hall to wind up, of course I am not going there.

I wish I had some news here to interest you. You have not told me whether your papa shows you all the letters I write him. [Perhaps this explains why we have so many letters from Richard to George — George passed them on to Emma, and never bothered to reclaim them!]

I am very glad to find that your dear mama is better.

With fondest love
From
Yours lovingly,
Dick

Rakaia
Apl 15/80

My own darling Nannie,

I only wish you were here to bother me, as you say. I think I could stand a deal of it. I wonder if you do miss me as much as I miss you, you have all your family to cheer you & here I am quite alone.

I don't suppose I shall see much of Mrs Maclean who is the lady I mentioned in my last. I don't know Mrs Elton yet.

I did feel nervous when I made my little speech, do you really think it would pay to get a licence now & another in June besides I fear that I should never make a good auctioneer. You must not pay much attention to the advts: they may come to nothing & do not be too sanguine wifie.

I went with Mr Darroch to Ch:Ch: today to arrange with an auctioneer about his place.

Oh! that I could have been with you on Saturday my own darling, did you wish for my company? You have not told me who escorted you home on Sunday evening. [Presumably some escorts are, then, acceptable?]

I wish Jones had not put in that local about me, respected citizen indeed. I suppose he wants an advt: I don't think he will get one just now.

When I say don't be too sanguine, you must not misunderstand me wifie, altho' you may be told that I am doing well, you must not credit that as it will be some time yet before I can say that, perhaps the end of the year unless I do better than I anticipate now, if I had my way you would be my wifie tomorrow but it cannot be helped; we must endure the delay.

So your papa told you that I seemed in good spirits, I am pleased to find that I can hide my feelings so well.

I want you to do me a favour next week & that is to address me the same as I did your last letter, if I am asking too much please tell me so & I will try not to mind.

Now I suppose I must write Harriet & Mary.

With fondest love my own wifie
I am
Yours lovingly
Dick

I won't tell you what I was thinking about as I passed a quiet family Hotel in ChCh today.

Rakaia
Apl 22/80

My darling Nannie

I did not know I was asking anything very dreadful or I should not have asked it, never mind wifie.

I suppose I may call you what I like.

So you think I am going to make more than the price of the licence in two months, how do you arrive at it?

I hope I may but I do not quite see it just now besides do you think I should make a good auctioneer? I fear darling that I am not suited for it, I am too sensitive & cannot make myself agreeable to every one.

I hope you will not think that I am taking a morbid view of things.

I shall have to make a good many £5 before I consider that I have made a fair start. I cannot explain all I could tell you if I could see your sweet face, oh! that I could see it if only for an hour.

Bother A Bristed & Atkins I say, don't you trouble yourself about them please.

McKerrow & I went to the Caradices. I had breakfast at the same table the next morning!

You need not address c/o McK & Co any more. Rakaia Canterbury is sufficient.

I wrote Mrs Filleul a short time ago, enveloped is an extract from her letter, is it not kind of her?

I have not heard from Rhodes for a very long time.

We do not sing a hymn at the beginning of the service.

I took Mrs McLean's class at the school last Sunday as she was in Ch.Ch. The class consisted of a dozen girls from 8 to 12 years of age. Sunday is such a terribly long day here, the time hangs so heavily on my hands, the past 8 weeks seem to be the longest I have ever known, when am I to pay Oakleigh a visit?

I expect I shall have to go to ChCh both on Thursday & Saturday next week & neither of the farms are likely to sell.

I am not surprised to find that Constance does not like Wellington, JGH is not there.

I see that there has been a picnic at Waianakarua, were you there?

Waianakarua appears to have been a popular picnicking spot for special occasions, although some considerable distance from Oamaru. Sometimes a special "Excursion Train" might be put on— it took an hour and forty minutes, with stops at Maheno and Herbert.

Rakaia
Apl 28th 1880

My darling Nannie

I have to reply to two of your letters. I was agreeably surprised to find a letter from you at the post office last Friday altho' you say that you do not know whether I shall care to get it.

I think I know the Dr Davies who Mr Martin refers to, if it is the one I mean he has left ChCh for home on account of ill health & from the description I got it must be an old friend of mine in South Wales. You tell Mrs Martin that the photograph flatters the original.

Mr Pascoe who preached here on Sunday week is both short & fair.

When is your papa coming up? He distinctly gave me to understand that he would be up this week, if he does not come I shall be very much annoyed & shall not fail to let him know it.

I do feel very lonely as you say & if you do not come soon I shall have to take you away by force, of course you will come if you care for me.

I miss Mr & Mrs Elton very much, Mr Chambers seems to be a good sort of fellow I don't know much about his wife yet.

I have just seen the doctors wife she looks almost as nice as my wifie or I should say she comes next to my wifie in Rakaia.

Lottie & Mary must be glad to get home again. There is no place like Oakleigh that I know of.

I enclose a few seeds of the American honeysuckle also a flower off it for Blanche.

With fondest love
My darling wifie
I am Yours lovingly
Dick

Rakaia
Apl 29th 1880

My darling Em

As I anticipated, Tiverton did not sell today, it may be sold privately but I am not sure yet.

If people ask you how I am getting on I think you may say that I am doing well. I have not done much yet but I have every hope of doing so.

Who are Mr & Mrs Derrett? I don't think I have ever heard of them before.

I rather liked the girls class at the school. I much prefer them to boys.

I was at the parsonage last evening (your evening). Mrs Elton wanted me to sing the Men of the Harlech. On the way however Mrs McLean, who will not be able to play the harmonium for a time, said I wish I could get someone to play as Mrs Elton is not strong enough to do so. I thought of one dear little woman that could do it if I were only able to bring her here.

Mrs Forrester is quite correct, this place is very bleak & cold in the winter, even now the nights are very cold.

You won't dance very often with the same one at these dances that the gentlemen are getting up will you wifie?

I don't think I paid sufficient attention to the Caradices to be able to tell you which I admired most.

I wish I had your dear cloth jacket here now with your dear self inside.

I saw two of the Misses Cole in ChCh today. I did not speak to them. The only two ladies that I have had any conversation with since I left are Mrs Elton & Mrs McLean, so you will see that you are a deal better off than I am.

How can I thank you enough for sending me such nice long letters?

I must now write a few lines to your papa & then bed

Fondest love pet
From your good for nothing
Dick

Rakaia
May 6th 1880

My own darling

Where did you get that beautiful piece of poetry you sent me?

There will not be much difficulty in keeping an account of what I make by auction sales in April & May, the first one was £6- & the one on Monday about £20. The land sales were not a success as farms cannot be sold just now. Not very encouraging is it wifie? Still I hope & pray for the best. I think you do the same.

I did not sing at Mrs Elton's, I don't care about visiting now & shall not go there nor to the Beach oftener than I can help.

You did not say you would be going to the dances, still, you will go, there is no reason why you should not enjoy yourself altho' I am not there to share it with you.

You say that you have made fifty one, please tell me what they are, perhaps conquests. I know you could if you liked.

I remember meeting Mr French I don't think I am much afraid of him altho' I am not so sure about Mr Heaton as you rather like him.

I had a letter from Jack today he seems to like Gippsland [a rural area east of Melbourne] but his Welsh wife is very unwell, he has had to send her to Melbourne, bush life does not suit her & she is homesick. I would not have a wife like that!!

Oh that I had come here 2 yrs ago when business was prosperous. I seem to have started at a bad time but I don't despair although it does seem cruel to try your patience so much.

Goodbye wifie; try & think the best of me at dances & every where else

With fondest love
Believe me
Yours lovingly
Dick

Rakaia
May 13th 1880

My darling Nannie

My letters seem to be bright & dull alternately, this week it must be a dull one, your papa's last letter is not very hopeful.

If I had come here 2 years ago I should have made about £500 thro' McK & Co's sales alone, now farms are simply unsaleable, if all the farms I advertised had sold I should have made about £200.

I don't think £20 in 2 months is very encouraging.

I am not a bit afraid of what my dear wife would be like, oh! that I could take you at once darling.

So that young monkey Bristed has commenced again, I am so glad that you walked away from them. It does annoy me to find that such fellows as Fercus walk with you although I am very much obliged to you for letting me know of it.

It is just possible that I may be asked to become Superintendent of the Sunday School, I don't want to do so until I know that I shall get along well here, please try & not let people see that you are down in the dumps wifie.

You will be my very own as soon as I can manage it, that is provided you do not get tired of waiting & meet some one ever so much nicer at the dances that will be coming on shortly.

I will let you know when I take cold. I have not taken one yet.

I have to go to ChCh on Saturday. I don't expect to make anything by it, I regret to say.

I received a letter from my married sister by last mail. She states "we have not yet received Miss Sumpter's photo we should like to very much". I suppose it had not reached Wales when she wrote on the 22nd March.

It is pouring rain just now. I can see that this is a bleak plain in the winter.

With fondest love my very own Nannie
I am
Yours devotedly
Dick

The sale I had on the 3rd was on a/c of a Mr Cleland a nice gentlemanly fellow who was on the point of returning to Tasmania to get married. He has today written a long letter to his lady love stating that he is not in a position to marry & that he is compelled to set her free. So you see that we are not the only unfortunate ones if that is any consolation

Rakaia
May 28

My darling Nannie

I only got your letter this evening. My handkerchief was going at a good rate although I could hardly see your house owing to the smoke.

Mr Mann paid me a great compliment, he said "I am glad you have come back as I have missed you very much" fancy Johnnie saying that.

No Signs of the new Bank yet darling.

I thought I had replied to Mary & George when I was down.

Tell Lottie that I did not call on her friend, I could not do so after what she said in the avenue on Sunday evening.

I regret exceedingly now that I went visiting on Sunday when you were so much against it, it must have pained you very much & it was very cruel of me, can you forgive me darling & think as much of me as you did before that unfortunate afternoon?

Please tell your dear Mama that I could not speak when she wished me good-bye. I hope she will not put it down to my rudeness. I feel all the better for the visit altho' I am suffering the pain of parting over again.

So you & Harriet have eaten my Indian corn, I will punish you when you are my wifie & Harriet in my letter next week.

I have telegraphed to your papa twice & written twice for prices of seed wheat, I suppose he has too much on his mind to be bothered with my little affair.

In haste darling as I am both tired & sleepy

I am
Yours for ever
Dick

Oh! that I could rest my weary head on your shoulder just now

Dick

Rakaia
June 10/80

My darling Em,

My sister's letter came duly to hand, she says you have such an amiable face etc etc.

I spent this evening at the parsonage. Mr & Mrs McLean & Pearson was there, Mr McL & Mann seem to have made it up again, the latter will be in Oamaru tomorrow.

Poor Dr Garland, I feel very sorry for him. Oamaru seems to be getting quite notorious for accidents etc.

I expect I shall now have to take Mrs McLean's class for 3 months, how inconsiderate ladies are, this is not the first time that I have been inconvenienced by them. Am I not selfish?

I saw Mr & Mrs Burnett in Christchurch last week, they asked me to go to lunch with them but I hadn't time.

I shall not be able to get a licence until next month. I think I cleared about £8 by yesterday's sale.

Winter still seems to think that we are going to join when he gets clean of his partner but I don't think so.

On Saturday evening, shortly after five o'clock, the people of this town received one of the severest shocks that they have ever suffered since its settlement. Dr. Garland had taken a number of his friends for a drive to Papakaio in his waggonette, in which there were four horses. In the vehicle, in addition to the doctor, were Mrs. Garland, Mrs. Lintott, Miss Fenwick, Mr. James Hassell, jun., and Mr. Medlicott. Everything went well until they arrived near Mr. John Hardy's residence, on the return journey. At this spot the horses were pulled up, so that Miss Wait might get into the vehicle. In pulling up, the bolt connecting the main tree with the off-leader's tree broke. The off-leader's tree becoming out of gear, fell against the animal's heels, and he became unmanageable, and took possession of the whole concern. During the struggle, the vehicle had been dragged to the kerbing, where it capsized, and the occupants were thrown out with great force. Mrs. Garland received such severe injury that, after lingering in great pain till about 10 o'clock this morning, she expired. Nor did Dr. Garland and Mr. Medlicott escape. The doctor was stunned by the force of the fall, whilst Mr. Medlicott received some ugly bruises. But fortunately both gentlemen have almost entirely recovered from their personal injuries. Mrs. Lintott was less fortunate, for that lady is suffering from a broken arm. Of the party, Miss Fenwick and Mr. Hassell, jun., only escaped with nothing more than the shock to their system produced by the fall and the sad occurrence. Mrs. Garland was taken into Mr. Hardy's residence, where she of course received every attention at the hands of Mrs. Hardy, the Misses Hardy, and the patient's husband, Drs. Wait, de Lautour, Fleming, and Duncan. The death of Mrs. Garland has created profound sympathy for her relatives and sorrow for her loss throughout the community.

You will think this letter rather a short one but they are just going to put out the lights & I have no more ink.

I hope your papa & Winnie are quite well again. I am glad that the [unreadable] did not trouble you on Sunday night. I won't say anything about that Sunday so please try & forget it wifie!

Goodbye darling mine
With fondest love & kisses
I am
Your good for nothing
Dick

Rakaia
17.6.80

My own darling Em

Bless you my darling for writing such long & interesting letters.

I am sorry you did not see Mr Mann as he is such a character.

Where were your thoughts last Sunday as you could not attend to your class? Perhaps in Wellington!!

I hope you have received the books, your book made the two first Sundays after my return appear shorter than usual, it is a very good book altho' you did not seem to care about it.

Who is the Miss Alice that you met at the Robinsons? Miss James (H F Millers governess) is staying here with some friends for a day or two.

Nannie darling, I wish you would not sit up so late, it cannot be good for you to sit up till one o'clock, if I had you here I should not allow it. Do you still live on next to nothing or are you trying to oblige me by eating a little meat each day?

I have no right yet to speak to you in this way, but I cannot keep feeling that I have a little.

Waitaki is now the most Radical constituency in N.Z. it does not say much for the intelligence of the people when they put such a man as Jones at the head of the poll. This is another reason why I should make haste & take you away.

I have just made out a balance sheet of my transactions from the 9th April the date of my first sale & it seems that the gross profits are at the rate of about £300 p auc: not very bad is it?

If Winter were to leave I should not mind, when he finds that I do not care about joining him I fear he will prevail upon Mann to assist him, then I should either have to join him or work in opposition which would not pay if he got all Mann's business.

Harriet is going to send me some more books, if you have any I shall be glad to have them.

I have no news here to interest you so my letter must be shorter than yours

With fondest love
Believe me
Yours devotedly
Dick

[first pages missing, but placed here because of the reference to Miss James]

I have seen Mr Mann for a few minutes & told him about Mr Winter. I could only get evasive answers from him, such as "you know best what to do" I hope your papa will write me soon & give me his advice on the matter.

Much to my regret I have an invitation to go & have tea tomorrow evening at Mr Makeig's house where Miss James is staying, isn't it an awful bore?

Good bye wifie!!
Dick

Rakaia
June 24th

My own darling Nannie

I am glad to find that the sight of me has done you good. I know that my visits to Oamaru make my life ever so much brighter.

I cannot keep misunderstanding you, how can your papa admire my going down to ask his advise [sic] if I had made up my mind prior to going down? As a matter of fact I had not made up my mind as I had told both Winter & Mann that I could not decide definitely for a couple of days.

So your papa has been fretting for fear that he had helped to put me in the way of temptation, what ever does it mean? I hope he has not such a bad opinion of me, as to think that I should be led into dissipation. I should not be fit to live if I were to give way in that manner when I have the hope of calling you my dear wife at no very distant date. I hope you will let me know what he did mean in your next letter.

Mr James Lees was standing on the platform of the carriage with me when I waved my h'chief, of course, I had to tell him why I did it.

I got half thro' Hurlock Chase [a book] before I reached Ashburton & had to give it up as it nearly made me cry.

Tell your Mama that Winter & I will soon part if things do not go on smoothly, I have not much fear about it.

It rained here on Monday only.

Burn your letters indeed, no thank you [Emma's feelings here perhaps explain why we have no letters from her; only those to her.]

Goodbye my own
Fondest love
From Dick

Rakaia
July 1 1880

My darling Nannie,

I only got your letter this morning as there was a break down with the north train y'day. You should see Winter now, he has a new suit of clothes & looks very gentlemanly, he puts me quite in the shade.

Mary is very severe, I cannot afford to keep a diary much less send a telegram like our West Coast friend.

I felt very down hearted coming up in the train that coupled with a pathetic part in Hurlock Chase set my tears flowing.

You did not tell me how you enjoyed the dances, who was the nicest partner?

So you still wish to be with me, well darling I sincerely hope you will have your wish before the end of the year provided business improves a little & you can exist with bread & cheese & kisses & a small cottage.

I hear that Maclean is going to start opposition however we have not much fear of his doing much harm. I am only afraid that business is going to be worse instead of better during this winter & as we have but very little capital we have not much chance of making a lot of money, you know money makes money & without it it is terrible up hill work.

So I am not to say anything more about my dissipation, alright I will pay you out by & bye.

I have sent the books back addressed to your papa.

Harriet's photo is very good, as she wants the proofs back I have to write her by return so don't be very jealous wifie, I know you have a jealous disposition like myself.

I often think of your eating cold meat in preference to the roast fowls on Sunday week, what a poor man's wife you will make!

Goodby wifie mine
With ardent love
I am
Your poor love
Dick

Rakaia
July 7th 1880

My darling Nannie

As I shall have a long day tomorrow I think it will be safer to write tonight.

I count the days also. I know I should be very much disappointed if my letter did not come to hand regularly on Wednesdays.

I cannot see any improvement in my writing, it will always be like myself not much account.

What did your papa say about my spelling "bachelorizing with a T? I don't want you to get fond of tobacco scent, then perhaps you will be able to break me of the habit!!

You are easily satisfied if the fare I promised you will suffice, I am trying to make it better than that.

Our sale y'day was not very good, no one seems to have any money here, at least for the present.

It rained here on Saturday Sunday & Monday, no school on Sunday nor Service in the evening, it is now freezing hail we have ice ½ an inch thick on the roads & cold winds from the snowy mountains sweeping over the plains. Are you frightened?

We are going to be four in the house. Winter Pearson "Jim" & yours devotedly, they wanted to come & I could not refuse them, we bought about £20 worth of furniture at the sale yesterday.

If all goes well I will ask Mr Mann to build a nice cottage on one of his sections in about 3 months.

Mr Roberts is far preferable to Mr Smith.

I saw Dr Fleming this evening on his way down from Ch:Ch:

Your papa told me that I had authorized him to advertise Darrochs' farm in the "Mail". I cannot see how this can be for the following reasons.

1st I should have sent the advt: direct as I did to the N.O. Times

2nd I remember being very surprised at seeing the Advt: in the Mail.

3rd The Advt: did not appear until after the obnoxious local about me had appeared in the paper, if you refer to my letters you will find that I said "I could not send him (The Mail) an Advt: after what had occurred as it would look too much like gratitude" or words to that effect.

Excuse me troubling you with business but I don't care about paying the Mail a/c when I do not remember having sent them an advt:

Thursday

I think our sale today will pay for the licence, at least I hope so.

Please thank Lottie for her letter. I will reply when I have some news to interest her.

I must conclude now or my letter will be longer than yours.

With fondest love darling
I am
Yours devotedly
Dick Davies

9th

I am afraid your papa must be very much offended with what I said about both partners signing the same cheque as neither he nor you have mentioned it. Please let me know in your next

Rakaia
July 14th 1880

My darling Nannie

You see I am beginning my letter before yours comes to hand (4 pm)

I fear that we shall not make more than £30 after all on Harrisons sale, as the sale did not come up to their expectations. They have decided to work the farm together again, such being the case it will be better to forego the profit on the land rather than be called a hard firm just at the start – is it not annoying?

This place is exceedingly dull during the winter months. I hardly know how to get thro' the time, I learn from Harriet that you had lots of gaiety last week, I hope you always think of me thro' it all.

July 15th

About the cheques, how can I propose to another what I would not have if it was proposed to me? Ronayne & Cotterill must stand almost alone I think.

You have not told me what part you intend taking in the "Pinafore"! Miss Robinson is very considerate, altho' it is very hard that you should not have more fun, it seems to be all work with you my poor darling.

I see by the paper that Mr Evans has started in Oamaru, I wish I could say that we had enough to do, I fear that things will not improve until next harvest. However, if we can average £250 p ann: each from now to Xmas I shall ask you to join me about that time. I said that I averaged £300 before I joined Winter, now we shall have to make double that to get me the same amount.

The new establishment is a long time getting ready, I shall be agreeably surprised if we get in before the end of next month.

Get fond of the cook indeed, I only wish you were coming instead. I am suffering from your old complaint today viz toothache & no one to say a kind word to me.

I have not yet heard from Mr Bristed I hope he will not keep his beloved waiting as long as I have done.

You naughty girl, what do you mean by writing to me in a cold room? Cannot you write in the dining room before you go upstairs?

I see that the Caradices & my friend Miss Deakin are to be here again this week, so I have something to look forward to, haven't I?

Goodbye Cara mia
Fondest love
Your
Good for nothing
Dick

Mr Kemp the landlord of the Hotel saw your papa on Tuesday. I wonder if he thinks more of him than I do.

Rakaia
July 22nd

My darling Nannie

I don't think Johnnie Mann has frightened us about Harrisons Sale, we have done nothing in the matter yet, but I certainly think it would not be wise too [sic] charge the full comm: as the farm is still in the hands of the two brothers, now if you were hear [sic] we could argue the matter pro and con.

I'll box Mr Tate's ears if he says that you are lazy, or rather I would do so if I had the opportunity.

Please give the enclosed to Milly, Mr Winter is sending a lot to some young friends of his & I asked him for one.

Tell me darling how much a year you think would be sufficient to start with & then perhaps I shall be able to form some idea as to how many more Sundays must pass before I can take you in my arms & call you my own wifie.

I don't think I shall go to the station to see Miss Lemon as she passes thro'

I must have a very quick temper or you would not hope that I would not be vexed with what you said in the beginning of your letter.

We intend holding a weekly sale shortly & selling potatoes, onions, chaff, chick wheat, oats & I hope it will answer.

The Banker has been trying to bring Miss Williams & Mr McKerrow together but I don't think it will come to anything as Mr Mac is not a ladies man.

At the Railway Station a few days ago I carried Mrs Elton's little boy, who has a bad foot, from the buggy to the train & then I went to the Church to get Mrs Elton's muff when it had been left on the previous Sunday.

You will be three old maids now at the Sunday School viz: your sweet self, Miss Gifford Miss Lemon.

Messrs Mann & Hartnell are talking of going to Oamaru on Saturday to get prices of flour. I told them I should be happy to go for them, they laughed & said that it does not do for me to go down too often.

I have just heard that Mr McLean is likely to be removed shortly then Mrs Elton will be the only lady left in the township. I hope you will be the next to come here

With fondest love
I am
Yours affectionately
Dick

It is so cold I can hardly hold the pen.

Rakaia
July 27th 1880

My darling Nannie

I am very glad to find that your face ache is better. I don't think I could get tired of nursing you.

I am in a bad fix about the section, I really don't know what is to be done. I am trying to rent a house in the meantime but fear I shall not succeed.

I am afraid you will have to put up with plain furniture at first as I cannot take much money out of the business, but I do not think that will trouble you very much.

Why should I write to Herbert unless he is to be best man? Please pardon my ignorance as I know nothing about weddings. Is it to be Herbert or James as best man? I don't care which or perhaps I should have two!!

I was in Ch Ch today I saw Cecil Moore, he is a nice youth!!

I wrote to your papa on Monday night & told him that I could not get Hartnell's section as Mrs H objected so strongly to parting with it, I suggested going to furnished apartments in ChCh or Ashburton sooner than wait 3 or 4 months longer.

Oh! Nannie wifie I do want you so much.

I hope you will not flirt very much at Dr Waits tonight. I expect you will be dancing as I am writing this.

I thought of writing to your papa tonight but unfortunately I have no news to give him.

With fondest love
My poor darling
I am
Yours lovingly
Dick

Rakaia
July 29th 1880

My darling Nannie

Our first sale at Methven only paid expenses as I anticipated. I don't expect any profit from there for 2 or 3 months.

Did I tell you that we are having a small sale room build in order to hold weekly sales? I hope it will answer after a little. The toothache has all gone thank you. Did I complain of the cold? I ought not to have done so as it is preferable to the heat on the plains.

You ought to have gone to hear "Maritana" you will not be able to have anything of the sort up here.

"MARITANA."
THE OAMARU PHILHARMONIC SOCIETY
Will give their
NINTH CONCERT
ON
WEDNESDAY EVENING, 21ST JULY,
In the Volunteer Hall,
Consisting of Wallace's Opera
"MARITANA."
To commence at 8 o'clock p.m.
Tickets—Front Seats, 3s; Back Seats, 2s.
To be had of Messrs. Ronayne & Gottrell or Mr. R. L. Rule. 862

George Alexander Cleland cannot be one of the family your mama knows, he only came from home 6 years ago, he has relatives in Tasmania.

I don't think Constance would like to speak to me if she were to see me in my wide-awake hat & old clothes.

We have had to return Harrison Bros £26/-/- if we had not done so, we should have lost it in other ways.

Why have you not answered me about the cost of housekeeping? I should like to have your ideas on the subject before anyone elses.

I am longing to have you with me wifie, I am so tired of our long engagement (Now don't misunderstand me whatever you do) & wish I could see my way to bring it to an end at once.

I hope to be in the cottage in about a fortnight, I should then be able to judge as to the cost of housekeeping in Rakaia.

I have telegraphed to your papa today three times about flour. I hope he will be able to manage it as it means about £13 to each firm.

Since writing the above I have received a telegram from your papa & from the tenor of it I fear that he cannot execute my order.

With fondest love
I am
Yours sincerely
Dick

Rakaia
Aug 6th 1880

My darling Nannie

I see that your letter is written on the day I left altho' I only got it this evening. I saw the h'chiefs waving quite plainly but I could not distinguish anyone

I am not in the least afraid of Mr Allan so I don't see why you should not sing his songs.

I had my meals with the Turks y'day, I spent 4/- in two raffles at the Oriental Exhibition & won such a nice tea-caddy made of olive wood & a card basket. I was offered £1 for the caddy. Mr Hartnell whispered to me not to take it but keep it for Mrs D. I did not mean to sell it but was amused by his remark.

THE ORIENTAL EXHIBITION will open at the Colonists' Hall, Lyttelton, Friday, June 18, at 2 p.m. For three days only. One of the most extraordinary Exhibitions that has never been brought to this Colony. We respectfully expect a visit from the public, and all are welcome. Admission 1s. A present to every visitor. N. Kaurt and M. Ali, proprietors. 2556

Our gross profits from July 1st to date are about £100, I hope they will continue like that, of course we are indebted to Harrisons sale for half of it. The Sale y'day was our monthly sale, the weekly sales will not commence till Sept.

I am very busy this evening making up y'day's a/cs. I like the work but unfortunately have a bad cold which hinders me a little.

You do not say anything about the earthquake. I hope you were not very frightened.

You seem to be very much afraid of teasing me, I wish you were not darling. It ought to be a pleasant change after I leave as I am not there to bother you.

We bought Dr Fleming's 3 horses at the sale y'day, I hope he won't back out of it.

I wish you were here to nurse my cold instead of being teased by the children at home. I wonder how you would like it.

Goodbye my beloved wifie
With fondest love
I am
Yours lovingly
Dick

I saw Mr A Bristed at your papa's office on Tuesday, of course we did not speak, what fun!!

10pm

I am just going to have some onion broth for my cold, horrid stuff I should think.

Rakaia
Aug 12th 1880

My darling Nannie

I should very much like to know how your papa & Lottie know that you care more for me than I do for you. I am very certain that I don't know that such is the case, do you?

Perhaps it is because my letter did not come to hand till Saturday, if that is the reason it is a very poor one I consider.

You ask your papa the difference between gross & nett profits, I fear you do not understand it wifie.

I was invited to supper at the parsonage on Sunday evening & I promised Mrs Elton that I would not leave the school yet awhile altho' I shall lose the Senior girls. Mrs McLean was the means of getting the class together & it would not do to ask her to take another.

Some days I think things are as bright as possible & other days I think we are only making bread & cheese.

There must be a resemblance between the Norwegian Captain & your beloved Dick.

Did Mr Tempest send me any message?

The cottage is not ready yet, I wish the others were not coming to it as I want my wifie there.

Can I buy you anything at the enclosed sale? It is only a small affair still it is better than nothing.

I have been reporting for Winter at the R.M. [Resident Magistrates] Court today, I cannot say that I like it very much.

Mind you tell me next time you write whether you are of the same opinion as your papa & Lottie.

Johnnie Mann is always at some practical jokes, he frequently takes the key away & locks the office door. A few days ago he took a stand with a jacket & dress on it from Hardys store.

With fondest love wifie
I am
Yours fondly
Dick

Rakaia
Aug 19th 1880

My darling Nannie

If ever you say again that I care more for you than you deserve I'll box your ears, it is impossible darling, much as I love you.

I had a letter from Conny on Monday she states "Herbert now sports a dress suit & looks quite Spif" also that she is going to Mrs Newtons Calico ball dressed as a "Sea fairy".

The Captain resembles me in being an old man with a young wife.

The office key is usually kept on a nail & if Mr Mann cannot find that he takes anything else that is sortable. We shall have to summons Dr Fleming if he does not settle with us in a day or two.

I like you preaching wifie, it does me more good than harm.

What on earth possessed Blanche & Clara to make them write to that vulgar little man?

Give my love to your Mama & tell her that I cannot afford more than 10/- to the Bazaar. I have guaranteed £5 p annum to the clergyman's stipend here.

It has been blowing a "nor-wester" the last two days & the table that I am now writing on in the office is all of a shake, it was all I could do to work against it this morning, if you were here I should have to lock you up for fear the wind would carry you away.

I enclose advt: of a sale which means £10 to £15 profit I hope.

I fancy Jim & Pearson will not come & live in the cottage now. I told them that it is possible I may want them to clear out by the end of the year, they say it is hardly worth while moving for 4 months & then perhaps have to leave. I shall be all the better pleased if they do not come as they are rather too noisy.

Our sale room is nearly completed we shall, I hope, hold the first weekly sale on Saturday week. I do hope it will answer.

I have just had Mr Elton in the office telling me that he wanted a good cheap cow & that he could not afford to pay cash. I am not the only poor man in the place, you see.

With fondest love my own Nannie
From
Yours devotedly
Dick

Aug 20

It has been blowing hard all night, please let me know if it is blowing at Oamaru

Rakaia
Aug 26th 1880

My darling Nannie

Thank you very much for the first paragraph in your letter. I don't see why Constance should be angry with me as she did not ask for my photo in her letter, besides I haven't got one.

Dr Flemings telegram was sufficiently binding, I wrote him on Monday threatening legal proceedings , he replied "I expected to have been at Rakaia some time ago or you would have heard ere this", he will be up in 2 days.

Poor little May [some relation of Mr Mann's], as you call her, has written to your sisters. Please tell me why they wrote I really am too stupid to see it.

Give my love to your Mama & tell her that I have requested your papa to pay the 10/- as we have an open a/c.

I am not sure yet that I have frightened Jim & Pearson, they appear to be quite undecided what to do. It doesn't matter as they will come in with the understanding that they are not to be there after Xmas.

Poor little wifie, I wish I could be with you every Wednesday, however you will have enough of my company by & bye.

So Mr Tate is going to bring you some music, I never heard of him before, I thought it was to have been Mr Allan. I am not sure that I am agreeable to his doing it, what will be his address in Dunedin?

Is your papa going to keep Peterkins ponies? I don't think they are safe for ladies to drive.

I feel very much flattered to find that Mrs Moore takes such an interest in our affairs.

I enclose a/c of the sale it was very good on the whole.

Tell Constance from me that if she does not want to be an old maid she had better go round & nurse poor Finch.

You have not said a word about the Assembly Ball.

With fondest love
I remain
Your devoted lover
Dick

We have just recd a list from Miss Wood containing 250 Lots of Bibs Tuckers & a number of unmentionables.

Rakaia
Sep 2nd 1880

My darling Nannie

I am sorry to say that our monthly sale today was a very poor affair. I hope the weekly sales which commence on Saturday will be better.

The Doctor has paid at last.

The Banker & his wife will be going on Saturday. I think old Johnnie is at the bottom of it. Poor Mrs Elton won't have a single lady in the township that she can visit now.

I think we shall be in the cottage on Saturday or Monday. Jim will be coming I think. It is a very nice cottage. I have only to complain that it is rather public owing to its being nearer the road than your old house & the Section is a small one, the house is much nicer than your old one, it has a nice verandah 5 rooms & a pantry. Oh! that you were coming in to it next week.

We were selling some of the Bankers furniture at the Sale today & amongst other things a perambulator, when it was put up a tradesman called out "Mr Davies you had better buy that as you will probably want one before long." I blushed like a schoolgirl, he then said look at him blushing it must be true.

I don't hear anything of Messrs Bristed & Atkins now, do they still accompany any of you home from town??

I suppose my friend! Miss Wait will be at Harriets party. I don't expect I shall be able to come down on Saturday again if we shall be busy at our sales.

You had better give Constance one of the photos you have!!

I see that Oamaru still holds her own in the way of Statistics?

Poor Anderson came to a sad end. I believe a young lady up North jilted him.

I expect I shall have the girls again at the Sunday School until you come then they must get someone else.

With fondest love my own Nannie
I am
Yours devotedly
Dick

Vital statistics of Oamaru for July last: Population (as estimated for 1st January last), 5098; total births, 26; total deaths, 5; proportion of deaths to the 1000 of population, 0.98. The deaths of persons not residents of the borough, occurring at hospitals, are excluded as is usual.

According to the last Gazette, Wanganui, of the fifteen principal towns of New Zealand, registered the largest proportion of deaths to the 1000 of population, being 1.92. Lyttelton registered the smallest proportion, being 0.55.

Of the total number of deaths in the fifteen towns, being 167, males contributed 104; females, 63. 79 of the deaths were of children under five years of age, being 47.31 per cent. of the whole number; 62 of these were of children under one year of age.

Rakaia
Sep 9th 1880

My darling Nannie

I was awfully grumpy last night as your letter did not come to hand until this evening, it must have been posted on Wednesday evening.

Tell Blanche that I do not understand colors but will endeavour to ascertain next time I write.

I never realised until now what a lot of work you have to do, we commence with the fires at 5.30 pm & never finish until 8pm although the joint is cooked at the bakery next door, the same in the morning from 7 to 9 altho we have only some porridge & bacon to cook.

I am sorry to find that A Bristed was at your house on Sunday night, why should I not ask about him? I don't think I should like to be at the party as I should probably meet both him & Miss Wait there.

The Sale on Saturday was a small affair. I hope it will improve by & bye.

I should have been glad to have heard Mr Stanford as from what you say I think his Sermon would have cheered me. I saw the notice of Mr Lewis's marriage. I see that JW Harrison Ashburton is also married, while my poor little darling has to wait, if we do as well as we have been doing I hope to take you away by the end of the year, unfortunately the few months before harvest are the worst months in the year.

Thank you for letting me see Miss Filleuls letter. Please try & let me have my letter on Wednesdays in future, if you do not want to worry me.

Poor Mrs Elton has too much work now on Sundays. Mr Elton says he will have to forbid her doing it unless someone comes to her assistance soon!

With fondest love & not with love, as you say,
I am
Ever your own
Dick

Sept 10. I have enclosed a little of the paint off the house. The windows & frames are white, top of the verandah iron, green & white alternately.

Goodbye wife
Dick

Rakaia
Sept 15th 1880

My darling Nannie

The enclosed was written by Mr Winter who is a capital newspaper correspondent. Please show it to your papa. We are not afraid of N Maclean as he spends most of his time at the Hotel.

Give my love to your Mama & say that I am very much obliged for the invitation altho' I fear there is not much likelihood of my being there.

"Entre Nous" Please forgive me wifie but I feel a wee bit vexed at being asked to meet A.B. after the cutting he gave me, how could I possibly come & avoid speaking to him? & I think I said he should never have the chance of doing it again. Now confess that you feel a little bit frightened at the prospect of living with such a crabby being as your humble servant!

Our sale on Saturday was a very poor one, in fact, I could have been away without any inconvenience. I fear it will be some little time before they answer.

I made a rice pudding on Sunday & had to dig it out of the dish, it was so hard. Jim says I had better get you to send up some recipes for plain puddings, Mrs Beetons book has more ingredients than we are possessed of.

The gum Seed was for Hardy & Co, I think it is intended for the Rakaia Domain, does not that sound grand?

Tell Mary that I am afraid to write to her now for fear somebody should forbid me to do it.

No you may not have the joints cooked next door when you come to Rakaia!

I am longing to pay you another visit darling but fear it would not be wise to do so just now, if I had you here the parties would not worry me very much.

Mr Mann has asked me if I would do his children the honor of presiding at a birthday party tomorrow, he dislikes the bother himself & has given me the unpleasant task. I cannot very well refuse as he takes offence so easily.

I saw little Martin a couple of days ago & he just confirmed what I have heard from two or three others viz: that Mr Harrison would lose his customers at his weekly sale if there were any opposition as he is so very irritable, he won't allow anyone to touch things before the Sale & if he is teased he threatens to stop the sale. He must be like me? I should like to start a weekly sale at Ashburton if I thought it would pay.

It was blowing very hard on Saturday & also today.

Now darling I must ask you to let me have a nice letter to read on Wednesday evening in return for my crabby one. I shall be thinking of the aristocratic Mr Grant <u>honouring you</u> with his arm for a dance, not to mention Atkins! & others. Oh! dear it will be a delightful party for me.

I had a letter from Jack a few days ago. I find that I have a niece born in Australia, he says that they intend returning to England in a few weeks.

Sept 16th

I see from Harriets letter that she takes it for granted that I shall be down next week. I am sorry for this as I certainly shall not be there. I hope you will not be very much offended with what I have said about the party. I suppose it is my nature to be disagreeable sometimes. I will try & atone for it when you are my very dear wife.

Goodbye darling, you will not forget me altogether on Wednesday evening.

With fondest love
I am
Yours lovingly
Dick

Rakaia
Sep 18th

My darling Nannie

I was agreeably surprised to receive your letter this evening & sorry to find that you think me unkind for not coming down on Wednesday. Of course your papa can invite who he pleases but surely I am justified in refusing to be present when he has people I don't care to meet, if I were there I should have to shake hands with A Bristed when at the same time I should be more inclined to box his ears, you know quite well that I am not good at hiding my feelings. In fact, I could not shake hands with him, is not that reason enough?

The cottage is infinitely preferable to the Hotel altho' Jim & Winter are rather noisy at times.

V Pyke is a son of the M.H.R. [Vincent Pyke was a Member of the House of Representatives, representing Dunstan]

If I were to come down just now I fear you would find me in a very bad temper, still, if it were your turn to go to Church in the evening on Sunday the 26th inst I should like to go down there, that is provided I recover by that time.

The party at Mr Mann's was most wearisome.

Our sale today was a small affair still I have some hopes of an improvement by & bye.

I suppose I may still expect my letter on Wednesday next, if I don't get it I shall send a telegram & spoil your party.

Another nor-wester today with lots of heat.

You don't say anything about the lay reader proposal!

10pm

I must now get some buckets of water for a bath in the morning & help Jim to make the supper viz a cup of cocoa.

With fondest love

I am
Your crabby lover
Dick

Monday 8.45 a.m.

I thought I would feel less crabby today, but I find that I am not so. I suppose it will go off when the party is over

Rakaia
Sept 25th 1880

My dear Emma,

I have to own receipt of the only unkind letter I have ever received from you.

When I have the pleasure of seeing you perhaps I shall be able to convince you that I did right notwithstanding what others may have said.

Please consider what I said in my letter of the 23rd about a visit as unsaid, I don't suppose you will care about seeing me for some time as you are so very angry with me.

With kind love
I am
Yours affectly
Dick

Rakaia
Sep 29th 1880

My darling Nannie

I am so sorry to have made you so miserable, please forgive me this time.

I shall be oh! so glad to visit you on Saturday now that I find you are longing to see me.

I will keep the scolding until I see you, then you may look out for squalls.

From the tone of your previous letter I did not think you cared particularly about my visit just now or I don't suppose I could have written to you in the way I did.

I am sending this by the afternoon train with the hope that one of you may be in the office at mid-day tomorrow so that my darling may get it at the earliest possible moment.

Good bye till Saturday
With fondest love
I am
Your crabby lover
Dick

Rakaia
Oct 7th 1880

My darling Nannie

I received your welcome letter mid-day y'day. It has been blowing a nor-wester for the last three days, this afternoon it changed to rain which I hope will continue for a day or two.

Finch said that you looked happier on Sunday evening than you have done for a long time & also that he had heard from 3 or 4 that we were to be married on the 15th Nov & that there was to be a party at Oakleigh the same evening. I wish it could be so, don't you? I told him that he must have got his information from Mrs Lemon.

I saw Mrs Webb in the train. Mr John McCaw waved his hand out of the window as we passed the manse.

I was awfully annoyed with Jim & Pearson on my return as they were standing in the passage just as the train arrived, making a most hideous noise with a kerosene tin etc. I was awfully grumpy the whole evening until Jim said I will make him laugh when I bring out my invention. He then brought out a piece of perforated tin with a handle to it which he said was a capital utensil for turning pancakes or for lifting poached eggs from the frying pan. I could not help laughing, altho' I did not feel like it.

Do you know wifie that every visit makes me feel that I am anything but good enough for you, never mind darling. I will be oh! so kind to you so that I may in some measure make up my difficulty in other things.

Goodbye darling mine
With fondest love
I am
Yours affectionately
Dick

Rakaia
Oct 14th 1880

My darling Nannie

I thought I had told you in my last letter that we are doing next to nothing. I am all the more annoyed as I should have liked nothing better than to know that the report was true, have you found out where it emanated from? I think it must have come from your Aunt.

I was only vexed at the disgraceful noise the fellows made, the neighbours must have thought that we were tipsy. Hartnell did not like it, he said that kind of thing would tend to depreciate the value of his property. I quite agree with him!

Poor little darling, so you are very much afraid that I shall be disappointed with you, I am more afraid that you will be shocked with me, the author of "Red as a Rose" is quite right I expect, the Welsh are a lot of savages. You ought to be a little frightened! [This probably refers to a book by Rhoda Broughton, called "Red as a Rose is She"; a love story set in Wales.]

I was over at Mr Eltons to tea on Sunday, his charming wife has now decided on giving up Sunday School the same way as Mrs McLean did, it is too bad I say! She told me that it was cheaper to live married than Single but that it was not always nice when both ends did not happen to meet. What do you say?

Perhaps your papa will not like a letter. I have just written him about some charges on my sisters money. I cannot keep it as I should write just the same to anyone on business.

If Mr Allan were to see more of me I fancy he would like me less, I am quite sure I could not agree with him.

I have just received a letter from Harriet in which she states that you have gone to tea at your Aunts. I expect you will now know all about our wedding tour & everything else.

With fondest love Nannie mine
I am
Yours devotedly
Dick

Rakaia
Oct 21 1880

My darling Nannie

I expect I have forgotten the occasion you allude to, do you mean the evening of the Indian Relief Fund? I was very fond of you then or I should not have tapped your hand or said you were a naughty girl when we were standing together near the buggy.

Who is Mr Wilson?

You should go to Robertsons party my darling as I hope you will not have many more opportunities of enjoying yourself in Oamaru.

I wish the harvest time had commenced it seems a long time to look forward to, still I am hoping to be able to take you away about the beginning of the year.

Mr C E Tempest will, I should think, hardly like being transferred to Leeston as it is a smaller office than the Hokitika Branch.

What have I done to Constance? I don't remember saying anything objectionable.

I am very much obliged for the box, so are the others. I don't expect there will be much cake left by Sunday.

Herbert Lemon also told me that I looked younger than of yore, I think I had better take off my beard before I see Oamaru again. Then I shall hope to look still younger.

We are now living at the rate of 15/- p week each including house rent, I don't think that is dear considering the quantity we waste.

I have been making a flower garden the last couple of days. I don't know what it will look like yet.

I wrote to your papa about pairs of cornsacks on Saturday, he has not yet replied, I suppose he can't be bothered with me any longer.

With fondest love
Carissima mine
I am
Yours devotedly
Dick

Rakaia
Oct 28th

My poor little darling

I do hope that your mama's indisposition is only for a day or two, more especially as it makes you miserable & I also hope that your toothache will have disappeared when this comes to hand. Oh! that I could have you with me to try & comfort you. I don't yet know whether we shall have to postpone our marriage until Feby. I shall be able to speak more definitely on the subject in another month.

You do not tease me wifie by writing as you do. I only wonder you have such patience with me.

Tempest drove over here on Sunday with the Leeston Manager, he was here about an hour & talked about himself the whole time, he did not ask after any of you or anyone else, he goes to Dunedin today & expects to be sent up to the goldfield district, perhaps he may call on you. I am only surmising this.

The two cakes have gone also the tamarinds.

Jim & I had a row this morning owing to my objecting to his sitting down to breakfast un-dressed. I am so tired of it all & intend to turn them out at the end of the year whether I can take you just then or not.

There is a vacant section next to the Bank. Mrs Pyke sits there for hours together playing with her boy, fancy doing that opposite Coggins Shop.

We have had splendid weather for the last fortnight excepting on Sunday when we had a strong nor-wester.

I am now hoping that there will be no more parties soon after letting you to go to Robinsons, you don't know what a jealous husband you will have.

How much furniture shall we want to start with? I have not the remotest idea as to what we should have, please tell me.

With fondest love my wifie
I am Yours Affect[ly]
Dick

Rakaia
Nov 4 1880

My darling Nannie

I am glad to find that you are in better spirits this week & that your Mama is so much better.

You need not be afraid that I shall get tired of you & your toothache, I think there is more danger of your getting tired of me.

I hope we shall manage to get married before Jennie Honour. [Alas no! Jane Honour was married on the 20th of the following January.]

I had quite forgotten having given Miss Gleeson a photograph. I know it was before I had any hope of winning your sweet self.

The idea of your Mama & one of your sisters coming up here seems rather formidable. I don't prefer getting things myself. I should much prefer having you with me darling but that would mean paying a lot of money at the time whereas if we got them from Hardy & by degrees, it would come easier not to mention 3 months credit, the profits of business are not easily got at & we have already a lot on the books.

The kitchen has a capital pantry and cupboard also table & chairs but not matting or oilcloth, I have nothing yet for the sitting room, of course we should want a sofa, I fancy you have forgotten some very necessary furniture is it not so? Never mind my naughtiness wifie.

I have taken my beard off, a neighbour said that he hardly recognized me.

I shall have Rakaia nearly all to myself for a couple of days next week as everyone seems to be going to the Ch.Ch. races & show.

Bother Mrs Filleuls parties, you will be able to pay me out & go there without me.

Goodbye wifie mine
With fondest love
I am yours devotedly
Dick

Rakaia
Nov 12th 1880

My darling Nannie

I don't suppose you will care much about getting my letter as my visit will have worried you enough for one week.

I had a talk with Mr Clowes in the train, he asked me when our marriage was to take place & said that you were one of the best girls in Oamaru & he hopes that I shall be as happy as he has been since his marriage, he said something about being careful not to give way at the first & then things will go on smoothly, he mentioned Edmund Gibson as one who had made that mistake & now he cannot brand a bale of wool without first consulting his wife, wasn't it fun? I did have such a laugh altho' I did not feel in a laughing humor. Of course this is "Entre nous".

I carried my headache back with me so it could not be the wail of a pipe as you imagined.

I think you should go to the Bazaar next week Nannie darling. It will look as if you were tired of the world if you do not go, at least I fancy so.

Pearson said at tea last night that he wished to goodness one of us would shoot him as he was tired of this world, I don't feel like that, do you?

Your papa came to the station to see me off, I had Mr Fidler for company all the way, he has gone to ChCh for his examination. [A teacher at the District High School; the exam being the University Examination. The North Otago Times records the Rector's complaint about the inconvenience to the school. You will be pleased to know Mr Fidler successfully passed his B.A.]

May Mann wants to know why your sisters do not reply to her letter, I hope they will not do anything of the kind.

I should not be surprised to hear that Harriet & Tempest come together after all, what loving brothers in law or rather relatives we should make, I mean Tempest Bristed Atkins & your devoted loving

Dick the good for nothing

Rakaia
Nov 18th 1880

My darling Nannie

I am exceedingly glad to find that my visit did not worry you as I was a little bit afraid that it had done so. My headache has quite left me thank you, if you fret about such a little thing as that, I fear that if I were ill you would become ill too & that would never do as I should have no one to nurse me. I do not know whether the account I gave you about E Gibson is true or not but I am quite confident that we shall not quarrel very often or in other words I am sure we shall be very happy.

I told Pearson & Jim that I should want them to leave the cottage at the end of the year, will you fix some time in January for the happy day?

You must let me have a couple of weeks after they leave to have the house cleaned out & to get some furniture into the place.

I am sorry that I should have had to ask you to come here in the hottest month as the flies & dust are so troublesome, last Sunday was a stifling day with us here. By the way, I should like Finch to be best man.

I had not heard of Fenwicks accident he will not be so conceited now I should think.

I do hope we shall have a good harvest, if not you will have to live on bread & cheese & kisses

With fondest love wifie mine
I am
Yours devotedly
Dick

Rakaia
Nov 30/80

My darling Nannie

I cannot keep saying it but I am bitterly disappointed to find that we cannot get married at the end of January. I was at the parsonage last night & told them that I hoped to be married about that time, what am I to do about the fellows in the house? Shall I tell them that they can remain for another two or three months?

Somehow I don't look forward to my visit at Xmas as much now as I did before I got your letter, please do not think that I do not care about seeing you as it is anything but that.

I haven't the heart to write a longer letter tonight

With fondest love I am still
Yours devotedly
Dick

What's the reason for the delay? The next letters suggest that George is annoyed with Richard.

Rakaia
Dec 4

My darling Nannie

I quite agree with you in thinking that your papas letter is very unkind. I think he might have replied in a different tone. You will notice that my reply is not a very long epistle.

I am so sorry for you my darling. It does not matter for me as I deserve it. Try & bear up wifie & we will have a talk about it at Christmas, that is, if I am down. I will then tell you more than I can write about it.

You must not blame yourself wifie as it is not your fault.

This also must be a very short letter as I feel awfully wicked.

Goodbye darling mine
With fondest love
I am
Yours sincerely
Dick

Rakaia
Dec 8th 1880

My darling Nannie

Please tell me how my letter was such a miserable one? I told the truth in the best way I could which is a very poor way in the best of times. I am very much afraid that I shall only mar all the gaiety which seems to be going on with you if I come down at Christmas.

I have written your papa a business letter this evening which I fear he will not like. I shall be sorry if such is the case, still I cannot allow anyone to hint that I have authorized anything unless I have authority for doing so. I am afraid that I have got to be more crabby than ever, being away from you, it certainly does not make me more amiable.

So you are going to have a nice trip next Tuesday evening & I suppose return at daylight next morning.

Jim says that I am enough to make a saint miserable as I never laugh.

I saw Lewis Morton [at?] Middleton Anderson & Rock the photographer at Ch Ch yesterday. [Lewis Morton was a senior officer in George's Volunteers.]

I hope I shall be in a better temper by Christmas or I declare it will be very unwise to go anywhere there.

I cannot write a very entertaining letter so I will conclude by asking you to love me more than ever with all my faults

With fondest love
I am
Yours devotedly
Dick

Rakaia
Dec 15

My darling Nannie

I am not vexed with you wifie only I cannot forget a certain word in your papa's letter. Others cannot read my face as well as you can so do not be afraid of your papa seeing it. I see that you fully expect me to come down next week. Sometimes I think it would be best to keep away & other times I am longing to be with you. Of course I always long to be at your side so don't misunderstand me. I wish I could be bothered with your letters every day.

I suppose you enjoyed yourself immensely at the Reeds, by the way why did you prefer going there?

I have just rec[d] a letter from Gerald Filleul stating that he will be passing Rakaia tomorrow & that he has been told to invite me to a party at their house this day week. I don't think I shall be there altho' I expect you will be there.

If I come down I intend leaving it until Christmas day as your seat at Church will be quite full enough without me, unless you can say that you are not going to Church then I should remain with you, that is always provided I shall be down.

I remember Miss D'Oyley she is another sweet girl!

You seem to have visitors more frequently than of yore, don't you feel very much in the way?

What will you say to me if I don't come down at Xmas?

With fondest love
My own darling
I am always
Yours devotedly
Dick

Rakaia
Dec 21st 1880

My darling Nannie

Your letter of the 17th came to hand last night. You were very good at the Reichs, better than I deserve in fact. I am surprised to find that you have not been invited to the Filleuls as Gerald in his letter states "Miss Sumpter is sure to be asked as she is one of Blanche's friends".

It isn't the prospect of a good Christmas dinner that will influence me <u>now</u>, you should see some of the meals we have on hot days, the fellows will not take the trouble to cook anything.

If you will <u>not</u> scold me for not coming down I shall have to come down as I want to see you oh! so much.

I expect you will be at the Otepopo bush as I am writing this.

Johnny Mann & Hartnell were at Haselmayer Entert^{t}. The latter said that he thought it might have been Miss Sumpter.

I am afraid you will have some visitors on Christmas day or rather I shall not care if I can have you all to myself.

If I thought the s.s "Grafton" which leaves Lyttelton for Oamaru on Friday evening would arrive before midday on Saturday I should prefer going that way as a sea voyage would suit me better just now.

I am now busy at the Rate Roll & business is improving gradually.

If I am not down by the express on Friday I may be in the Steamer on Saturday or may be dining with a "Mermaid".

With fondest love
I am
Your good for nothing
Dick

Professor Haselmayer gave his farewell entertainment last evening at the Volunteer Hall to a fair house. His card and other tricks, particularly the drum tricks, were highly appreciated, the time of the drum's accompaniment being kept admirably while the Professor played a march upon the pianoforte. For his performance on the stylocarfe he was encored. The principal feature of the evening was the crystal cabinet, in which—after it had undergone the closest scrutiny of two gentlemen who had been selected from amongst the audience--Madame Haselmayer was fastened down in a kneeling position by the wrists. The loops through which the wrists were secured were locked by and the keys kept by the scrutineers. After that had been done, the lid was put down and also secured by means of a padlock and key which were kept by one of the gentlemen on the stage. A curtain was then drawn over the cabinet, which was just large enough to contain Madame Haselmayer, and in about 15 seconds she appeared from behind the curtain. The cabinet was then uncovered and the locks were found in the same position as before, and the manner in which Madame obtained her liberty completely mystified the audience. Professor and Madame Haselmayer leave for Waimate to-day, at which place they perform tonight. Their entertainment is an admirable one.

Rakaia
Dec 30 1880

My darling Nannie

It has just occurred to me that the Post Office will be closed on Saturday. I must therefore write tonight altho' I did not intend writing until tomorrow.

I enjoyed this visit more than any, I think, altho' your sisters seem to be very tired of me, I don't blame them it is very natural, I don't intend at present to visit you again until I come to take you away. I mean if I feel later on as I do just now.

The train was full so I haven't a good chance of waving my h'chief.

I am afraid that you are a little bit disappointed with me the more you see of me, if you are not it is more than I desire, I know that I am not half good enough for you & I shall always think so as it is quite true.

The writer of the enclosed must have been thinking of you when he wrote, it is exactly what you will be when I shall have the unalloyed happiness of calling you wife.

Mr Winter told Mr Harvey that he had received a telegram from me stating that they were to clear out of the house at once.

I am going to ask Mr Harvey the cost of furnishing the cottage, your papa, it seems to me, does not wish me to have you for a long time.

If we do have a good harvest I mean to have you by hook or by crook. That is provided you care for me as much as I think. It was so miserable tumbling into my blankets last night with everything topsy turvy & no signs of loving hands having been about.

With fondest love, wifie
I am
Yours fondly
Dick

Rakaia
Jan 6th 1881

My darling Nannie

Don't you tell me again that you cannot write nice letters as the one I received last night is simply charming.

Please forgive me once more for saying that I am not good enough for you, I should have said you are not good enough for me (what a fib!).

It is only my conscience that makes me think you are disappointed with me, however, I am very glad to find that it is not true.

Mr Hardy called me a duffer on my return. By the way I asked him what it would cost to furnish the cottage just nicely, (he has been for some years in a large furnishing warehouse) he said that it could be done for £60! Of course this does not include a piano.

I also wish I had been with you over New Years Eve. I went to bed at 10 o'clock & had to get up at 2 as Mann & party came & roused us up.

Has Mr West & his bride returned yet?

As I am writing this I expect you will be feeling a little tired after the School treat.

How could the article make me feel that there was some good in me. I think it would take more than that to make me feel anything of the kind. I don't fear for a moment that you will fall short of the ideal I have pictured you to be, so there!!

Do you mean to say that it was simply laziness that kept you from the pic-nic?

You naughty girl, I think I must come & rouse you. Still I am selfish enough to be glad that you did not go.

With fondest love
I am
Yours lovingly
Dick

Rakaia
Jan 12/81

My darling Nannie

This will have to be a hurried scrawl as I am busy assisting Mr Elton at the Church. I have been made Superintendent of the Sunday School much against my will. I dread next Saturday as I shall have to dine with the Bishop. I have been to the parsonage to tea 3 times this week. Don't be frightened but there is a Miss Walkern staying there. I think she knows that I am engaged so there is no danger.

Mr Elton told Miss Walkern that I was such a good fellow & of great assistance to him. He doesn't know me yet, does he?

I won't forget about the dining room table. Hardy said I was a duffer because I did not bring you back with me.

Please give my love to Mary & say that I hope she has quite recovered from the accident. Harriet in her letter apologizes for the way in which she treated me & says that she could not help it!! D Moore seems to be the favorite now.

Business seems to be improving & if we have a good harvest we shall do very well.

Tempest has written me stating that he met West who told him that I was to be married soon. He wants to know the date. I have not replied to his letter & don't feel inclined to do so.

In haste
With fondest love
My own sweet love
I am Yours fondly
Dick

Rakaia
Jan 20th 1881
George Sumpter Esq
Oamaru

Dear Sir,

If you should hear of a parcel of grass seed I shall be glad to have samples &

prices. When may we expect a/c sales of flour?

We are now going in for Station Stores, Machine Oil, twine etc as there will not be much doing in Auctioneering until after harvest.

The crops in this district are looking splendid.

McKerrow & Co have already got 300 Bales of sacks in their stores.

In haste
Yours truly
R Davies

Rakaia
Jan 20th 1881

My darling Nannie,

I had rather a hard day's work on Saturday & was very glad when it was all over, more especially as it was very warm & I had to keep a large fire going to boil the water for the tea. There was only one young lady there, a Miss Passmore 16 yrs of age, tall & silly.

I enclose an account of the proceedings. After dining with the Bishop I went to the Church & worked there until midnight. On Sunday after morning Service I drove home with Mr & Mrs C N Mackie (he is a squatter living about 8 miles from here) & stayed there until next morning. Then I went to Ch Ch on business.

On Wednesday I went to the funeral of an old lady related to the Mackies.

What a number of aristocratic visitors you have calling. You will surely miss them when you come up.

We are now taking orders for Station Stores of all sorts as there will not be much doing in Auctioneering until after harvest.

Jim & I had a row this evening as I did not approve of his conduct in the house.

I shall be so glad to get rid of them.

I am afraid Mr Hardy thinks we are interfering with his business. I cannot help it if he does think so. I mean to do anything I can in a legitimate way to get business.

I don't think I have much to interest you this week. It makes me very happy to find that you look forward to Friday.

With fondest love wifie
I am
Yours devotedly
Dick

I wonder if the "aristocratic visitors" are the Larnachs? George and Susannah are on record as visiting the Larnachs at their famous "Castle" in Dunedin.

Rakaia
Jan 26 1881

My darling Nannie

I received your letter on Tuesday this week.

The parsonage is about 10 minutes walk from the centre of the township.

I have had charge of the Sunday School for 3 Sundays. I can not say that I care much about it.

I am afraid that I must have offended Harriet as she has not replied to my last letter. It seems that I give offence to every one sooner or later. However, I don't much care as long as I don't offend you.

It was fortunate for your cricketers that there was not time to finish the game or I think they would have been badly beaten.

I wish we had a lot of capital. I can see a quantity of business going past us for the want of it.

Everyone seems to be getting married but you my poor little darling. It is an awful shame of me to have kept you waiting so long. I think you must know that I am doing my best to bring it to an end. As the fault is on my side I ought to feel it more than you do. Cheer up darling I hope we shall not have to wait very much longer.

I don't see that I am more unselfish than Burbury, it would be easier for any one to leave Nelly Wait than it would be to leave you.

Mann & Hartnell put me on the School Comm: altho' I asked them to nominate someone else.

You have not told me whether you are making the most of your aristocratic friends?

With fondest love
I am
Yours Sincerely
Dick

PS

Who does Jim Hassell come to see? Not you I hope or I shall have to call & see about it.

Rakaia
Feb 3rd 1881

My darling Nannie

I am sorry Harriet should have stayed up to write to me. I think I must give her a scolding for doing so.

I only guessed that you wanted cheering up. I know that I do & that I shall not have much happiness until I have you with me.

There is not much chance of my putting Johnnie Mann in the shade, if I have the use of some of his money I think it might be managed.

I am glad to find that George escaped so easily, if I had anything to say in the matter I certainly would not allow any of you to ride Rose.

There seems to be no end of amusement going on at Oamaru, it makes me feel rather envious as I have not got you with me.

The heat has been intense here also since Sunday. I cannot say that I like cooking in this weather it is very unpleasant work.

Harvesting is pretty general here now. I hope it will bring us some sales ere long.

I saw young Maude & Walls passing thro' by the express a few days ago.

I wish I could write a longer & more interesting letter but I really have no news to interest you my darling.

Mr Mann has been in the office the last few minutes & this must account for some of the mistakes.

I don't think you finished your last letter quite as affectionately as usual.

With fondest love
I am my own Nannie
Yours lovingly
Dick

Rakaia
Feb 10th 1881

My darling Nannie

Your letter came to hand as usual. I suppose Miss McCaw must have posted it.

I don't much mind or rather I should not mind living in such a lonely place if I had you with me.

Did I tell you that I acted as proxy for Mr Eltons baby who was christened a few days ago?

Harvest seems to be a month later this year. I have just been making up the profits to date & I find that my share is at the rate of £300 per annum. If your papa still insists on my having £300 for furniture he might just as well say that we cannot be married for another year. I want to have you about your birthday if I can. I declare I shall not care about life much longer without you. I have just drafted a letter for your papa & want to know if you think it will do. Please help me with it & send it back with corrections in your next.

The postscript on Mary's letter is as follows "Please let it be soon for E's sake". I cannot tell you how much that moved me.

I don't suppose you will mind doing with a little furniture for 12 months, it is not the same as if there were a lot of society here.

I had to go to Ch Ch today. I wish you had been with me & that we were going to stay there for a week.

With fondest love
I am
Yours fondly
Dick

You say "Mama Bertie & I walked into town today. I think I know how much walking fell to Berties share.

Rakaia
Feb 17th 1881
George Sumpter Esq
Oamaru

Dear Sir,

I have just been making a rough balance sheet to date & find that my share of the profits is at the rate of £300 p ann nett & as far as I can see it is more likely to increase than diminish.

I understood you to say that I should have £300 for furniture. As I cannot possibly manage this I hope you will reconsider the matter. There is next to no society here & I thought we might commence with a little & increase it by degrees.

I do hope you will allow me to take dear Emma in a couple of months.

Yours truly
R Davies

Rakaia
25/2/81

My darling Nannie

As I did not receive your letter until last night I was afraid that I had made another mistake. I am very glad to receive the message from your papa. I have written to him giving him all the information I can think of. I should like to run down very much. The last 2 months seem to have been longer than usual.

I am credited here with writing the enclosed letter to the Lyttelton Times. Archdeacon Williams is Mrs McLean's papa.

Mr Elton is going to preach on married life next Sunday.

Mrs Elton asked me to show her your photo as she did not expect to have the pleasure of seeing you.

Who sent Harriet the watch? Someone must be terribly in earnest.

It is blowing a gale just now & the desk I am writing on is shaking very much.

As Messrs Milne & Hassell are making themselves so agreeable you won't want to see me just now.

I hope your papa will reply early next week & that he will let me have you some time in April.

With fondest love darling mine
I am
Yours fondly
Dick

If I should muster up courage to go down tomorrow I hope you will be glad to see me.

RD

Rakaia
Mar 10 1881

My darling Nannie

I don't think I could have written you an interesting one Saturday. I always feel cross for a day or two after my return.

Give my love to your mama & say that I have truly recovered from the bee sting.

I told Finch about my visit he said that he would not have waited any longer until I told him what your papa said about coming up etc etc he then said that it would hardly be wise to quarrel for the sake of 2 or 3 months.

Is Charlie Baker your old admirer or the young lad? If the former I shall be very angry.

On the way home from school last Sunday I got a loaf for Mrs Elton & carried it home for her.

Fancy Johnnie Mann being impudent enough to ~~write &~~ ask me to invite you up with your papa & to stay at his house.

Your papa says in his letter of the 8th inst "I shall be glad to hear about the land & if possible to pay the visit I spoke of". If he does not come up this month I shall have a row with somebody whether it be wise or foolish of me.

I saw the h'chiefs waving on Friday. I had the carriage all to myself until we reached Waimate junction.

There is to be a muff cricket match here tomorrow & I think Mann & Hartnell are going to play. [A "Muff" cricket match seems to be an informal affair, that often involved the wearing of funny or odd costumes.]

Tell your papa that I hope he has sent off the wheat I ordered today. It should leave by the 4 pm train tomorrow.

With fondest love my darling wifie
I am
Yours devotedly,
Dick

Married at last!

Richard's hard work pays off at last! Or perhaps George softened his heart with business seemingly on the up. Oamaru now had some 5800 residents and was building as fast as it could — not realizing that this figure would mark the peak.

A coy note heralds the happy event:

> Mr Parker presents his compliments to Miss Sumpter and in reference to a coming event requests that she will do him the kindness to accept the accompanying trifle.
>
> Oamaru,
> 11th October 1881

MARRIAGE.

On the 19th inst., at St. Luke's Church, Oamaru, by the Rev. A. Gifford, assisted by the Rev. E. Eliot Chambers, Incumbent of Rakaia, Canterbury, Richard Davies, eldest surviving son of the late John Davies, Carmarthen, South Wales, to Emma Katherine, the oldest daughter of George Sumpter, Oakleigh, Oamaru.

And so, on October 19, 1881, Richard and Emma are at last married. Emma is now 22; Richard 36.

The wedding was quite a swell affair! Emma was, after all, the oldest child of a prominent citizen. No less than two separate, and lengthy, reports appeared in the local newspapers (on following page), and "The proceedings were on a scale that may truly be termed magnificent and imposing." "The town was here and there gaily dressed with bunting, and the flags on Flagstaff-Hill and on the shipping made a grand display." Recall George's involvement with the Harbour Board.

Public interest was great: the church was "crowded to the doors, while the avenue was densely lined by the public"; "Tees-street., on both sides in the vicinity of St. Luke's Church, the scene of the event, was crowded long before that hour [of the ceremony]". Perhaps, too, part of the public interest can be taken as a sign that Emma was well-known and well-liked.

Emma was supported by six bridesmaids, five of her sisters and one cousin (I believe the use of the term "Miss Lemon", rather than a first name, signifies that this is the oldest Lemon daughter, namely Connie).

The happy couple honeymooned in Christchurch.

To-day, Mr. George Sumpter's eldest daughter was married to Mr. Richard Davis, of South Rakaia. The proceedings were on a scale that may truly be termed magnificent and imposing. The hour fixed for the performance of the marriage ceremony was 12.30, but Tees-street on both sides in the vicinity of St. Luke's Church, the scene of the event, was crowded long before that hour. The town was here and there gaily dressed with bunting, and the flags on Flagstaff Hill and on the shipping made a grand display. Vehicles bustled to and fro, and it seemed that they had been brought into requisition in full force. The ceremony was solemnised by the Rev. Algernon Gifford, assisted by the Rev. E. E. Chalmers, the church being crowded to the doors, while the avenue was densely lined by the public. Miss Harriet Sumpter, Miss Lemon, and the Misses Lottie, Mary, Blanche, and Clara Sumpter were bridesmaids, and Messrs. Bristed, M'Kerrow, and Herbert Lemon were groomsmen. The service was opened by the choir singing "The voice that breathed o'er Eden." They also chanted the 128th Psalm in the course of the ceremony, and the organist appropriately played the "Wedding March" at its conclusion. The wedding party then proceeded to Mr. Sumpter's residence, where they partook of that gentleman's hospitality.

On last Sunday afternoon, the Rev. Mr. Gifford presented Miss Sumpter, on behalf of the teachers and pupils of St. Luke's Sunday school, with a very handsome and valuable collection of books, intended to form the nucleus of a library in her new home. In making the presentation, the Rev. Mr. Gifford bore testimony to the long and valuable services which Miss Sumpter had rendered in her dual capacity of teacher and Sunday school organist. Mr. Sumpter, with evident emotion, replied on behalf of his daughter.

St Luke's Church was filled to overflowing yesterday on the occasion of the marriage of Miss Sumpter to Mr Davis. The signal station and the vessels in the harbor hoisted all their available bunting in honor of the ceremony – the bride's father being chairman of the Harbor Board – which was performed at half-past twelve o'clock. The church was decorated for the occasion, as also the gateway in Tees street. The ceremony was performed by the Rev. Mr Gifford, assisted by the Rev. Mr E. E. Chalmers. The bride wore a white pearl silk dress trimmed with Brussells lace, and orange blossoms; no jewellery being worn. There were six bridesmaids (five sisters of the bride and Miss Lemon), whose dresses were of white cashmere, trimmed, three with heliotrope, and three with rose satin; veils and wreaths to match being also worn. The groomsmen were Messrs Bristed, M'Kerrow, and H. Lemon The bride and bridegroom left in the afternoon for Timaru, *en route* to Christchurch. On Sunday last Miss Sumpter was presented with a collection of books by the teachers and pupils of St. Luke's Sunday School. The Rev. Mr Gifford, who made the presentation, referred in complimentary terms to Miss Sumpter's long connection with the school.

Now that Richard and Emma are married, there are no more letters between them for a while. Let us turn, then, to letters from the family at Oakleigh.

Letters from the family begin in 1882. Let's start with a quick headcount of the siblings: Harriet is 19; Lottie 17; Mary 15; Blanche 13; Clara

12; John 10; Walter 8; Millie 6. We also now have Winnie (4) and Bertie (2).

Emma & Richard's first child was also born in this year, in around July-August: Richard George Llewellyn (called Llewellyn). No doubt George's remarks about Emma's health in the following letter are in response to her pregnancy.

The year in Oamaru is marred by an outbreak of scarlet fever. Happily it is of a "mild type", but most of Oakleigh seem to succumb.

Oamaru
April 20th 1882

My dear Emma,

I was pleased to receive your letter & glad that Blanche's visit gave you pleasure — I should much like myself to have been able to have had a peep at your premises.

I was glad to see you looking better although I think there is plenty of room for improvement & think a few hearty meals of fowls, chicken foie, etc would assist & I would strongly recommend you to be wise in time.

You did not give me a hint that there was any chance of your going to Christchurch or I should have been much pleased to have made arrangements for you there.

Tell Mr Chambers he did not keep his promise of seeing me there or giving me the opportunity of saluting him. Had he let me know about the trial? I would have sent him up a balloon. I am sorry to hear that Mr Winter is still unwell ask Richard to remember me to him & tell him I hope he will soon be better — nothing like hot baths & [unreadable] porridge. You were right in your surmise as to John Gifford etc. I am told he has made a small fortune in Auckland, having sold out for £7000 leaving him clear £4000 This is pretty well considering the short time he has been away if it be true.

He also has a lot of money left him through his wifes relatives & has been advised to go home & arrange about it. He has taken Mr Restall with him I believe.

I am very sorry that Richard missed the train as it was the only chance I should have had for a chat with him for I could not get an opportunity of talking to him at the Exhibition as I had more company than I wanted at the time.

I don't know when I shall be able to come up again as dear Mama has not got strong enough although I am in hopes she is now really on the mend.

The weather has not been so very pleasant lately.

There is an exceedingly brilliant Aurora here tonight I presume you will see it also, I must now say good bye my dear Emma & with best love to yourself & Richard from Mama & myself,

I am
Your loving Father
George Sumpter

Shall expect a long letter from Richard by way of apology for his desertion.

Now that Richard has given George a grandson, I believe I detect a softening of his attitude toward his son-in-law. After all, they're committed now, and George, I'm sure, wishes him well most earnestly.

Oakleigh
July 26th 1882

My dear Emmie,

I think I shall write you a short letter as I have not written since I was at the Parsonage and that letter was gratis.

Mr Finch is up tonight; he is in one of his jolly tempers and has kept us roaring all the time. Clara, George, Walter, and I went to Charley Roberts' party on Thursday; Edgar Finch was there he is so nice! We acted a charade Tea-Spoon. Perhaps you would like to hear about it. In the first scene Constance had an afternoon tea-party and Agnes Todd & I, who were supposed to be sisters, went to it. I was "dreadfully aesthetical" and when I was offered a slice of cake leant back in my chair; I held it gingerly between my fingers, & eat the tiniest possible morsels off it. Then I was so insulting that I had to be turned out of the house; but returned after a while to ask Constance haughtily if she had "abducted" my card-case out of my pocket. Of course she indignantly said no, & then I picked up my unfinished slice of cake (which I had in reality returned for) & asked her if I might take it; she had to say yes out of politeness.

In the second scene Laurie & I; Jim & Agnes were "spoons"; and Constance & Charley (my papa & mamma) came into the room suddenly & found us flirting outrageously. She gave us a severe scolding but could hardly keep from laughing at our lover-like signs to each other.

In the last Mabel had lost a tea-spoon, fork, and knife. Constance a servant had her hair untidy & face blackened. She was great fun & after telling a lot of fibs about the spoon calmly produced it out of her pocket & said she had found it in her box but had not put it there. Then we other servants brought forth the fork & knife which we had found somewhere else.

Constance was up on Monday she yarns an awful lot about "Cousin Dick & Patience". I think she has improved but I always liked her the best of the Lemons.

I am going to have an excuse for my lessons to-morrow they were awfully difficult. I hope Baby & you are quite salubrious. Mabel is going to send you some "dalicus" seeds. Please remind me of any of my broken promises & please excuse the scribble & blots. With love from all to all

Believe me to remain
Ever your loving little sister
Blanche.

Oakleigh
August 12 1882

My dear Emma,

As you will have seen for yourself by this time I have a robe for the Baby, it was the prettiest I could find, the price of it is 35/. I hope it is not too expensive but the prices of the good ones were nearly all between 30/ & 40/.

I have really had no time to write to you before to-night for we have had visitors one of the evenings & there have been two or three parties this week, & of course I have had to attend to the clothes.

Mr Finch & Herbert came up on Tuesday evening & stayed until about twelve o'clock, Mr Finch was telling some fearful tales about Mesmerism. On Wednesday afternoon Miss McCaw sent a message asking Lottie & me to go down there in the evening, she had meant to have her party to-night but the Todd's were engaged Mrs Todd, Agnes, Brute, Jim, Miss Huxtable, Miss Annie Gillies, Constance, Herbert, Mr Bannerman, Mr Morris, Mr Fergusson, Mr McAndrew (Jeannie Trotter's friend) & a Mr Norreys were there so it was quite a large party for them, we were dancing most of the time.

Yesterday afternoon I drove Blanche & Clara out to the Gilchrist's to a party & they stayed all night and Lottie & Mary went to another party at Mrs Todd's so Oamaru is waking up isn't it? Edith is going to have her party on Tuesday Lottie & I are going I am going to wear my bridesmaid's dress it will be the first time I have worn it to a dance since the night of the Wedding.

The bursary you speak of is the one George Gifford was trying for.

Mrs Jackson was getting so anxious about Willie that he only stayed here a week, but even that seemed to have done him a great deal of good.

I will send you the petticoat in a day or two I had sent the robe before your letter came.

They are all very well again now. Blanche seems a good deal brighter the last few days.

I should like to strangle that cat more than ever there must be something "wrong" with it.

We are having lovely weather again just now though the mornings & evenings are still very cold I hope it intends to last for a while.

Mrs Todd & the McCaws were kindly asking all about you & the baby the other night, Miss Maggie says if its eyes are like Mr Davies' they must be pretty, be sure & tell him that.

Please remember me to any one who asks about me, especially Mr & Mrs Chambers.

Toodie says I am to tell Mr Davies with her love, to keep his promise about writing to her, & Millie sends her love to him, the baby & yourself [from what I can work out, "Toodie" must be a nickname for Winnie.]

With much love from all of us
I remain
Your loving sister
Harriet C Sumpter

Oakleigh
August 15

My dear Emma,

Thank you very much for your nice letter. I am glad you like the little shawl, but I wish it were prettier. Edith has her birthday party tonight. Harriet & Lottie have gone. Harriet has worn her bridesmaid's dress with mittens to match the darkest shade of the satin. Lottie has got a new dress for the occasion. It is pale pink nun's veiling (like your light dress) trimmed pink satin & lace. It is sweetly pretty & Lottie looks splendid although Mamma thinks that blue would have suited her better. Mr Ruddock (the minister from Melanesia) came up yesterday with Mr & Mrs Gifford. Harriet & I walked out to the Reservoir with Mr Gifford & Mr Ruddock. We do not care for him very much. He says that most of those curiosities that came from Auckland are from Melanesia. You know those nuts that make that dreadful noise that Dick is so fond of? Well, Mr Ruddock says they are used at dances. The gentlemen tie them to their knees. Only fancy wearing those things while you danced the Highland Schottische. Papa says it is no worse than "yelling out like they do". Mr Gifford says that Charlie is fourth in the first class. I hope he (Charlie) will not get too conceited.

There is not very much news to tell you, but I will tell you as much as I can.

I hope you & baby are both getting on well. Lottie & I went to a party at the Manse last Thursday. Blanche Filleul was there & she asked me all about you & the baby & what his name was to be.

She says she likes Llewellyn very much. She sent her love to you & told me to tell that you certainly ought to give him the three names. I like the three names very much. Mrs Burbury said that her boy was to be called Edward, so this is his name, Edward, Percy Harold Burbury.

Now dear Emma I must say goodbye so with love to you all,

I remain
You loving sister
Mary I. Sumpter

Oamaru Sept 16 1882

My very dear Emma

I do not like to let this morning mail go without writing a few lines to you to let you know before Sunday how we are all getting on – I am exceedingly thankful to say that so far the invalids are progressing wonderfully & have had two or three outings all except Mary whose time for lying up is not over – Mr Finch & Moore returned to play a game at Lawn Tennis with Lottie but of course would not come in – We are to have the opening match at Cricket between President & Vice today & it bids fair to be a very fine day for it. The British troops have been very successful in Egypt at last – so at parade yesterday I formed my Battalion into line & got the Band to play "Rule Britannia" which sounded very well – Gordon Millington has caught scarlet fever & gone to the hospital. It is I believe of the same mild type – Oakleigh has just begun to put on its spring dress & looks beautiful & the trees bid fair to give a large crop – & I hope we may all be spared to partake of the fruit together.-

The weather here is beautiful but the times are miserably dull hardly anything doing at all – I hope harvest time will make up for it if we can paddle along till then – The mole [at the breakwater] is creeping out at the rate of 30 feet or rather yards a month – how is my grandson getting on: has he made his Father feel uncomfortable any more by his screams – I have not made him his christening present yet but shall not forget

With much love to all
Your Father George Sumpter

Oakleigh
September 25th
1882

My dear Emma,

Thank you very much indeed for the nice book you & Dick sent me; please give him my love & thank him. I began it yesterday & think it is very nice. Have either of you read it.

Blanche, Clara, & Walter came down to dinner for the first time on Sunday. Poor Mary was the only one upstairs, but I hope she will be with us all next Sunday. She sends her very best love & says I am to tell you she has made two little flannels for Llewellyn & begun the third. Mamma thinks he will be able to wear them quite well when you put him into his short clothes. We are all very glad to hear Baby is getting better.

Poor Papa has a nasty sty. It bothers him a great deal. He has been unfortunate he has had two or three boils on his face lately.

The rain is coming down in torrents tonight. It reminded me of the day I left Rakaia. I expect you are having the same. Had you dreadful duststorms on Saturday & Sunday? We had.

On Sunday morning Mr Finch & Herbert Moore came up to wish me "Many Happy Returns". Herbert sent me such a lovely bracelet with my name & the date engraved on it. Jessie Gilchrist sent me a very pretty bracelet too. Harriet gave a pair of sweet little vases. Papa gave me £1 & Mamma ten shillings & I got six cards. Harriet & I got a very nice letter from Sophie tonight for our Birthdays. None of the Lemons seem to have remembered us. They keep away from us more than any one. They will not shake hands with us even edith says she only hopes they don't get it.

Mamma sends her love & says she hopes it will not be very long now before she is able to write to you. We hope to be able to go to Church next Sunday week.

Miss Cole lives in Aunt Mary's street now. In a new house of Papa's just opposite the Milne's.

Mr Moore's Service of Song on Friday evening was a great success. There were 100 singers (from all the choirs in Oamaru) & more than a 1000 people in the hall. It was held in Colombo Church hall. I do not expect you know where it is. Above Mr Smith new store opposite the Union Bank. The proceeds were to be divided among all the Sunday Schools.

Millie & Winnie have not written to you for a long while. They do not have lessons now & so they do not get so much practice. I expect Millie will write to answer your letter soon.

I hope it will not be very long before we shall all be able to see our dear wee nephew. You will see a change in Oamaru. It seems such an age since we saw you.

But now dear Nannie I must stop.

With very much love from all of us. Believe me to remain,
Ever your loving sister Lottie

Oakleigh
October `6th 1882

Dear old Emmie,

I am just going to answer your kind letter, thank you very much for the anemone seeds, Mary and I were admiring some lovely red & white and purple & white anemones in Reed Street last Thursday, I love them.

I have such a dear little curly headed blue eyed doll to dress up as a boy for dear wee Bertie. Miss Cooke cut the suit out for me in ruby velvet & she put a stiff white sailor collar round its neck which sets it off splendidly.

It was so strange being at church on Sunday, we (at least I) escaped the disagreeableness of walking into church when nearly every one was seated as Papa took the service we were naturally about the first.

I can't help being sorry to hear that Baby Llewellyn is getting "fat" of course I have no need to be so if he is well. Clara & I took Millie, Toodie, & Bertie down to town today, it was so lovely. Bertie did not get tired at all he said & we drove home with Papa, he was so pleased; there was rather a cold wind (not one of Dick's favourite "north-westers") blowing as we drove up Thames St. Bertie made me laugh so when I was in Bulleid's, he was talking away so loudly to me about the door & lamps.

I am going to stay on Wednesday with Jeannie Mitchell till Saturday it will be Bertie's birthday so I will not go until four or five o'clock.

It is very good of Jeannie to ask me is it not? especially just now.

There was a jolly game of cricket on Saturday between the "Bankers" & "Lawyers", and the "Oamaru Cricket Club". It was such fun watching Mr Millar & Mr Clarke playing, the first one caught Papa & Mr Walker out splendidly.

So it will be the anniversary of "Our Darling's" Wedding day on Thursday. I will not forget to drink Dick & your health on the 19th although I will not be at home.

Please Emmie write as much about yourself in your next letter, you write such a little about either yourself or Dick not that I am finding fault with you only I can never hear too much of either of you dear ones.

Mamma likes me to drink wine "three times a day" just fancy! I hope I will not "cherish a love for alcohol" as it says in Patience.

As I am afraid I will not get Bertie's doll dressed in time if I do not stop I must do so, with my very best love to Dick & yourself & a kiss to Baby (if you don't mind giving it).

Believe me to remain
Your loving sister
Blanche

More next time I write dear Nannie which will be next week I think.

I put the paper round this letter because the envelopes are so thin & my epistles are not so very beautiful that I like to have them read —

My dear Emma

Thank you very much for your nice present but the dear little box was broken we went down fishing and we got one hundred and thirteen fish I suppose you heard about the rechs [wretches?] in tinuru [Timaru?] now I must end this short letter I remain yours truly W Sumpter

My Dear Emma

Edgar caught a robin on Monday Edgar made some splendid things for a ship he gave George a billiard table in the cabin, with little cues, and balls a little ladder leading to the pantry and he bought a box of furniture for it. Douglas gave Bertie such a pretty pink kite. Blanche and Clara have left school.

With love to Dick and dear wee baby and to you

I am your
Loving sister
Milly

dear Emma

I think Topsy is a nice name for the kitty.

My dear Emma

I am very sorry that I did not write to you before.

Bertie sends his love and a kiss to baby.

I went to Mrs Sutherland's on Wednesday and I enjoyed myself very much.

Fred and Florrie Sutherlands come to school and I like school better now when they are there.

Mr Sutton is very ill, and so Amy is staying with Miss Cole. Is it not kind of them to have her? And now I must say good night with love to All

[from Walter?]

[PS]Dear Emma

Please do not hesitate about sending for Lottie, unless you would rather she did not come, best love from your loving mother and all of us.

Oakleigh
October 10th 1882

Dear Emma,

Thank you very much for writing to me.

I had a great many letters while I was ill (I mean when I had the scarlet fever, for I was not ill). All ~~my~~ the girls in my class wrote to me; besides Herbert Moore & you.

Blanche is almost quite well, she looks better than she did before she got ill. She went down town yesterday with Lottie for the first time. She was so glad to go.

Herbert says he asked Gracie Lemon if she knew how we were, & if she had come to see us. She said "Of course not! I won't go for months, it won't be safe." (It will not be much loss to us will it? But, although they don't write or ask after us they go & tell people how we are!)

Doctor Wait has not been here since the Saturday before last. I suppose he wants us to go out of quarantine on our own account & then if any one catches it from us he can say it is not his fault.

Mamma wants to know if you got the parcel for Llewellyn safely on Saturday. She should so like to see how Llewellyn looks in the bonnet.

Fancy! All our apples have not gone yet; we have a few winter ones left.

You would laugh if you saw me write a letter. I write a little then I stop & think, or tell Milly "what comes next" for her to write.

She is writing to you; but I am afraid her letter will not be very nicely printed. Papa has promised Miss Cole to have Milly. I suppose she will go after Christmas. I teach Toody & her just now.

I hope you will excuse the writing, & everything bad in this letter please. But now, dear Emma, I think I must conclude. With love to yourself & a kiss to Llewellyn,

I remain,
Your loving sister,
Clara Sumpter

Oakleigh
Oct 11th 1882

My dear Emma

I am sorry not to have written to you before but I could not. One of my Ducks is quite lame, and I think I will get it killed tomorrow.

Oct 12th

Papa made us do sums last night & so I could not finish my letter. Mr Benett sent my ducks eggs home tonight. I did not get my duck killed today.

16th Oct. I saw Mr & Johnnie Mann today & I went and was going to shake hands with him but he did not know me and then Mr Mann asked me my name and when I answered he told Johnnie to shake hands with me.

And now dear Emma I must say goodbye. With best love to all,

I remain
Your loving brother
G Sumpter

Oakleigh
October 21st '82

My dear Emma,

Thank you very much indeed for your letter.

I asked Bertie what message he had for you for sending him the cup, he says – Bertie's love & thank you. He was so delighted with it, you could hardly have chosen anything better. Harriet used to give him a saucer with his mug before because he used always to ask for one.

It was great fun on his birthday he got such a lot of presents he did not know which one to take first.

Papa, Mamma, Mary & I went to the Cricket Concert last night I am sorry it was not a success. Sophie, Mr & Mrs Williams Edith & lots of others refused to help much to Papa's annoyance. There was a very poor audience & the programme was not very lively. Constance's piece was very pretty but was too good for an encore. The bands played very well indeed.

Harry Thompson is in Oamaru just now. He goes North on Monday so I expect Dick will see him. He & Mr Clarke, Mr Finch & Herbert were up playing lawn tennis yesterday afternoon. We are going to play every Friday I believe.

I am sending up Mrs Rutter's shawl at last. It is not made of wool as thick as I should like but I could only get the same as yours is made of, so I would not use that. She is quite welcome to it as a gift if she likes but if she would rather pay for the wool it is 5/6.

We have got to work as hard as we can for this bazaar now. Harriet is not going to have anything to do with it. We are to have fancy dresses. I think Mary told you though.

It looks rather like rain today we have had two or three showery days this week.

Blanche comes home from Mrs Mitchells today. Papa saw her yesterday & thought she was looking very well. Mr Finch said she looked quite blooming. I think her illness has really done her good. & now with love to you & Dick from all of us. & kisses to Llewellyn

Believe me to remain
Your loving sister,
Lottie

Oakleigh
October 28th 1882

Dearest Emma,

I am at last going to pester you again with a letter, which I hope you will not object.

I enjoyed myself very much at Mrs Mitchell's, Jeannie and I went for a walk up to the Boundary on Thursday & Friday and on the night I arrived there (Wednesday) we went to the Church Practice. While Mrs Williams was singing a solo in "As Pants the Heart" Sophie made a sign to Jeannie that she felt a spider at her neck. Jeannie pulled Sophie's frilling about and out crawled a fat brown spider. Jeannie knocked it on to the floor, and then went to one end of the pew, and Sophie went to the other end. Then Mr Vincent (a bass in the choir with an awfully deep voice) wanted to see what the fun was so he struck a match, and leant over the pew. At this noise the trebles turned round, & they saw Jeannie & Sophie nearly in fits with laughing but they had to wait patiently until the solo was finished to hear what was the matter. Then they turned eagerly round and Sophie, with tears in her eyes, told them of her fright.

We are so excited about the Fancy Dresses for the Bazaar; Mary & Clara have not decided yet on their costumes although we have hunted up all kinds of books. Lottie is either going as a "Cracovienne" [a woman of Krakow? The word also signifies a popular dance, and a famous piano piece], or in a "Stuart" Costume they are both extremely pretty, and would suit her to perfection. Mamma is going as "Mary of Lorraine" I think and I am going as "Marguerite" in Faust. I am to wear a white & blue cashmere dress caught up at one side so as to show a white petticoat trimmed with blue; my sleeves are to be tight with two puffs, and round my waist I am to wear a blue velvet girdle with a small bag attached to it. My bodice I am not quite sure of, nor of my shoes or stockings; my hair is to be done in two <u>long</u> plaits down my back.

Mr, Mrs, and Annie Finch are coming up to Oamaru tonight by the ½ past nine train. We were going down there this afternoon to play Lawn Tennis as Mr Finch expected them this afternoon but this morning his gardener brought a letter from him (Mr Finch saying that "his apple-cart was upset as his people were not coming until ½ past nine so he was afraid he must defer the lawn tennis until some day next week when he & Annie would fix the day." Please tell Dick that our gardener Colman met that deaf & dumb man, he & I had such fun about, (the cracks on the ceiling etc) at a boarding house & he is really so afflicted.

I am going to look for the announcement of Nellie Honour's marriage to enclose in here as Mama asked me too. I am afraid I will not have Llewellyn's petticoat finished as soon as I meant to, as I have to do some bazaar work.

On Friday all of us are asked out except Millie, Toodie, and Bertie; for Mrs Roberts has asked Mamma, Papa, Harriet, Lottie and Mary to a grand dance and

Mrs Clowes has asked Clara, George, Walter, and me to another dance. Harriet is the only one who is going to refuse.

Poor little Millie has not been very well lately. She is quite hoarse tonight with a cold. Herbert has been in Dunedin at an examination; he will not know the result of it until Christmas. What does that last word remind you of? it reminds me of a happy reunion with our dear ones. But now dear Nannie with best love & kisses I am ever

Your loving sister Blanche

(I hope you will not be unable to read this letter as it is so crossed.)

For those who, like me, have ever wondered what exactly was meant by letters being "crossed" (something referred to in historical novels of a certain type), I have put an image of this letter, among others, on the website.

Oakleigh Oct 21 1882

My dear Emma,

I had intended to write two or three evenings before, this week, but some-one else was going to.

We are going to have a sort of "At home" for Lawn Tennis every Friday, yesterday Herbert, Mr Finch, Mr Clarke, and Harry Thompson came up.

Poor Constance's engagement was broken off three months ago, and she has been very unwell, she has been staying in Napier since that, but is going home with him, and promises to write to me again as soon as she gets back I hope she will.

I was astonished to see Harry Thompson in town the other day but knew him at once, he has "grown a beard", & we all think looks very like Henry Honour, he is just as "soft" as ever.

The Concert was a very poor one last night both the Entertainment & the audience; Papa Mamma, Lottie & Mary went. Blanche came back this evening she looks much better for the change.

They have all been hunting up histories and books of all sorts to find descriptions of fancy dresses for the Bazaar, Blanche wants to go in an Oriental costume.

Mr Finch is going to preach in our Church both times tomorrow, and on Monday night there is to be an Organ Recital Mr Finch says it is going to be a very good one.

I hope you got your parcel safely tonight, Mamma drove down to send it, & that Mrs Rutter will admire her shawl, is it not a beauty?

It is not "our" Mrs Leslie who keeps the Boarding-house she lives in Severn Street still.

There was a good deal of excitement over the election, as Councillor, yesterday, Mr Hassell & Mr Connell were the candidates & Mr Connell got in by one vote, Mr Burbury drove about six ladies down to vote, in a big wagonette, just before the polling closed but it did us good.

I can think of no more news so

With love from all
I remain
Your loving sister
Harriet E Sumpter

Oamaru Oct 31 1882

Dear Richard

I duly received your note with cheque for which I am much obliged. How is it you did not deduct your commission? I did hope some one might have been tempted to have given a higher price as really the house I think is likely to turn out a very good one –

I am glad to hear you are better & that Emma & little one are flourishing – I hope we may as you say have a merry Xmas, together – I am almost afraid to ask whether Emma or you have any idea of coming down to the Bazaar or Show as this might interfere with Christmas & the journey twice be too much – The invalids that were are now beginning to recover their health & strength & not to look much the worse, & I think all danger of infection must now be past.

Business does not seem to improve much although I hope it will shortly. The weather also is very dry & there is already a little fear expressed as to grass & crops. With best love to all I must now close this scribble.

Your aff Father
George Sumpter

Oakleigh
November 12th 1882

My dear Emma,

If I do not write to you this morning I am afraid I shall not be able to this week so you must please forgive a hasty scrawl.

We shall, of course, be dreadfully busy this week so you must not be anxious if you do not hear from us. Mamma and all of us are very well indeed, Blanche's illness has done her a great deal of good, I think, she looks ever so much better than she did before it.

Papa & the boys went down to the Dunedin Review. Harriet, Mary & I went down to the station to see them off at one o'clock in the morning & stayed up till two for them on Friday morning. Mr Walter Finch was up here nearly all day & Mr Finch came up to play lawn tennis in the afternoon. The Moore's were going to have a picnic had it not been for illness. On Friday we were all quite hopeful for poor little Gwladys [the Gifford's 20-month-old daughter], as Charlie told us she was better, but on Saturday George brought home the sad news that she was dead. It must have been a happy relief for her as she was suffering a great deal. They must all feel her loss very much. They have always taken such care of her. All the others & Annie Finch are getting on as well as possible.

They allow Mr Finch to play the organ & I think, attend at Philharmonic all the same, but he will not go into any one's house although he is covered with disinfectants.

I hope you, Llewellyn & Dick are all perfectly well, we shall be so delighted to see you at Christmas time.

There is such a thick, damp fog all over Oamaru this morning. I do hope it will not be like it all the week. It looks very much like it did that Easter the volunteers were here.

The bazaar people are having nice old rows. They have not called a committee meeting ever since we were well, Mrs Hislop, Mrs Forrester, Mrs W.I Smith, Mrs H.W. Robinson & Mrs Bulleid meet & arrange everything as they like. The hall is engaged for the night before the bazaar & they threaten if they cannot get it that night to give it up. They did not engage it for that night & if they chose it would do quite well the next morning for Papa promised to get the stalls all ready for them.

Douglas sent us a big bunch of bananas, we used to go into the greenhouse & eat as many as we wanted & we are so dreadfully sorry they are all gone!

If the blossoms are as good as they look we shall have more strawberries than we have ever had before splendid isn't it?

Blanche & Clara went to Miss McCaws picnic to the Sandy Beach on Saturday they enjoyed themselves.

[not signed but looks like Lottie's writing]

Growing bananas in Oamaru! Perhaps these hot days they complain of really are a sign that the weather was warmer then.

Oakleigh
November 23rd 1882

My dear Emma.

Thank you very much for your letter. The bazaar is at last all over & I am glad to say we can once more go on with our proper work. I hope you Dick and Llewellyn are all perfectly well. Are we not having dreadfully hot weather? I wish we might have a thunderstorm to clear the air.

Mary and I began our singing lessons this week. I went this morning. Neither of us like her altogether but perhaps she will be nicer after a while.

Mamma went to the Guild today and Mary, Blanche, Clara went to play lawn tennis at Mr Finch's. Annie is able to sit up & is getting on very well. The Moores are all getting on capitally too, but poor Frank Williams has it now. They say he caught it from those wretched people at the bazaar. His case is very slight indeed. He had not even to go to bed.

Mrs Newton is going to have a carpet dance tomorrow evening. Harriet and I are asked. We have accepted & I suppose we shall go.

We have had two or three strawberries already. I hope this weather does not scorch all the blossoms up. I am afraid there is not much to tell you but I do not like letting much time go without writing some kind of a letter & I know you will not mind a rather hasty letter.

Did you hear the nice story about Bob Balmer he has not been heard of since Monday. They say he has gone back to Sydney.

Yes; Mr Brown is Mr Herdman's successor for a while at any rate [I assume this is the Mr Herdman who was manager of the Oamaru Branch of the Union Bank of Australia]. I do not think he is very nice. I bought a rose tree, at least Mamma bought it for me, from the bazaar. It was only in bud the first day & I was rather disappointed when it came out it was not nearly as pretty as I expected.

An entertainment was given last night in the Volunteer Hall, the proceeds from which were for the benefit of St. Luke's Ladies' Guild Fund. The programme consisted of a mixture of vocal and instrumental music and representations of a number of the tableaux vivants which had been given at the Athenæum bazaar. These were again capitally represented and well put on the stage. "What are the wild waves saying?" in which the character of Florence and Paul were taken by Miss Gertrude Lemon and Miss Ethel Mitchell respectively, was perhaps the best, and certainly the most taking, of the tableaux part of the programme, which included the sleep-walking scene in Macbeth; "Queen Eleanor and Fair Rosamond"; "The Kenwigs family," and "Jeannie and Effie Deans." The glees, solos, and part songs, were all excellently rendered, and were received with applause and occasional demands for repetition. In this part of the programme, "Two's Company," sung by Miss Gifford, was very enjoyable, an encore being demanded, and Mr Weymouth was loudly encored for "We tars that o'er the ocean sail," which he sang in character. The instrumental music consisted of pianoforte solos and duets by Mrs Lemon, Miss Lemon, Miss E. Lemon, and Miss Mitchell. Miss Mitchell acted efficiently as accompaniste. The Philharmonic Society's piano, which was lent for the occasion, had been put in excellent order by Mr Oakden. The whole entertainment passed off smoothly and successfully.

Please give Dick my love and tell him I should very much like to come and look after him thank you but I am afraid I could not do it well enough. But I shall not be able to come because of the Confirmation. Mary comes to the classes too. I think she will be confirmed this year with me. I am very glad Mrs Rutter likes her shawl. We all saw the eclipse of the sun, we smoked glass to look at it.

Aunt Mary is going to have the tableaux over again soon for the sake of the Guild. I hope you will be able to see them, they are quite worth seeing.

But now dear Nannie it is getting late

With very much love from us all to you & Dick,
Believe me,
Ever your loving sister,
Lottie

We are all well. When I leave this out do not imagine we are ill.

Oakleigh
Jan 9th 1883

My dear Emma,

I am going to keep my promise to you.

I had not a bad journey down. Milly was very good. Some more people came in at Timaru. We saw Douglas & Herbert le Cren at the station. When we reached Oamaru Papa, Lottie, Mary and Blanche & Mr Weymouth were there to meet us. I do not think that Blanche's hair being cut makes her look any different.

They never got the letters I wrote on Friday night till yesterday evening. Mr Davies must have posted it too late for the train.

Bertie is very pleased with the stable. Toodie did not care for it much, so Milly gave it all to him. I do not know what colours you wanted the gloves. As soon as you tell me, I will get them. Blanche sends her love & thanks you for ~~her~~ ~~your~~ the letter, which you wrote for Milly. She will write soon.

I keep on calling Bertie 'Bubs' & 'Baby' because of Llwellyn.

Milly gave me a card in Rakaia & said it was mine from Mr Walter, but I think it is yours. I brought it down here. I will send; but if it is not yours, you can keep it.

Please remember me to Mary & say good-bye to her for me.

Blanche did not mind my knowing that about her ride, she only told me not to tell Mary. Remember me to Mr & Mrs Chambers & Mrs Pyke please, & tell Mr Chambers Papa can't tell who the gentleman was.

Florry Muir is such a cheeky girl! I suppose Lottie told you they were up. She made a man out of her handkerchief, & when any one played, she made this man dance first on one leg then on the other.

Please excuse the shortness of the letter & the writing. With love to Llwellyn & yourself,

I remain,
Your loving sister Clara

Mama sends her love, & says she is quite ashamed of not writing.

Oakleigh Jan^{ry} 10th 1883

My very dear Emma

I shall not try to excuse myself for my long silence though I feel very much ashamed of it. You were very good to write so soon, it seems almost wonderful to me, that you, and Dick, and the two children should have travelled up and down so often in safety and Papa too! I am afraid from what I hear, that Millie must have been rather troublesome, she looks all the better for the change, however, and I can only thank you for all the care you have taken of her and of Clara who seems to have enjoyed herself very much. I suppose you have now settled down again, we can hardly do so until after tomorrow although we are altogether now. I received a letter from Mrs Chambers last night and am glad to hear that she thinks both you and herself benefited by the changes.

I hope Dick is quite well, and darling wee Llewellyn still growing and thriving as he did when here. Please do not be afraid to tell me all about him when you write. Dick's visit was so short that it seems like a dream but I do thank him for sparing you so long, and hope he did not suffer too much discomfort during your absence. Papa is all the better for his little trip and on the whole does not seem to be so much worried. I am very well indeed and feel quite glad to be able to help in giving the children their treat this year. Harriet has been very busy since you left making jam, but there are <u>plenty</u> of Gooseberries left. I only wish I could transport you into the midst of them by some magic power.

I will write to Mrs Chambers after the Treat as I shall then have something to tell her about. We are all very sorry to hear that poor Mr Chambers suffered so much with his finger and also that he should have gone home unnecessarily, as the New Year week was certainly better than Christmas week as regards weather. Please give our kind regards to Mr and Mrs Chambers and thank Mrs Pyke for her kind remembrance of me. I hope I shall see her again some day.

Millie says perhaps she will write tonight, if not she sends her love and so do every one of us. Your visit has left me some very happy memories I am only sorry that it was not brighter and more cheerful for you. I fear it was dull like this epistle which I must now close with fondest love to all of you.

Remaining always your loving Mother

P.S. Mrs John McCaw has a little son born on Thursday last I think Lottie said.

Oamaru Jany 16 1883
My very dear Emma,

Thank you for writing to me I am sure I do not deserve it as it is a long time since I wrote – I have not much news to tell you – I am still having plenty to do to keep things moving & shall only be thankful if able to do that – I could not comply with your request as to Mrs Chambers book as I did not get your letter in time to do so – I learn however that it was posted – I have got the photograph of the harbor to day for Mr Chambers which I will send by first opportunity & also the lawn tennis set – Have you got one? – I am very sorry I could not stop as I passed as I might as well have done as although by going on was to try & do something with Barnes but I understand it has all been upset or most likely will be & so the time & trouble was wasted – The town is looking a little livelier just now being full of harvest workers I do hope the good harvest will do something to make business better – Mr Jas Hassell Junr has decided to take out an auctioneers licence & I think will probably make a pretty good one. Did you notice that Mr Jas Murison is dead – The Sunday school treat went off very well although we had several showers – We are very badly off for teachers – The girls have lots of invitations to parties & I think work a great deal too hard in consequence and I really do not know how Harriet manages to do it all. After waiting for about two months for decent weather the contractors Miller & Smillie have at last to day been able to put down the caisson at the head of the breakwater with the three hundred ton block – You will have noticed that we had a very large majority as to the Harbour Board loan - Have you told Mr Chambers. I must now conclude with much love to yourself, & Richard & best remembrances to Mr & Mrs Chambers,

Your loving Father
George Sumpter

Oakleigh
Feb. 5th 1883

My dear Emma

I paid Sargeant for the Photographs & am sending you the receipt, he says he is very glad you like them so much, & will let us have the others on Saturday; the gloves are paid for too. Llewellyn must be getting on famously I expect we shall find him quite altered when next we see him, (when is that to be?)

PHOTOGRAPHY.

ALBT. SARGEANT, Tees street, Oamaru, is now taking ALL PHOTOS by the INSTANTANEOUS PROCESS.

Special attention is drawn to his new Cameo Oil Photo, which is confessed to be the nearest approach to life yet introduced. With this process the real color and complexion, hair, dress, etc., can be given and cannot be equalled for beauty and softness.

SEE SPECIMENS IN WINDOW.

sr25

I hope Mr Chambers is quite well again now he cannot be very strong.

Charley will get on very well at the College I expect, he is in the third division from the top now, & he is very quick.

George & Walter have found a new amusement lately, they have got a barrel-sledge & harness Nelly or Solomon to it & ride all over the place on it (of course a few tumbles, more or less, are nothing) they spend nearly all their spare time that way.

Poor Mr Newman has been rather badly hurt to-day, they were loading some of the Woollen Factory's machinery at Papa's store & a pillar belonging to it fell on him hurting his arm a good deal & fracturing two or three of his ribs, however they hope it is not a very serious hurt.

A serious accident occurred yesterday morning to Mr Mark Newman, who was employed in carting the Woollen Factory plant from Mr Sumpter's office to the building site. It appears that Newman was standing on the front part of his dray, while loading some of the iron pillars for the building, when his foot slipped, and he fell to the ground. In falling he tried to save himself by catching at one of the pillars, and the pillar, being insecurely loaded, rolled over and fell across the unfortunate man's breast and arms. Newman was at once placed in a cab and conveyed to his home, being met on the way by Dr Garland, who accompanied him. He was found, on examination, to have had two of his ribs fractured on the right side, besides having his right arm severely bruised and torn, and being otherwise shaken by the accident. He is doing as well as can be expected.

Of course you heard of Mr Finch's Fancy dress Ball some of the costumes were splendid a good many of them wore their "Bazaar" dresses. Kate Finch looked as well as any of the girls, she was dressed as "Snow" in white muslin with a little swansdown about it, my dress (Lady in George IV's time) was a rather short red skirt with two poufings & a deep flounce of white lace round the bottom; square-cut bodice with short sleeves, old-gold belt & sachet; & a wide white hat trimmed with red silk & cream & red ostrich feathers, Mr Murdoch's was the most ridiculous among the gentlemen's dresses it was a regular clown's dress in pink & white with bells at each point, about fifty I should think, which twinkled every time he moved & at the end of his long pointed cap he had a rather large one tied to a string.

Mamma sends her love to you & wishes me to tell you that she was getting some gloves for herself & thought she would get a pair for you as well before Clara came down, she wished to give them to you so we did not think it worth while to get another pair.

We are having splendid weather for the Harvest here now it rained a little last night but there has been a splendid drying wind all today so it will not have done the least harm.

Milly seems to get on very well at Miss Cole's there are only nine of them she likes it very much on the whole though at first she used to get very tired of being still so long.

With love from all
I remain Your loving sister
Harriet C. Sumpter

Oakleigh
Feb 17th 1883.

Dear, darling Emma.

I am awfully angry with myself for not writing to you before, and I should not say I have not time, because I suppose if I had chosen, I could easily have written some afternoon after school.

This is Saturday morning & I am writing this before breakfast.

We have had such wretched weather lately, Oamaru seems to have changed its character altogether. It is a great pity for the farmers & merchants is it not; Mr Finch says heaps of them will be ruined.

Has any one told you in their letters about the engagement (~~or~~ if not that yet it soon will be) between Mr Finch, and Gracie. It is so funny to see <u>him</u>, above every one, being spoony.

He is often at the Lemon's now, & on Thursday Constance & Gracie stayed to tea, with Kate & him. He took Gracie home at ten & then went to a spree the Roberts' were having (Mary & Lottie were there).

Bertie was delighted with his valentine he showed it to us all round, & at tea-time kept on saying, "Millie have you seen my "balentine"? "Blanche have you," & then he would "Oh Harriet you have not have you"?

We had such a lovely flower in the Greenhouse a little while ago; it was one Mamma bought from Falconer who told her it would not bloom for three years. Soon after Mamma had got it Lottie accidentally broke off the top of it. Papa put the top in a pot and it grew; and the other half flowered. The flower was four inches in length, and was of a large white trumpet or bell shape. Papa took it down to the Office & he said it scented it at once.

I suppose you like having a perambulator for Baby very much, it is a good thing he likes it. I showed Mrs Gifford your letter (I hope you do not mind) and she was so pleased at your asking after her after the School Treat. I like having my hair cut off very much; it is so cool, and I can wash it in cold water every morning.

Oh Emma I wish you had not asked me to pay you another visit for I should [omitted] to so much, but I am afraid it is not my turn to go to Rakaia, and besides school will prevent me.

I am the only one in my class but I learn geography and "Merchant of Venice" with Clara. But I think a girl of eighteen, Jessie Borrie, is coming & she may be in my class, if she is not too alarmingly clever.

<u>Jennie</u> Borrie has been at school for a fortnight; she is fifteen; and is in Gertrude Lemon's class.

I suppose you know that Clara & I learn dancing after tennis on Fridays; it is so jolly. It was not very fine yesterday but Mr Penrice, (the first time he has ever been up) Mr Clarke, Mr Waymouth, Mr Finch & Kate, Herbert & Douglas, Miss Leech and Edith Robinson were up.

Douglas gave Clara and me a lot of transfer pictures and he showed [rest lost]

[from Blanche]

The courtship Blanche refers to seems (particularly in contrast to poor Emma's lengthy engagement!) surprisingly short. A mere two months later, Grace Lemon marries James Finch.

MARRIAGE.

On the 24th April, at St. Luke's Church, Oamaru, by the Rev. Algernon Gifford, James George, eldest son of James Finch, Dunedin, to Grace, third daughter of John Lemon, Oamaru.

Oakleigh
May 12th 1883

Dear old Emmie,

Thank you very much for writing to me, I was so surprised and delighted when Papa gave it to me, I thought you were not going to write before you came down.

I wish Wednesday would hurry up, it is getting on for six months since we saw you, and Llewellyn, (except those that have been up) I am awfully sorry Dick (dear old fellow) can not come.

Would you like to have my room when you come down? If you would, please say so, in any letter you write before Wednesday if you do not mind.

The Juvenile Opera Bouffe Company has been in Oamaru since Wednesday. It is a really splendid company, Papa, Mary, Millie, George, Walter, and I went on Wednesday evening to see H.M.S. Pinafore acted. I enjoyed it awfully, Ralph, and Josephine were capital! The former (Amy Childs) sung magnificently and the latter (Laurie Graupner) acted splendidly. Mary and I were so disappointed that "Ralph" was a girl, she has such a merry face, and lovely voice.

This afternoon Clara took Toodie to see "Jack the Giant-Killer" acted, Toodie was perfectly enchanted with it, at tea-time she was trying to tell Papa about, and she did not know where to begin, or to end. What struck her particularly was about the Giant hitting a stick with a coat over it, by mistake for Jack. She said to Papa "the old giant thought he was killing Jack, and he wasn't at all; it was a log he was hitting all the time." While they were at the Pantomime I took Millie, and Bertie down to the Chinamen's. Mary was drying the tea-things at Aunt Mary's one Saturday after tennis, and she unfortunately broke one of the Chinese afternoon tea-cups. She was in a dreadful way about it, and is going to replace it so I went down to see if the Chinamen had got those they promised to obtain from Dunedin, but they had not. Bertie's courage failed him at the gate, and he would not go in, so poor little Millie, who wanted to go in awfully, had to stay outside with him. Millie wanted to go in particularly, to see the little Chinese boy who interprets what we say; he has been to the North School to learn English. Rakaia must be a little lovelier now, as from your letter there seem to be several children-visitors. Poor Mr Makeig must miss his wife very much. Please give my love to Mrs Pyke, she is a darling, we are all awfully fond of her.

"Councillor" Allan wrote a letter to the paper the other night begging to be excused for his absence from council, but he had been unwell, and he told them, he is going to propose that trees should be planted in Thames Street. Do you think it will be an improvement?

When I was out at the Parsonage I wrote a letter to Florry McLeod, and I had an answer from her last night, such a nice letter.

I suppose you know Annie Finch stayed with us from Saturday night till Tuesday, and then she had to go to Mrs Mitchell's, and came back to us last night but she has gone away today. Gracie did not go to church last Sunday, as she did not want any callers last week; when Mamma was calling at Aunt Mary's and asked after Gracie, Edith said hastily "Oh she receives no callers". Aunt Mary is dreadfully particular about everything to do with the newly married couple. But now dearest with best love to Dick and yourself I will conclude this gossiping trash — I remain

Your loving sister Blanche.

Oakleigh
May 2nd

My dear Emma

I remember quite well seeing the Engine. I expect Lewllyn is quite a different boy to what he used to be when I saw him last. I have nothing at home to do but loaf about the trees. I think I am going for a ride to morrow with Fred Newton, on Bessy. George will have plenty of riding to do these holidays. We had such fun on Papa's stacks pushing each other off we only caught one mouse the whole time we were there, and I dident like to keep him shut up so I let him go into a hedge so that the other boys couldent catch it on my birthday. Is there any butterscotch flying round up there. Papa gave me a splendid paint box and the boarders gave me one exactly the same. Thank you very much for the pretty card you gave me. Mr Moore fell down and broke his finger. Now dear Emma I must say good night.

I remain Yours truly
Walter

My dear emma

I wish I could see the baby. Milly says she will write to you soon. Mama and papa are going to Mrs reid's big dance. Mama and Milly and Lottie are going to the concert tonight. Harriet wanted to go to it so she has written to ask leave to stay till after the dance. Now I must say good with best love to all I am your loving sister Winnie

My dear Emma,

I am going to spend a week at Mr Lees on Monday. Lottie thanks you for your letter you sent her. Bertie sends his love to you and dick. We are getting holidays now for three weeks. I am doing cruel [crewel, one imagines!] work for Harriet. I like the book that you gave me. Walter got two paint boxes on his birthday. Mama sends her love to you. George is gone to the Sutherlands Station. Lottie and Mary are going to the Robinsons on Friday. I am trying to keep my locket and chain as long as I can. Mary sends her love to you. Clara sends her love to you.

Now I must goodbye with love to all
I am Your loving sister
Milly

Oakleigh May 29th

My dear Emma,

I really do not know whether it is my turn to write, but at all events I am going to do so. I expect you are glad to have Constance with you at last.

I am very sorry she did not say she was going to Rakaia on Wednesday because then we should have seen you as well as Dick. We were surprised to see him. What a lonely holiday you must have spent!

All of us went down in the morning to see the Volunteers. Lottie, Blanche, Clara, the boys, & I went over to see the Football Match. I did not see much of the game for I stood with my back to the players, most of the time, for you know I said I would not watch another football match, but Lottie & Clara got quite interested. We had a few fire-works in the evening. It was a splendid evening, & the rockets went off beautifully, especially one with coloured stars.

In the afternoon Papa, Mamma, Millie, Winnie, Bertie, & I drove up to Mr Allan's & then up to the Waitaki High School. We went all over the School. It is a splendid building both inside & out.

There was a Concert at Ngapara last Friday. Papa was going to read but his throat was too bad. I was going with him, so I was rather disappointed. Fanny Gifford met me in town & took me home with her, so I got an unexpected pleasure. Papa's throat was very sore indeed, but it is a little better tonight.

Edith has gone up to Duntroon for a fortnight, & Miss N. Hardy is going to Dunedin for a month, so we have lost two Sunday-school teachers.

Now dear Emma I must say goodbye, so with best love to Constance, Dick, & yourself,

I remain,
Your loving sister, Mary I. Sumpter

P.S. I wrote this letter for school but you must not be angry. Mr Finch & Mr Walter, Mr Duthie, Douglas & Herbert, Mr Allan, & last & least A. Gifford were up on the Queen's Birthday. Douglas has been sent to Timaru. He heard that he was to go last night & he went today. He came to say goodbye.

Mamma sends her love to you & she wants to know if you have tried any knitting for the Bazaar. She says you ought to for the sake of letting Dick see the needles he was so fond of. I wish you had not spoken about the paper for I cannot get into the way of sending it again not that it is any trouble. I am going to keep a Post office at the Rifles' Band Bazaar & Herbert is up here writing some letters for me. Mrs Finch is going to write some too. Please do not say anything about it to Constance.

Now dear Emma I must say good-night so with best love

I remain, Your loving sister, Mary I.S.

Oamaru June 4 1883

My dear Emma

You cannot think how disappointed I was not to have been at the Station when you & dear Mary left. Of course I intended otherwise but was relying on some of you calling for me at the office. I was fully occupied with visitors on business – Robert asked me whether I was not going to the station as I had mentioned to him stating that there was little time to spare – I immediately rushed off, but was only in time to see the back of train but neither of you – I hope you arrived safely & comfortably Mama wishes me to say that she was none the worse but all the better, for her walk – notwithstanding the terrific scolding!! I gave her for not calling for me "en passant" – I enclose a letter for Mary from Lottie & shall be writing to her myself in a day or two –

I find the pen & card case that I brought down in the buggy & thought Clara had dropped were for me from you dear Emma – I thank you very much for them & shall be well reminded of you when I use the pen which I shall do constantly – I hope Richard has received my polite message & that it has been duly considered by him with a view to amendments –

I must now close this with very best love to all of you

Your loving Father
George Sumpter

Oakleigh June 8th 1883

My very dear Daughter

I am sure you need not speak of thanking any of us for anything we can do for you – we are only glad to have any opportunity of giving you pleasure. I am sorry to hear that Baby has a cough but hope it will not last long. Has he cut any more teeth yet? I miss the dear little fellow very much and for two or three evenings I kept on hushing the children when they made a noise in the hall. I am glad his Father thinks he has grown.

Bertie looks so funny with his hair cut short. Winnie tried to write a letter to you last night after her party but could not manage it. She is just going with Harriet now to meet Milly and go with her and the boys to Mrs Hislop's for Bessie's party. Are they not gay! Mrs Newton accepted my apologies on your behalf very graciously and said she was glad to see you looking so well. She asked if you were not very proud of the baby as she thought you looked as you were. Mrs Gifford sends her love to you and is sorry she could not see you, she sent Winnie a "Chatter box" on her birthday [This appears to be a "serial volume" such as a children's annual].

Did Blanche tell you that Winnie and I went to Mrs Christie's after I had been to Mrs Newton's we went down the "Horse's Paddock" and through the Chinamen's ground and came back through the orchard so we had no steep hill to climb.

Please send word when you next write whether you would like your cards left at any other houses than Mrs Roberts and Mrs Hislop's. Mrs Christie has a little boy of five and a little girl a year old with dark eyes and pretty hair.

I forgot to notice in the bustle of your starting whether your tickets were for the whole distance — were they? or had you to get fresh tickets at Ashburton? As in that case you must have lent Mary the money for hers, will you please deduct it from the money which I think, Harriet is going to ask you to give Mary instead of sending to her.

My cold is almost gone, but poor Aunt Mary and Constance have very bad ones again. How is Mary's cough? The weather is dry now but too windy to be pleasant. I must now close this rather rambling epistle asking you, please, to give my fond love to Mollie, Dick and my Grandson (keeping a full share for yourself.

I am always Your loving Mother
S.S. Sumpter

Oakleigh
June 26 1883 [dated 1882, but this seems impossible from the contents]

My dear Emma

I wish I could have Romeo down here to catch some of the wild rabbits that are about here. Yankee caught one the other day and eat it.

I am so glad Llewellyn can say some words now. Mama and Papa have gone to Aunt Mary's tonight. How did Dick like the fowls. I hope they were not tough. Douglas Moore is up here tonight. Harriet Blanche Mama and Lottie have done two seams of the carpets and begun another.

How are the Bruces have you seen them lately. Do not bother about answering me because I know you have not time. Ask Dick when he is going to answer my letter tell him I will give it to him when I next see him. I suppose that you will not come down with Mary tell her not to bother about writing to me. I saw Mr Mann on Thursday he was down here. Tell Mary that our old buggy is splendid Papa has got the man to change its colour it is brown and kind of pink. And now dear Emma with best love to all at home and kisses to Llewellyn

I remain Your loving brother
George Sumpter

Oamaru Augt 4 1883

My dear Emma

I hasten to reply to your letter received to day in case there should be any mistake as to Lotties visit! neither does she nor do we at all wish her to stay at home for fear she should not be comfortable with you as if she can really be of sufficient use to you to make the journey worth while all of us are not only willing that she should go but desirous that she should & if you really think so telegraph & she will come up the following day – Our wish was that Richard would have visited us & that the whole arrangements could have been fully discussed before any final action was taken – and we are still quite puzzled how it can possibly be that he cannot arrange to come down on a Saturday returning on a Monday – & are much disappointed that he cannot do so – I can with you only hope that the decision as to going to Wellington is the best one although I fear it is only the temporary dryness that has alarmed Richard as it does almost every one else – Of course my dear Emma we shall be glad enough to have you with us whenever it is convenient for you to come & with our best love to you all from Mama & myself

I am Your aff Father
George Sumpter

Oakleigh Oamaru
Aug 7th 1883

Dear Emma

It is such a long time since I wrote to you but I don't get much time in the evenings as we have a good deal to do now. We read Don Quixote in school. They have all gone out except Lottie blanche and Clara and george and myself. Blanche wrote a letter to you for school and put alott of news in it and Miss McCaw hasent given it back to her yet she is so sorry because she meant to send it to you because she hasent time to write another. I caught such a pretty toihey [tui?] on saturday it was ~~a~~ blue with grey feathers on its neck and so white under its head.

Now with love to all
I remain your loving Brother Walter

Tough times for Richard & Emma

As intimated in George's recent letter, things are going badly for Richard. It's clear from the following letters that Richard is in debt, and Emma and the baby are sent down to Oakleigh while Richard goes north. Richard has got a position with the N.Z. Loan & Mercantile Agency Company in Wellington.

The family are parted for some four months.

Important changes have recently been taking place at the Rakaia. The business hitherto carried on by Messrs M'Kerrow and Mann has changed hands, and for the future will be carried on by the New Zealand Loan and Mercantile Agency Company, Limited. Mr Richard Davies, of the firm of R. Davies and Co., has left, or is about to leave, that locality for fresh fields and pastures new. The scene of his future labours will, I understand, lie in Wellington, and the monthly sales which he most pluckily continued to conduct, though meeting with so little encouragement, will, for the future, be held by Mr E. G. Staveley.

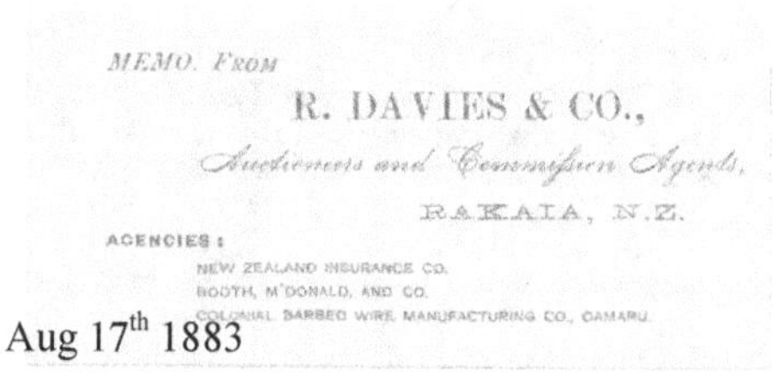

MEMO. FROM
R. DAVIES & CO.,
Auctioneers and Commission Agents,
RAKAIA, N.Z.
AGENCIES:
NEW ZEALAND INSURANCE CO.
BOOTH, M'DONALD, AND CO.
COLONIAL BARBED WIRE MANUFACTURING CO., OAMARU.

Aug 17th 1883

My darling Wife

I hope this will find you & the boy safe at Oakleigh. I enclose £10. Mr Mann has got his back up again & I don't know how I shall get on.

With lots of love
Your affect husband
Dick

Aug 18th 1883

My dear Wifie

I am glad to find that you & the boy arrived safely. I am going to Ch Ch on Monday, there is a small boat leaving for Kaikoura & Wellington in the evening but I do not know if the Compy want me to go by that. I thought you knew I could not possibly go down much as I should have liked it. Mr Coster wants two of your sisters at the Ball & to stay at Somerton. Please write Mrs Coster at once to let her know if they can come.

With fondest love
From your affect Husband
Dick

Mrs Smith will send the clothes on Tuesday

[Please thank Lottie for the nice letter & say I will write from Wellington]

Wellington
Aug 22/83

My darling Wife

I arrived at this horrid place @ 5.30 this evening just too late to send you a telegram. I feel dreadfully miserable at being so far away from you & the boy.

I am staying at a quiet Hotel but shall look out for a nice lodgings in a day or two, tomorrow I must present myself to my chief & get into harness I suppose.

I enclose cutting from Tuesdays Times. I don't suppose any of your sisters will be going to the dance. I hope you will not forget to write to Mrs Coster.

I see that a farmer named Smith at Papakaio has failed & that he owes your papa over £700, it is, I think enough to drive one out of his mind.

I must now conclude with fondest love to all

From your
Affect^{te} Husband
Dick

V. R.

IN BANKRUPTCY.

THIS is to Notify that at the first meeting of the creditors of JAMES SMITH, of Papakaio, Farmer, a debtor, held at the Courthouse, Oamaru, on Monday, the 20th day of August, 1883, JOHN SHENNAN, of Oamaru, Commission Agent, was appointed Trustee of the estate of said James Smith; and further, that the said John Shennan has duly declared his acceptance of the said trusteeship.

Dated this 22nd day of August, 1883.

J. L. TAIT,
Deputy Clerk of the Court.

J. O'MEAGHER,
Debtor's Solicitor. 964

Wellington
Aug 27th 1883

My darling Emma

Your welcome letter reached me this morning altho' I might have got it on Saturday if I had the Post Office key. I hope you got the £10 I sent you from Rakaia. I am in capital health & sorry to find that you have had such a bad toothache.

I spent y'day afternoon & evening at Dr Lemons, the electric light is splendid & he spends hours with his gas engine etc. [John Lemon's brother, Dr Charles Lemon, had been in Wellington since 1867, when he took up his position in the Telegraph Department.]

I don't know whether I shall be able to find the card plate, however, I will try my best & send you the cards.

There is not as much scope for business here with the Comp[y] as they have in Canterbury but I suppose I must make the best of it.

It is strange that Llewellyn will only take to Harriet; I suppose he must know that <u>his pa</u> is partial to her.

With lots of love
From
Your affect husband
Dick

House rent is something dreadful here

Wellington
Sept 4/83

My darling Wife

I suppose your papa will have told you that I am not getting on well with the Agent. I can honestly say that I am not to blame, the Agent now states that he does not object to me as an Auctioneer but because I do not sell more flour & potatoes. He does not seem to understand that this is a limited market & that the Comp[y] are working at a great disadvantage for various reasons which I shall explain to Mr Cooke when I see him. [John Cooke is the Manager in Christchurch.]

I haven't been to see a Doctor as I am all right. I have been to the Lemons once.

The nibs were sent in mistake.

I am now waiting to hear what the Auckland office have to say about me, of course, I take it, they will confirm their Agents action.

With lots of love to all
Your affect[te] husband
Dick

I miss you & baby very much

Wellington
Sept 13th 1883

My darling Wife

I am very sorry to tell you that I do not seem to suit the Agent here & I expect to be in Christchurch in about a week. However I think Mr Cooke will give me an appointment in the South Island.

I cannot write much as I am so thoroughly upset & all thro' no fault of my own.

I hope you & the wee boy are not missing me too much. The Ball went off well, Clark & his wife were the only foreigners.

With lots of love to all
I am
Your affect[te] Husband
Dick

Metropolitan Hotel
Cashel St
Christchurch
Sep 20th 1883

My darling Wife

You will have heard ere this reaches you that I am down here. Mr Cooke is away & will not be back until tonight. I shall call on him tomorrow & hope he will be able to give me an appointment in this Island. I shall have to go to Rakaia in a day or two as Mr Oxley writes to say that several creditors will have to be sued.

I am staying at a Temperance Hotel & cannot even get a bit of blotting paper.

My poor darling I expect you are pretty miserable. Tell your papa I will write to him after I have seen Mr Cooke.

The last letter I received from you came to hand on the 15th, if any others go forward I shall get them in due course.

With lots of love to all
I am
Your affect[te] Husband
Dick

Christchurch
Oct 1st 1883

My darling Wifie

I have just received your letters of the 15th ult addressed Wellington & yours of the 26th ult: addressed ChCh. I came here today from Rakaia. I could only see Mr Cooke for a short time as he will be leaving for Melbourne tomorrow, he had just received a letter from the Auckland office stating that they could not understand the action of the Wellington office & also stated that if I liked they would withdraw from the Auctioneering at Rakaia or give me six months salary.

I told him that I did not want either but that I should prefer remaining in the Companys service, he then said that I had better go to Rakaia & Leeston for a month & work up the business until he returned from Melbourne. He also told me that if the head office have confirmed the report from the Wellington office he would have resigned his position, so Mr Cooke is not as bad as some people make out.

I will try & get down to Oamaru in a few days. I do want to see you & the boy. It is just possible I may have the Sales at Rakaia & Methven. But I don't know where we are to live. I enclose £5 – which I trust will help to pay off some a/cs.

With lots of love
I am
Your affect[te] Husband
Dick

Rakaia
Oct 11th/83

My darling Wife

I have been travelling about for the last 3 days & shall be going to Leeston tomorrow. I told Turner I wanted the buggy, he did not seem to like it very much. [C.W. Turner was the Company's agent in Rakaia.]

I think I have done fairly well for the Company since my return.

I have not been to see Dr Ross as I feel quite well in health.

Someone went and smashed up Oxleys buggy the night before last, both shafts are broken in the middle & a spoke out of each wheel.

Theres going to be a big shooting match (rabbits) down the ?land next Tuesday, all the country side will be there.

I hope you & baby are quite well

Lots of love to all
From
Your affect[te] Husband
Dick

Please tell your papa to send particulars of your Banker per return without fail

Rakaia
Oct 13th 1883

My darling Wife,

I saw you waving your h'chief on Monday. I understood the boys to say that they would not be along the railway so I did not look for them.

I am quite well darling in fact the riding & driving seems to be the very thing to suit me. I want you too my darling oh! so much but I don't know how to get you until Mr Cooke returns from Melbourne. In fact, I could not afford the expense of taking a house here & then perhaps have to move in a week or two & I very much fear I shall not be able to pay all my debts as I now find that several of the a/cs are not of much account.

Mr Mann is going to the farm to live on Monday thank goodness but I expect he will be down every other day or so, however, I shall not see much of him. Pyke & Oxley are still bachelors so the three of us have to condole with each other. Things are very dull here & seem to be getting worse.

With lots of love to all
I am
Your affect[te] husband
Dick

Richard has mentioned this waving as the train goes past before. I don't understand why he would be passing through Oamaru, which would seem to be well south of any of the territory he would be covering, but there it is. It would seem he, on occasion, ranges further than one would assume.

Rakaia
Oct 19/83

My darling Wifie

I don't know whether there is a letter for me this evening as I have not seen Pyke.

I enclose a letter from my sister with a photo of two nieces, I think they are anything but nice looking.

I sold about £220 worth of sheep etc y'day & Matson & Co sold about £5 worth.

There is to be a concert at the Town Hall this evening in aid of the Library. Mr & Mrs Chambers arrived last evening.

I shall be starting for the Methven district on Monday & don't expect to get back until the end of the week.

I hope you are all well.

With lots of love
I am
Your affect[te] husband
Dick

Rakaia
Nov 1st 1883

My darling Wifie

Harriet sends her love what does that mean? I have not had such a message for many a long day. What time was up on the 28th ult?

I hear that Mrs Holmes' little boy is not expected to live. [I found no record of his death, so hopefully he recovered. The eldest daughter of a John and Elizabeth Holmes did die on the 6th, aged 2 years 2 months, but this was very sudden, after eating a quantity of match-heads.]

The goods sent for from home have not yet come to hand. Do you still want to go to Leeston in preference to remaining here?

I saw Mrs Chambers yesterday. She told me to call round whenever I liked & not wait to be asked. I have not been yet!

As this is written at Howells Hotel there is not a good pen available. [The letter appears to be written in purple pencil!]

I had a sale last Thursday at Methven, Tuesday at Ashburton & here today.

I rather like travelling about as it seems to agree with me. Altho' I am longing to have a home of our own again.

I have not seen Mr Mann for a week. I fear he will be about today as the Road Board meet.

Is Mr Cooke partial to one of the girls? [This appears to be the brother of the Mr Cooke of the Company.] If so, it will be a good thing for us provided they treat him kindly!!

With lots of love to all
From your affect Husband
Dick

Rakaia
Nov 5th 1883

My darling Wife

I hear that Mr Cooke returns tomorrow so I hope to get some news at the end of the week.

I am told that Mr & Mrs Chambers may be going to Lyttelton shortly. The offertories y'day morning amounted to 2/6.

I have not had my beard cut off & do not intend to have it taken away just now.

Whats wrong with Gracie? Has Finch been illtreating her?

Business is very dull just now & I have not been able to do much lately.

Mrs Coster is the only country lady that has called on Mrs Turner & I don't think there will be many more to come.

I think I shall call at the Parsonage this evening. I shall have to go to Ch Ch on Friday (Show Day) much as I should like to go to Oamaru but as I expect to get several orders I must reluctantly go North.

I am so sick & tired of bachelorizing.

With lots of love to all
I am
Your affect^{te} Husband
Dick

My darling Wifie

I am quite well only awfully worried. Mr Mann will not pay his customers orders so I shall have to sue them all this month.

Mr Cooke will be home tomorrow, I believe. I hope you are not getting fond of his brother, your remarks make me feel quite jealous. I only hope I shall be able to get down at Xmas but until I know where I am to be stationed I cannot say anything about it.

I do so long to see you & baby & I am very tired of the Hotel.

The Williamses drove thro' today to South bridge as Mr Lee is dangerously ill. I saw Tom Hislop this evening on his way to Christchurch.

With fondest love darling
I am
Your affect^{te} Husband
Dick

Rakaia
Nov 15/83

My darling Wifie

I am still bothered with my old business worse luck. [A reference, I assume, to the debts still owed him.] What has Mr Pyke done to you? I know he has been a friend of mine.

I am getting very tired too darling. I mean to go to Ch Ch on Saturday & see Mr Cooke.

I managed to break the splinter bar (between the shafts) of the new buggy a few days ago, you should have seen Turners face when I told him.

I went to the Show at Ashburton y'day & made £15 for the Company.

Your papa seems to be in trouble like myself.

I hope you & the boy are keeping quite well. I will try & send you a few pounds in a day or two.

With fondest love
Your affect^{te} Husband
Dick

Richard's reference to George's "trouble" may relate to George's advertisements: for storage of "Grain, Wool, and other Merchandise", he now offers "Expenses very much reduced, no cartage being required, and low rate of insurance." George, too, it seems, is feeling the pinch of these hard times.

Rakaia
Nov 19/83

My darling Wifie

I saw Mr Cooke on Saturday & got instructions to go to Ashburton & work up that district as the Company are not doing much business there. I think Turner is jealous of my being here as the farmers come to me & not to him. I shall go down tomorrow or Wednesday & try & get decent lodgings. Can you manage to live in lodgings for a little until I know where I am to be fixed permanently?

Good bye Wifie mine
With fondest love
I am
Your affect^{te} Husband
Dick

Rakaia
Nov 30th

My darling Wife

I called on Mrs Chambers this evening. She is going to write in a few days. Mrs Pyke will be going to Dunedin shortly & will write you to meet her. Could you manage to ask her to stay a night.

Turner is writing to Mr Cooke today to know where I am to go to. I don't know how to do without you any longer darling but what can I do under the circumstances.

I hear that Cookson at Methven is about coming to grief, every one, almost, seems to be in the same way.

I will try to lease the section from Robinson. I don't know whether he will do it.

With fondest love *etc*

The Press records in January a meeting of 74 creditors in the estate of Messrs Louden Bros., well-known farmers of Kyle and Methven. The principal creditors were our friends the N.Z. Loan and Mercantile Agency Company, and Messrs McKerrow and Co. The principal unsecured creditors also included some familiar names: Messrs Hardy and Co., and

Matson, Cox and Co., plus the afore-mentioned C.W. J. Cookson. In February, we see Mr Cookson advertising a "Timber, Coal, Grain and Wholesale General Store in the rising Township of Methven" for sale.

Hard times, for everyone.

Rakaia
Dec 8/83

My darling Wifie

I suppose your papa will have told you that I have got my congé from the Company thanks to Turner I believe.

I hope by the end of next week to know whether I shall remain here or not.

I want to do so for several reasons which I will explain to you when I have the pleasure of seeing you, at Xmas I hope.

Mrs Pyke does not go South until Xmas. I have nothing to write about as I feel so upset.

With fondest love
I am
Your affect^{te} Husband
Dick

Rakaia
Dec 11th 1883

My darling Wifie

I don't know whether there is a letter for me tonight or not as I told Clark to put my letters in Oxley's box. I could not go to Ch Ch on Monday but hope to get away tomorrow. I expect you feel rather miserable my darling, I know I do. If Stead will start an Agency here I will show Turner that he is not going to have it all his own way.

I shall have five or six court cases next week, it is so annoying but it can't be helped. [Presumably this relates to the debts owed him.]

Mrs Chambers has called a Parish meeting this week to know whether they intend keeping on a Clergyman or not.

With fondest love to you & Baby
I am
Your affect^{te} Husband
Dick

The idea that Rakaia might not be able to support a clergyman surely shows how tight money is all over.

Rakaia
Dec 12th 1883

My darling Wife,

I saw Mr Stead today, I have to see him again on Monday, he says that if I can show him that the Agency can pay expenses for the first year he will try it.

Please don't say that perhaps you are better away from me as every thing seems to have gone wrong since you have been away. I fear your papa is annoyed with me as he has not written.

Mr John Holmes has bought Waihorunga for £82.000.

I expect to have a small sale tomorrow of Mutters Stock [Thomas Mutter, "Under Distraint for Rent"].

With lots of love to all
I am
Your affectte Husband
Dick

Rakaia
19/12/83

My darling Wifie

I have joined the Grain Agency [the N.Z. Grain Agency] & hope to get the Doctors house as I learn that altho' it was taken for Hartnell he is not likely to want it.

Poor Mr Chambers fell off his horse y'day & was badly shaken. He will have to remain in bed for at least a fortnight.

You might write to Mrs Chambers & ask her if you could go there for a week. You might help to cook so as to give her more time with him. Besides I don't know what we have got in the way of furniture etc.

In haste
With fondest love
Your affectte Husband
Dick

From left, clockwise: Richard, Llewelyn, Emma, Reginald, Gwendoline

The family in 1884-5

It's clear from the adults' correspondence that times are not getting better — quite the contrary. Indeed, one of the Lemon girls (Edith, then 24) left Oamaru to take up a position as governess at one of the rural Stations (in 1887 she is advertising as a singing teacher; in 1895, at age 34, she's getting married). In February, George tells his daughter: "as to business & business matters they seem to get worse & worse every day & I cannot get any settlement & fear that I shall only be able to get any relief except by doing what I should be very thankful to be able to avoid but I must live in hopes although I am having all the energy taken out of me".

There is also a lot of sickness — whooping cough, measles, influenza — reminding us of the constant toll of infection in those days.

But it's not all gloom and doom! There are Entertainments and Excursions, and Emma has a new baby.

We also hear repeated mentions of Emma's grandfather, Richard Smith Newell, who is now with them at Oakleigh (his wife died in 1877).

Emma's older siblings are now young women: Harriet is 22; Lottie 20; Mary 18; Blanche 16; Clara 15. John (George) is 13 (and showing himself to be quite the chip off the block!); Walter 11; Millie 9; Winnie (Toodie) 7 and Bertie 5.

Oakleigh
January 14th/84

Dear Emma,

Thank you very much for your letter it seems bad of me not to have answered it sooner.

The holidays do not seem to be over yet. Last week the children were at two parties on Thursday at the Taylor's & on Friday George drove them out to the Gilchrist's. We had a splendid day for tennis, and had about ten visitors. Clara did not go to the party but stayed to keep me company. In the evening Papa, Harriet, Clara & I went down to the final performance of the pirates. [The Pirates of Penzance, put on by the Oamaru Amateur Opera Company]

On Saturday, Charlie came up & asked us to go down at seven o'clock & go for a row. Harriet, Clara Walter & I went. It was so lovely. The sky was beautifully clear & everything looked glorious in the moonlight. We seem such a small family now. Mary & Blanche have written once or twice & are enjoying themselves very much. Papa thought he would have to go down to Dunedin last Saturday but will not go till Thursday.

Today the Primate is to be here. There is to be a service at half past 7. I do not know whether any of us will be able to go down because Mamma has asked Mrs Forrester & all her visitors to come & spend the day. Tomorrow Clara & the four children are going to a party at the Newtons and on Wednesday the school treat is to be at the Parsonage so we shall have plenty to do as usual.

I have given up teaching in the Sunday School now. I cannot altogether like doing it but it is better every way. I think Mamma will take a class after a while. She would like to.

I am sorry poor Llewellyn is not very well but hope it is only through his teeth. It would not be very nice if he were to get whooping cough.

Please forgive such bad writing but Bertie keeps on shaking me – Give my love to Dick please & tell him I have not forgotten that I owe him a letter & will write <u>someday</u>.

Bertie is such a young monkey: He is a regular boy there is no keeping him still a minute. How do you like your new house. Perhaps I will come & see it after a while. We are all quite well except Harriet who has a horrid cough I wish she would be [bothered?] to go away.

And now I must say good-bye.

Hoping you are well & with much love to you all from all

Believe me
Ever your loving sister
Lottie

Oakleigh
Feb^{ry} 20th 1884

My darling Girl

I would have written yesterday to thank you for your loving remembrances of my birthday, the Card is very beautiful, the Thimble fits exactly and completes your other gift while the letter is best of all. You and I my dear Emma do not [need] to be assured of each other's love, but I do quite understand because I feel how much you must wish that we could see you and you could see us sometimes. Of course we can do that without in any way slighting those dear ones whom we have with us. For myself I am very glad you have not gone to Wellington as I can now hope to come up and see you some time. I am very glad to hear that you are all well and that Master Baby has been taught his first lessons. I only wish it had been done before he left here – for I am sure when the battle is over you will both feel better for it. [weaning? toilet training?] Millie and Toodie were very pleased to hear of his looking at their portraits when he is going to bed. Bertie says I am to tell you he has a new slate and is trying very hard to write he says he has no Portrait. I have not seen Gracie yet but Mr Finch says she is visible now to her relatives [Grace gave birth to a daughter on the 8th]. Constance came up on Monday to bring me a pretty little pair of Vases with her Mamma's love and stayed for the evening but unfortunately Papa brought Mr G. Jones home with him, and he rather spoiled things. Blanche gave me a larger pair of Vases of Irridescent Glass. Mr and Mrs Kerr sent two dear little New Year Cards to Papa and me from Paris. On the back of Papa's was written in French "To Mr Sumpter, the Father of Oamaru who has devoted himself heart and soul to her interest, a happy and prosperous New Year," and on mine Good wishes for the New Year from Mrs Kerr. Harriet sends her love to you and says she will write to you some time but some one else always seems to be writing when she has a chance of doing it. Lottie and Blanche went to the Parsonage on Saturday morning and came back after Church, and Lottie and Clara have gone out there this afternoon for Lawn Tennis. Douglas and Herbert had dinner here on Sunday and last night Papa and I, Grandpapa and Blanche & George drove down to see the Bicycle Procession start while Harriet and Walter rode down on Rose and Solomon. In case I cannot get the Advertisement to send I had better tell you that Viola Edwards was married on Valentine's day to Mr Densham, so they are not all going to be old maids. Mrs Roberts is beginning to send her belongings to the New House to-day. I hope you will not make yourself too tired with the work and Llewellyn. I think Lottie would really like to come to you if she could be of any use but if you and she think anything of it you had better ask Papa direct. Only do not let us stand in Connies way if you wish to ask her. Poor girl she says she has had a cold for a fortnight. By the bye our colds have not quite gone yet. Harriet's has gone and Papa's and mine, the others are slowly taking their departure. It is tea-time so I must conclude, thanking you for both your letters again and sending you, Dick and Baby as much love as a letter can carry

I am
Always
Your loving Mother

The next letter indicates that Emma's grandfather, Richard Newell, is returning to Adelaide (the "Richard" referred to here must be Emma's uncle). The reference to marriage is intriguing, but nothing presumably came of it, for he is back at Oakleigh by May of the following year.

It is also clear from the letter that Emma is expecting again. Her daughter Gwendoline was born in September, so she must be about four months along. It's worth remembering, as Emma's mother delicately refers to some garment she is sending down, that Emma's youngest brother is only three years older than his uncle Llewellyn!

Oakleigh
April 18th 1884

My very dear Emma

I had begun to write to you yesterday, when Mrs Finch Senr came up saying she would stay to lunch if convenient, so as I have since then received your welcome letter I will begin a new one. I thank you and Dick very much for your kindness to dear Grandpapa. It was such a pity we missed the train on Saturday as he had set his mind on spending one Sunday with you, but Harriet poor girl, was completely overworked between Church Decorations, Review, and all the rest and then to crown all our clocks and watches were slow. Did Llewellyn remember Grandpapa? I knew you would not mind seeing about the clothes, and for the other I will enclose it as soon as I can get to town. My Father's presence has become so natural to me again that I shall miss him very much, in fact I could not bear the thought of his going were it not that I feel sure that he really wishes to go and that he could not bear our winter. You have helped him on his way here and I have written to Richard to look after him at Port Adelaide. You know he still has hopes of marriage when he gets there. We can only ask that his voyage may be safe and pleasant. Now for yourself, dear Emma, as this letter is private and confidential and may be burnt if you like I am going to talk about all sorts of things. It is very good of you to accept my parcel as I wish – & oh, I sent it in fear and trembling but the one I had felt so comfortable that I could not help doing it. I scarcely think it will need washing all the winter, indeed you can if you like wear a white one under it to change. Then you must be careful and not overwork yourself if you cannot make any better management. I am sure Mary or one of the others will come and keep you company for a longer time than Lottie did. I think she would have stayed longer under other circumstances. She looks, I think, a great deal better for the change as it is. One more thing, or rather two things in one do not hesitate to send down to me for anything I can get for you, and if you would not mind taking all the "little things" I have I shall be very glad to send them to you so that you may make what use you can of them. Mrs Udall did knit the little socks and is very proud of being able to do so, as she says she never tried to knit Stockings till last year. Lottie sends her love to you and says she will write to you soon. Papa's arm is he thinks gradually getting better. Harriet, Mary and ourselves were at Mrs Roberts' dance on Thursday night, it is a splendid house. I meant to have written you a long letter but visitors have prevented my doing so this time, and now I must stop or you will not get it before Sunday. With fondest love to you all and kisses for my boy

I am always Your affectionate Mother

Oakleigh
July 11th 1884

My dear Emma,

I am at last going to answer your kind letter which is dated June 30, and mine is July 11th so I have had yours more than a week.

I am glad Llewellyn liked the mittens; but I am afraid he will soon lose them as they must be too loose for him. You say that the young monkey appreciated Lottie's present; I expect he did, as nearly all boys like cake don't they?

I suppose the reason Llewellyn does not call Toodie "Aunt" is because he thinks he thinks she is "Too" young. N.B. This is a pun.

He was very well remembered in Rakaia, taking all in all, I should think. Lottie told us how careful he was with his books. I wrote a French letter for M. Ledez last Tuesday, and as it was to you I spoke of Llewellyn in it; and he could not make out the name, and was forced to ask me what it was.

Mamma says that I am to please give you her love, and tell you that she can get the bootees done for you at 3/6 per pair, and would you like "threes" or "fours" pairs, varied colours, or all done in one?

If you would like them in different colours please let Mamma know as soon as possible.

Papa had a nice letter from Herbert yesterday; and he speaks very highly of Auckland in every respect. And his best news is that his face is nearly well again. Is it not a good thing? He says he is not sorry.

On Tuesday Mary and I went to lunch at Gracie's; and we enjoyed ourselves very much. I never could have imagined either Gracie or Mr Finch going into such raptures about a baby; the former calls Irene "Girlie", and the latter "Bups"!!! We meant to leave "Kahuru" at three o'clock, but then Kate and Sylvia Gifford called, and stayed till half past three so we could not get away; and then Gracie begged us to keep her company for a little while and so I nursed Irene (who was awfully good) and Mary played the piano until a quarter to five. Mr Gifford came up to see us today at half past two, (although it was Thursday) as he felt better than usual, and it was a lovely day. Lottie, Mary, and I stayed in the dining-room with him, and we had afternoon tea, but he only stayed until three. He is hardly ever well now I am sorry to say, and he says he has begun to think that bronchitis is part of himself.

Mrs Gifford told Mamma to ask whoever wrote to you next to give you her love & I happen to be that one. But now dear Emma I must say goodbye as I want to write a 'short note' to Dick (which I hope he won't mind) so with love to Llewellyn & yourself

I remain "ma Cherie"
Your loving sister Blanche

Oakleigh
Aug 26th 1884

My dear Emma

I have just written to little Llewellyn. Milly & Toodie have got the measles. I think little Bertie will have them soon. The Steam Ship Elderslie came in on Monday morning at ½ past 5, Harriet, Lottie, Millie, Toodie, Papa, Mama, Walter, & I went down to see her come in.

Please excuse the writing out of line but I can't see them very well. Don't trouble to write to me often because I know you have to answer a lot of letters.

You tell Dick that he should start up a Chemist's Shop, but still go on with his Auctioneering but get someone to go on with the shop in his name. I went to the Royal Hotel with Papa for lunch today. And now dear Emma With very best love to Dick Llewellyn & except the same yourself

I remain
Your loving brother
George Sumpter

It's clear that George has been picking up the way of business from his father!

September 9th 1884
Oakleigh
Oamaru

My Dear Emma,

Bertie sends his love to you. Bertie and I had such fun when Toody was in town. Bertie has the measles only he is going to get up to-morrow.

Marjorie Robinson has got the measles. Mrs Robinson had Marjorie out to-day and the rash was not gone.

Toody and I have got such a big garden with Violets, Primroses, and Forgetmenots, we dug it on Monday. Mama bought me a new doll just like Joe Hislop.

I am all right now again just as I did before. Bertie got such a nice garden with Roses, Violets, Primroses, Lilac, they are all coming out.

I have read the book you gave me. Papa gave Walter a scrap-book.

Harriet made me a night cap to keep my ear from aching.

Now I must say good bye with love to all

I am
Your loving sister
Milly

West Oxford
Sep 10/84

My dear Wife

I called on 6 people today & only found one at home, if I cannot do better than this between now & Saturday I fear I shall have to remain here till Monday & Tuesday.

I don't know what my address will be from day to day or would let you know.

I hope you & baby are keeping well.

I will send you a telegram on Saturday to let you know whether I shall be back at the end of the week.

With lots of love
I am
Your affect[te] Husband
Dick

Emma's second child, Gwendoline, is born.

Oakleigh
Sept 15th 1884

My dearest Emma

George came home about 4 o'clock this afternoon with a very beaming face, and asked me to guess what news he had brought, bursting out, before he had given me much time to guess, with, "You're another Grandmother". Emma has another kid, a little girl. But even after that announcement, Mr Davies' telegram "Emma and Miss Davies send their love" looked very puzzling. I, of course felt quite overwhelmed especially as Mrs and Miss Gull at that moment came to the door. Millie and Toodie were delighted. Millie cried out 'Oh do let me go up to Emma I am sure it is quite safe now some of us must go up." This, I suppose is the feeling most of us have I know it is mine but I am most thankful to hear that you and my dear little Grand-daughter are doing well, and pray and trust that you will continue to do so, although you may, perhaps not feel so strong as you did after Llewellyn was born. I have the comfort too, of knowing that you will be well and kindly cared for, and the hope that you will soon be able to come and see us even if I cannot go to see you just now. Poor old Llewellyn he is not "Ba'y" any longer but most likely his Father will be able to comfort him. Please give my fond love to Dick and thank him for sending word, and ask him to give my boy plenty of kisses for me. Thank you, so much for thinking of a way to give Bertie so much pleasure. He is, I am thankful to say doing as well as possible and was running about the ~~house~~ nursery when George brought the parcel and very quickly undid it and began eating an orange saying "it is kind of Emma". He is very pleased with his pretty book, too, and the children are charmed to have some more robes and patches for their dollies. George sends his love and says he is awfully glad, in fact everybody sends love to you all. Mary is much better, indeed she says she is quite well now, though she looks greatly shaken. Dr Wait says her attacks are not of a nature to cause any alarm, and that he hopes, if by care and medicine she can keep them off for two or three months she will get rid of them altogether. I will tell you more about her another time. I am so sorry I could not write before but last week we had visitors again and with Mary upstairs, Bertie in the nursery and visitors we could not get any time. Dr Wait has given the boys a certificate for the 17th [something to do with having a contagious illness?]. Edith and Mabel are going to stay with Mrs McDonald's sister Mrs Raffaelle! at Mornington on Wednesday. They came up today to say Goodbye, and Cecil Moore came up this afternoon I must now say Good-night my darling girl. May God bless and keep you and your dear ones is the earnest prayer of your loving

Mother

Oakleigh Sept 19th 1884

My very dear Emma

I was delighted and so was Papa to get your letter, but am almost afraid to answer it for fear you should be tempted to write again before you are strong enough. Papa says he is quite proud of your being able to write. It does seem hard that we can only write, but as I feared, you see, it would scarcely be safe for me to come to you. So for a while I must bear as patiently as I can the great longing I have to see you, my own dear girl, and your dear little, new baby. Cannot you persuade baby's Papa to write to some of us and give us a description of her!!! Dear Bertie is very well indeed. I am glad to say, I had the pleasure of taking him for a walk about the garden this morning Millie and Toodie do not look a bit worse for their illness in fact, I think they look better and Bertie is getting fearfully wild. Mr Allan came up to tea last night and Mary and I had the pleasure of playing 3 rubbers of Whist with him and Papa. He brought some new songs too. I went to the Guild yesterday. Mrs Gifford told me to be sure to send her love to you. Mrs Clarke brought some socks which he hopes you will accept for Llewellyn I will post them with this. The bad writing is Bertie's fault.

Saturday morning

I went down last night with Mary Blanche and the boys to the Elderslie Concert, there was such a crowd that the street looked quite black when we went down just before the doors were opened, and the Hall was packed, even the Orchestra space was filled with chairs. Papa read, "the lass of the Drake" beautifully I do not think I ever heard him read so well, and Mr and Mrs Williams sang, the Siren and the Friar very well, they had to repeat the duet part. Old Sims actually recited again and interpolated some flattering remarks about Papa. Lottie sends her love to you and says she is sorry she has not written to you but she has really not had time. Mary did not help in the Concert, as we did not think she was strong enough for that. I must say good-bye now my dearest girl with best and fondest love to you, Dick, and the little ones remaining always

Your loving Mother

Oakleigh Oct 10th 1884

My dear Emma,

I am very sorry but I do not think I can possibly come to you next week for Lottie is most likely going to Dunedin with Jeannie about the end of the week and of course we could not both be away together. I hope you will not be vexed with me but I did not say anything to her about your writing me for fear she would say she would not go and I think the change will do her good.

If you would like to have the christening on the 19th, is not that the date, please do, & if Lottie does not go until the next week I will try to come up for the one day, I do not think I could make up my mind to stay longer at any rate. I might possibly bring Millie if I do, but as I told you I have not spoken of it yet, except to Mamma, until I know Lottie's plans, she is not very decided about it as yet.

They have not a very nice night for their trip to Elderslie, it has been raining every now & then but fortunately it was fine when they drove down to the Station. Jeannie is madly excited about it, it is the first large dance she has been to.

Please Emma do not put off the christening for me if you would like to have it before Mr Chambers goes.

I must stop now & go & send the girls to bed as I am in charge. The others are coming home by a "Special" at about three.

With love from all
I remain
Your loving sister
Harriet C. Sumpter

Saturday morning. Jeannie is not going next week, so I shall be with you on Saturday night if that will suit you and I hope you will not be very vexed with me if I come back on the Monday, for I could not make up my mind to leave my work any longer. Harriet C. Sumpter

More of young George's entrepreneurial talents are on display in the next letter.

Oakleigh
Nov. 11th 84

My dear Emma

I always thought that it was your turn to write to me but tonight I was thinking it over & I think it is my turn to write to you. The Waitaki High School sports are going to be held on the Wednesday before the show. What does Llewellyn think of his little sister is he very proud of her. He is much braver than Bertie is about going out to Parties but Bertie went out to one the other day to Mrs Mitchell's. I am going to act in this coming Cantata I suppose I will be a ragged Boy.

Please tell Dick to get a fowl house built and get some good fowls such as Bramahs. You tell him that if he gets a pair he will make a lot of money by them. A sitting of eggs even is worth 5/- or 12/-. Walter got a setting from Mrs Every for 5/- but she said she had just sold a dozen for 12/- shillings the same day. I have got an awful lot of Bantams now. Please excuse the Bad writing because I have to be quick or I wont have time to write any more. And now dear Emma I must say good night. Hoping to see you all in about 5 weeks.

I am Dear Emma
Your loving brother
George

Oakleigh
Jan 14th 1885

Dearest Emma

Are you quite well. Does Llewellyn remember me at all. I was so sorry to find that you had gone. Is Dick glad that you are home again

I expect he is. Mama Mary Lottie & Clara have walked down to the Mirror of the World tonight. What sort of weather are you having up there it is horrid weather that we are having.

Please excuse my bad piece of paper but we haven't got any more in the house and also excuse the bad writing. Please give my best love to dear little Llewellyn and keep the same yourself. And give it to Dick if he will accept it.

I remain
Your loving brother
George Sumpter

At Mr Clifford's "Mirror of the World" last night the views shown were for the greater part representative of celebrated scenes in Scotland, and the islands round the northern and western coasts of that country. Some very fine statuary was also exhibited, and was very justly admired by the audience. All present were pleased with the Scottish views on account of the beauty or grandeur, or the historic or literary associations of the scenes they represented; while they, of course, had a peculiar attraction for those of the audience who claimed Scotland as their native country. For these reasons the applause at the Public Hall last night was pretty frequent and pretty hearty. To-night Mr Clifford will exhibit an interesting series of views illustrative of "rambles round the world."

The "Mirror of the World" afforded a delightful evening's entertainment on Saturday night, when "The River Thames from its source to London" was exhibited. Those who know little of the scenery of the Thames would be surprised at the natural beauties that are shown by the mirror. The scenery is of the most charming nature. No doubt Mr Clifford has chosen for transference to his pictures all the spots that would be most calculated to attract and please the eye. Starting at the source of the river the audience are brought down by rather a pleasant process to London. The Oxford colleges are shown, and a short description given of each. The scenes of the boat race between Cambridge and Oxford, and numerous fine bridges that span the Thames at London and at other parts of the river are also exhibited, and interspersed with these views are others showing the principal public buildings of the city. Mr Clifford has decided to exhibit the Mirror on Wednesday, Thursday, Friday and Saturday next,

Oakleigh
Jan. 21st 1885

My dear Emma,

I think it is about time that I should write to you. I have intended to do so ever since you went away, but have never found time yet.

Millie is a splendid little correspondent is she not? I am so sorry our letters crossed; please tell her not to trouble to answer my last because I think I shall write again soon.

Papa, Mamma, Lottie, Mary, Mr Allan and I went to "Remenyi's" Concert last night, and I enjoyed it so much; in fact I felt awfully sorry when it came to an end. We made up a party with the Giffords, Mr Brittain (an awfully nice Melanesian missionary), the Forresters, and Fred & Carrie Bicknell, and went to the "stall". The tickets there were quite dear enough, being three shillings; but Mr Allan took two of us, very kindly, so there was not quite such a strain on Papa's purse.

Mr Luckstone, the pianist accompanying "Remenyi", is such a splendid looking fellow, about twenty five years of age and he plays oh so beautifully! Mr Himmer the tenor, is such a queer looking fellow; I do not care for his voice much. In one song he sang "When the flowing tide comes in" he pronounced the second last word in such a peculiar way, just like "komins" (I wonder if you can understand that.) Miss Mattie Downing, the only lady, is rather "vulgar" looking. She was dressed in cream colour, no sleeves, and a almost entire skirt of "Spanish lace". She sings awfully swell, but puts on all kinds of airs. But "Remenyi"! I can not possibly describe his playing in the least. To begin with his violin is a little beauty, silver plated, and all. Some little runs were so soft and sweet that you had to listen very attentively to hear them. When he played his own arrangement of "Scotch Airs" you could almost fancy you heard Jeanie crying "Wae me". I shall enclose you a programme with the "encores" marked. I will tell what they were (the encores I mean) hoping I am not wearying you, but when once I start on a subject I can hardly stop myself. Miss Downing's first one was "I wouldn't would you?" a half comical song. Then for Remenyi's first, he played a "Barcarole" by Schubert, for his second "Tis the last Rose of Summer", his third the "Marsellaise", and then recalled again! he played the "Australasian" his own composition, and then "God save the Queen". For Miss Downing's second encore she sung "Comin thro' the Rye". Mr Himmer only bowed he was not in good voice. I wanted Mr Luckstone to be encored awfully, but instrumental music is hardly ever appreciated by the public, is it?

Lottie has told Millie about his (Remenyi's) coming up to breakfast I think.

Have you short-coated Gwendoline yet? The little blue dress Harriet has made for her is such a nice simple little thing. Mrs Waymouth is coming down to Oamaru from Ch.Ch. on Saturday, and she is going to stay with Mrs Roberts. I wonder if you, or Dick, will see her passing through! I should like to tell Mr

Waymouth that you had awfully.

Tell Millie that Miss Cole's school re-opens on Wednesday next, the same day as the Waitaki High School, so I am afraid that she will soon have to cut short what must be a very pleasant visit to her.

But now, dear Emma, as M. Ledez is coming up, & I have some French to do, I must say good-bye. With love to all from dear Mamma & myself Believe me to be your loving Blanche

This is the second mention of a Melanesian missionary. As the next letter makes clear, the church appears to be involved in sponsoring mission children.

Oamaru Feby 3 1885

My dear Emma

I must write a few lines to you for fear you should think I was neglecting you – I am sorry I have no good news to give you, except as to all of our healths – We have much to [be] thankful for in this direction indeed but as to business & business matters they seem to get worse & worse every day & I cannot get any settlement & fear that I shall only be able to get any relief except by doing what I should be very thankful to be able to avoid but I must live in hopes although I am having all the energy taken out of me – The weather has been & is very bad the crops although good are terribly beaten down & my little crop of wheat & oats has been eaten half away by the birds – I think they have destroyed about twenty bushels to the acre – School has begun again & Milly's male schoolfellow that used to knock her about has left so that they have gone back to Miss Coles who is very glad to get them again – The Loch Fergus another wool [he means perhaps another supply of wool carried on the Loch Fergus] has just come in – The Elderslie is expected about 15th March – The children are all busy in making preparation for the concert & waxworks & Harriet as usual is distinguishing herself, making dresses armour & even a horse for Joan of Arc (Clara) to ride – I have been allotted Blue beard & Lottie is to be my wife whose life I am not to spare – but I dare say you have been made acquainted with the arrangements by some of your correspondents – You must have been surprised at my telegram re Constance. I hope it will be for her benefit – I don't know what my poor chicks may have to do: it almost breaks my heart to think of it – Mr Brittain the Melanesian missionary left today – He is a very nice person & has made a great many friends here – He gave the children an address & showed them a number of curiosities – Did I tell you that our last scholar is dead & that we have now another given us by Mr Brittain named Thomas from Penticost Island one of the first Santa Cruz boys.

I must now close this disconnected epistle & with best love to yourself & Richard & kisses for little ones

I am Your loving Father
George Sumpter

I would infer from George's "You must have been surprised at my telegram re Constance. I hope it will be for her benefit – I don't know what my poor chicks may have to do: it almost breaks my heart to think of it" that Constance may have been forced to leave Oamaru to seek employment elsewhere. A woman of her name is recorded as being appointed postmistress at Newborough in 1908, and of course her uncle Dr Lemon was in the business. Perhaps he got her a job, or training.

For a man like George, with so many daughters (whose employment prospects were of course extremely limited), his reducing circumstances must have been fearful indeed.

Tuesday Feb!! 1885
Oakleigh
Oamaru

Dear Emma.

Papa Mama Lottie and Mary are going to a dance to-night. Mama sends her love to you. Please thank Maggie for the petticoat and give her my love and ~~for~~ Toody thanks Maggie for the petticoat she send Toody. We went to Mrs Gilchrist on Friday. Harriet has mended Toodies old doll. I have read nearly all the book that you gave me. I got the cups down quite safely and Bertie sends his love to you and Llewellyn and thanks him very much for the cup you send him and so do I. He likes the whistle very much. Please give my love to Llewellyn and Gwendoline and give them lots of kisses. I miss them very much and you and Dick. Please give everybody my love that I know. I am going to get my hair cut soon. Bertie said that his hair was down to his neck so he must go to Proberts to get his hair cut. Thank you very much for sending my box down but you did not send down my little book named The butterflies at home. The cape you gave me just fites Toody's doll it shows it is very fat does not it. Please excuse the smears. Harriet says we must go to bed unless I would write a longer letter.

Now I must say~~s~~ good-bye with love to all

I am
Your loving sister
Millie

Oakleigh Feby 23rd 1885

My very dear Emma

At last I write to thank you very very much for the dear little Vases you sent me through dear Millie, and for your loving letters. Thank you and please tell Dick that I thank him very much for all the kind wishes you both sent to me. I am so glad Llewellyn is better please kiss both the darlings for me. I hope Gwendoline is still as good tempered as ever. I suppose Miss Edwards has told you all about the Waxworks, we hear nothing but praises of them in all directions. I wish you could have seen them.

Did you hear of the Ball which Mrs Sutton and Mrs de Lautour got up for Miss Murdock and Miss Gleeson? They had arranged to hold it on the Friday evening we had taken but put it off until the next Tuesday. The batchelors provided the room, music, and drinkables, and I was invited to a meeting of ladies at Mrs de Lautour's to consider what each married lady would supply in the shape of provisions. We sent Tongue sandwiches and Blancmange and so many ladies contributed that they had far too large a stock approvisioned. Papa, Lottie, Mary and I went to the dance. Wasn't it wrong [perhaps she means wrong to be dancing in the Lecture room?] the dancing-room was the Lecture room of the Atheneum and the supper was laid in the room opposite, the ladies room being used as a Cloak-room. It was a very pleasant party in its way though a large one. Lottie wore her blue and white dress, and Mary had a cream-colored Cashmere with no other colour except her Fan-card and some crimson Roses for a button-hole.

My birthday was kept in a strange fashion for Papa, Harriet, and the two little girls went to Timaru by the excursion train. Papa went up to play Cricket and, as Mrs Gun and Lemon went up too, Mr Gun got a carriage and drove them all round about the downs, which I think Harriet liked pretty well, poor old girl, her cold is better though it is not well, yet she says she does not care what becomes of her! Fancy! she actually went to Alverton y'day to see Ally (entre nous of course) .

You will be surprised to hear that Edith left home this morning, poor Aunt Mary says from absolute necessity, to be governess at Galloway Station, to Mrs Gunion's two little girls age 8 and 6. She seems in very good spirits and Lottie Blanche and Mary and Clara went down to see her off. Blanche had the three gentlemen and Edie and Gertie Robinson to play Tennis on her birthday. Mr Bishop and Gertie remarked that she looked very well, and Mr Caldwell complimented her on her roses yesterday. We are all quite well Bertie, I think, is getting a little fatter, George is growing taller and as there is to be a Confirmation after Easter he is seriously thinking of presenting himself as a Candidate. I do not know whether he will be considered too young. Since all our dissipation has been over I have been resting myself by reading a very nice book which dear Lottie and Blanche gave me on the 18th and by hunting for hen's nests as usual. Hoping to send you a better letter next time. I remain with fondest love to you all Your most loving Mother S. S. Sumpter

Oakleigh March 4th/85

My dear Emma,

Once more I have kept your letter a fearfully long time, but excuses will take up too much space so I will not bother you with them. There is not much news for you – Blanche sent you such a long letter I expect she told you everything.

We miss Papa so much. I expect you were surprised to hear of his going. We had a telegram to say he had arrived safely, tonight. If he were not very ill I think the rest will do him good. We are enjoying a change of weather. It has been raining since Monday.

Clara and I have been very busy today in the greenhouses. To surprise Papa we are going to wash all the pots & stands. It is dirty work.

Blanche does look so well now – better than she has done for ever so long. She and Mary were going to Lenten Service tonight but it is far too wet. Something has come in the way every Wednesday.

So Miss Raine has really married Mr Reid! I hope they will be happy. I do wonder if she was Mr Caldwell's friend. Mr Holland was in town today. Last night Mr Bishop, Mr Waymouth and Mr Weston came up. We hadn't a very jolly evening. We were very sorry they came because Mamma has not been quite herself. The changeable weather seems to have upset her. Mamma did not want me to say anything about it but I must keep my promise and you need not think it is anything serious – She is much better today.

Did anyone tell you that Miss Headland was married to Mr Piper. They were married at half-past-eight in the morning & it was fearfully quiet. It is said he is not a nice fellow and her parents did not half like the match. She had been engaged three times to him.

Mamma went to a meeting about the ball at Mrs de Lautour's on Monday. Mrs Milne made a fuss because the gentlemen were not introduced to strangers. Miss Crompton, her friend, was under Mamma's care & can't dance a little bit. They say Mrs Connell is going to give a dance in about a month & is not going to make every other dance a waltz.

Please give Dick everybodys love & wish him many Happy Returns of his Birthday. I hope George's present will reach him safely.

Mr Lees brought Mary a little basket of such lovely plums on Monday. I have not finished Clara's skirt

[rest lost; appears to be from Lottie]

Oakleigh April 3rd 1885

Dearest Emma

Good-Friday is just over. We have spent it very quietly & pleasantly. It has been such a lovely day. We began by getting up very early & I do not think any of us will be sorry to be in bed – our volunteers more glad than any I expect.

Mary & I went to Church. Mr Finch walked up to his corner with me. Gracie took Irene to Dunedin for change yesterday so he is all alone. After dinner Mary, Bertie & I went over to the hay-stack near the gate & read. It was so nice.

It would have been jolly if you could have come down. But I expect it is a good thing really as Millie shows signs of mumps.

Mr & Mrs Chambers leave Rakaia very soon now I am sure you will miss them. Is another minister to take his place or will you be without?

I wonder if Dick saw Mr Weston & Mr Waymouth. They went to Christchurch by the special. Mr Bishop is left all by himself – poor fellow!

It is no use trying to tell you any news so many are writing but of course you will understand. Please accept my very best love & "many happy returns of your birthday". The years are going quickly are they not. It does not seem a year since I was with you but yet such lots of things have happened since then. Poor old Bertie was going to write to you. He says he will in the morning, but if he has not time you will take the will for the deed. I wonder if he will get the mumps too.

I was half afraid I should have to tell you Mamma was not well. She did not seem to be herself. She would go to town but Harriet would not take her till pretty late. I believe it did Mamma more good than harm & she is all right today except that she is naturally tired after being up so early.

It will seem so strange without Papa & the boys I do hope they will [have] fine weather & enjoy the trip.

This is fearfully written but I cannot help it.

And now dear Emma

With best love to you Dick Boy & baby,
With very best wishes from your loving sister
Lottie

Please accept the knife box with my love. It is very plain but I hope it will be useful.

Friday April 3 1885
Oakleigh

My dear Emma

I am just going to write a short letter ~~I~~ bacuse I have not much to say.

We are getting a few holidays for good Friday and Easter Monday but the waitak high school does not get Monday.

Mr Norman Gurr is down now Lottie and Mary saw him when they went to church.

Now I must say good bye with best love to all I remain your loving sister Winnie I wish you a ~~happy~~ merr

* Happy retins of the day for your birthday

[Winnie, I think]

Oakleigh May 20th 1885

My dear Daughter

I am very glad to hear that you and your dear little ones have recovered from your colds. Unfortunately our house is not yet free from the Influenza or whatever it may be called for poor Blanche has been in bed since Monday evening having evidently the same illness as Millie had only not quite so severe. She is very feverish with bad headache and swollen throat. I think she is a little better to-day at any rate she seems brighter and has eaten better. Millie is nearly all right now though she looks a little shaken and seems to have grown while in bed for her school-dress which she had made for her only a week or two ago is quite too short Winnie and Bertie are well again but both look a little paler. George, poor boy, is struggling hard not to "give in to bed" with his cold though his head and throat are evidently bad. Walter has grown very fast lately and is now about as tall as George and weighs 1½ lbs more. Papa has engaged a man to do the milking for a month, as he is working in the garden but the boys have to get Bessie and clean Papa's boots. They have gone down to see if there is any fun about town with the Election – poor fellows they have had very little "fun" these holidays as we have had so much sickness in the house. Happily Papa is very well so far and Grandpa seems to be shaking off the cold he had when he came. I am very sorry poor Dick has so much worry I do wish I knew how to help him effectually but I fear I am only the reverse of helpful to anybody. Does Llewellyn seem stronger now dear wee boy? I do wish I could see him and his little sister. Bertie says I am to tell you that he is "mad and has a fit." I suppose Capt. Creagh had one when he refused to obey the order to fire at the Sham Fight – he sent two insolent messages by the orderly and when Papa rode up to him he repeated his refusal. He apologized afterward though not until a day or two had passed and in the meantime Mr O'Meaghen had written to the paper about it and sent the Waimate Times with an untrue account of the affair to Wellington so we do not yet know how it will end. You will be sorry to hear that Mrs Forrester is ill. I fear seriously so, as she seems to get repeated attacks of Bronchitis and Inflammations of the Lungs. I have not seen poor Mrs Clowes yet – poor thing it must be a sad affliction for her. I fear I must stop scribbling now, please give the darlings plenty of kisses for me and believe me to be with fondest love

Your loving Mother

S.S. Sumpter

Susanna does not dwell too much on the infamous insubordination incident, but it was regarded quite seriously, by some at least, at the time. There were a number of passionate letters in the newspaper about it (you can read some of them on the website). One correspondent remarked: "The eyes of the whole colony are at this juncture on the volunteers, as at present they are our only defenders. Once let confidence be shaken by permitting recalcitrant members to snap their fingers at the regulations and set authority at defiance, and we may look for an epidemic of insubordination in the ranks". It was felt by many, we are told, that George should not have accepted the man's apology, but taken action appropriate for the "rank mutiny" it was held to be.

An upsetting incident for George, I'm sure. Richard, too, was having his troubles. Money may have been tight for George (the reference to George employing "a man to do the milking for a month, as he is working in the garden but the boys have to get Bessie and clean Papa's boots" is surely a sign that he can little afford any extra help, cheap as it was in these desperate times), but it appears that Richard is feeling the pinch even more.

Oamaru June 1 1885

My dear Emma,

Thank you for your kind brave letter – I cannot however glean sufficient from it to enable me judiciously either to advise or help you – If you certainly think that £50 would pull you through your difficulties I will give Richard my promissory notes at three & four months for £25 each which I have no doubt would under the circumstances meet matters with Hardy & Co for with the exception of my indebtedness to the Bank I am thankful to say I have so far met all my bills & have less currently now altogether than I have often had to meet in a day. I do not at all like the idea of mortgaging the property particularly as by what I can fathom from what you say I do not see that your doing so would free you from your indebtedness – or prevent your getting into future troubles & thus you could have nothing left to protect you – It would therefore in my opinion be much better to have this to fall back upon in case of anything happening so that you might have something to live or start upon – In fact of the two it would be much better if it were possible to sell if anything like a decent price could be obtained for it than to borrow on it – The money would have to be used for trust purposes for your benefit – I notice that the London shareholders recommend that the Grain Agency Co should go into liquidation & although this may not mean that Richard will at once lose his situation I presume it will not be his for long & it will then be for him to consider I suppose as to whether he should try & get a situation or commence business again on his own account – I fear there is not so much hope of Stead getting him a situation at Ch Ch as he thinks as I feel sure it is overdone there & he is almost sure to have more particular friends of his own to help in that direction – There is nothing like trying however – I am not at all sure that nothing could be done here – It might be worth his while to run down & see what chance there is – before making any definite arrangements. I suppose you let Richard know the contents of these letters & ask him to consider them as written to both of you & do not be afraid to speak freely for you never know what a little advice might do if given on full knowledge of facts – With much love & hope that there may be better times in store for both & all of us

I am
Your loving Father
George Sumpter

Oakleigh
June 2nd 1885

My dear Emma,

Thank you very much indeed for your kind letter, and wishes about my health; I am sure I am not worth either.

I am quite right again now thank you; I had my first walk into, and from town today, for a fortnight.

Friday night was the night of the "St Luke's Entertainment" got up by Mrs Mitchell, & Aunt Mary. Lottie, Clara, George, & Toodie had a little acting to do, and Papa, Mamma, Grandpapa, Mary, and I went to see it. Mamma had given me leave to go out then for the first time if it were [dry? omitted] and I was well wrapped up, and at tea-time I was reconciling myself to a supposed disappointment because there was quite a heavy shower of rain but at half past seven it had cleared up beautifully so we all went. The two charades were "Home-ward Bound", and "Tea-spoons."

When we arrived at the hall Mrs Booth and Gertie Lemon were playing a duet, (in a stage drawing-room) Mr Allan and Aunt Mary were having a game of chess, and Bertie Robinson, and Amy Lemon were playing about. Presently, Mrs Mitchell came in to give her brother Bertie a birth-day present, and then went to have a look at her Papa and Mamma's game of chess. Then, her husband, Mr Finch came in, and so as to have a little fun on Bertie's birthday

Mr Allan put on a mask, and ran about for a little while after Bertie and Amy looking exceedingly foolish. Then they sang (or murdered) "White Sand, or Grey Sand", and "There Blind Mice", and lastly Mrs Mitchell sang "Home, sweet Home", and the curtain drew down on the first syllable "Home". When next the curtain drew up a "ward" in a Hospital was in view with six patients in stretchers. They were Messrs G. Jones, Oswald Borton, Mr Gurr, George, Mr Bishop, and Gussy Robinson, Mr Caldwell made an amusing doctor, Edie a jolly matron, and Jeannie Mitchell, Lottie, Clara, Gertie & Mione [Mildred Hermione, I assume] & Mabel Lemon were nurses dressed in white aprons (over their dresses of course I mean) mob-caps, and red crosses on their arms. Some of the patients were great fun; Mr Bishop kept on shuddering all over and nearly throwing the bed-clothes off.

I have not your letter with me so please forgive me if I have not answered any question. Oh Emma, by the bye, have you sent the Dictionary or not? There is no hurry but Papa went to see if it had come & it was not there

Your loving
Blanche

June 13th 1885
My dear Emma,

You like getting letters on Saturday, and Monday evenings don't you? I thought you did anyway so I determined ~~to write~~ after tea that I would write one to you. I am afraid that as Mary wrote last night I will not have any news.

So you are going to have a grand ball in Rakaia. We were so surprised to get the invitation to it. I should think it would be awfully jolly for one of the girls to go up to it.

I suppose Mr & Mrs Reid will be the chief guests; it will be fine fun for them.

I hope the little stockings Clara has made for Gwendoline will fit her. They would be a great surprise for you tonight I expect. Clara was rather afraid that the first one she made, was too bad to send; and she talked of making a third one.

Poor little Millie had a bad headache this morning, and she has been lying on the sofa nearly all day. It must have been a very lively Saturday for her. Papa brought home some Sunday School libraries last night, and I opened them this morning to show Millie, and we found among them that old story (which you remember I daresay) "Daph & her Charges; or the Babes in the Basket." Millie was delighted with it, for she has never read it all through, so while I made my bed Clara read the first two chapters, & then I read on all the morning. I had finished the book by dinner-time.

Ought I not to be glad? I have not used my board to lie on since I had my cold!

Mamma does not think it necessary; at least not for such a long time.

Mr Allan told Marian, & me last Sunday, that we were to have our German lesson on Tuesday evening instead of Monday; and so we were quite prepared for him. Then, you can imagine how astonished we were, to hear on Monday evening, that Mr Allan was going as delegate to the South Sea Islands, and we were to have two months; at least, holiday. — Thank you very much indeed for sending down that parcel today, especially for the Dictionary which looks a splendid one. Monsieur Ledez arrived in Oamaru yesterday as French teacher to the older [rest lost]

[from Blanche, I think]

JULY 1ST 1885
OAKLEIGH

DEAR EMMA,

I AM GOING TO WRITE YOU A LITTLE NOTE TO THANK YOU FOR YOUR LETTER

LOTTIE IS GOING TO TAKE US FOR A WALK NEXT WEEK. HUGH LEES WAS TO NIGHT.

I REMAIN
YOUR LOVING BROTHER
BERTIE

MY DEAR EMMA it has been raing so much this week one day it was to wet for me to go to school now as Harriet calls me I must go to bed

Milly

George's brother-in-law, John Lemon, is also struggling, it seems.

Oakleigh July 9th 1885

My dearest Emma

I heartily wish we could see you or Dick for a little while letters being as you say very unsatisfactory as a means of consulting about anything. It really seems as if the more pains one takes to make things clear, the thicker they become so I do not think I will try to talk any business but only say that we shall be delighted to see Dick or you and the dear children or all of you for any length of time that may suit your plans. Surely Dick could manage to come to us from Saturday to Monday without troubling the Oamaru people to look at him much. (I hope you will understand that) I should be only too glad to have an excuse for getting you and any wee pets with me for awhile. But I will leave you to settle your own plans about all that. We all thank you and your dear husband for your care of Blanche, we are quite looking forward to seeing her with roses again; only we do not feel sure about her coming tomorrow now that the weather is so bad. I have just waded through the mud to Aunt Mary's to say good-bye to Mabel, the sky looked a little brighter just then but now it is as misty as ever. Harriet, Lottie and Clara went down to the Steamers, they hurried down as we had been told she would leave at 3 o'clock but Harriet has just come back having left the other two with Mabel for an hour as the time of sailing is put off until ½ past 8, poor Mabel has had enough of putting off, has she not? She seems in very good spirits and a bit of blue sky actually showed itself just as she had gone on board!! Poor Uncle John too is hoping, I believe, to do some good for himself in Sydney for things are very bad with him here (this is of course "entre nous") I am glad to say we are all very well now Walters cold has almost departed. We get on very well without a man. Anderson milks the cows and looks after the cows and George likes getting Bessie in the mornings though she sometimes plays him tricks. This morning she had got out as Papa could not shut the gates and the poor boy went almost down to the Rifle Range to look for her, and Papa went out to look for her in vain and had just made up his mind to walk down when Clara came in to breakfast and told us that Mike had caught Bessie and was putting the harness on. He said that when he took the food to the stable at ½ past 8 he found her there eating as fast as she could!! Grandpapa does not seem to feel the cold so much as I do even. Mr A.B. Booth has not left Oamaru. Mrs Roxby told us that he had been put down a step or two, and is only a clerk now. I wish Dick had got that place, what do you think about his helping Papa? This is not much of a letter but I must stop now. Please give the darlings plenty of kisses for me and believe me with fondest love to you, Dick and dear Blanche if she is with you

Your loving Mother
S.S. Sumpter

[lacking the first (or more) page, but put here on the basis of the following letter, which refers to Blanche's visit]

They are all quite well down at Oakleigh, I am thankful to say, Lottie perhaps does not look as brilliant as she might perhaps, but she was up till half past one last night as Mr Cuttell, Mr Waymouth, and Mr Weston were up in spite of all the mud.

I hope to goodness dear Emma that neuralgia did not trouble you after your cold walk to the station. Oh I do wish you were not troubled with that horrible toothache. Mrs Pyke told me last night that she thought weakness from nursing Gwendoline too much, might cause it in a great measure.

They were all so astonished when I told them that Baby could not crawl, and when I told Mamma about her only having two teeth nearly through Mamma was quite astonished. She says when Lottie was a baby she could walk when she was ten months old, and crawl when she was eight. [NOT what a mother wants to hear!]

Oamaru did seem so bustling after Rakaia, as I told you. I thought it would, but I should like to be back in the latter place again. I may never never have the chance to stay with you again, & I don't think you have ever been so dear to me, since the time you went away to be married, as you were this time. Oh I do wish I could have the stay over again, and be a little more thoughtful, and unselfish than I was. Lottie sends her love, and says she intended to write to you as usual last night only the visitors prevented her from doing so.

Mamma also thought that her letter would reach you after I had come home, when she began it.

We had last week's washing done on Friday, and this week's done this morning if the weather keeps fine. Yesterday, after a lovely morning, we had that misty rain again.

I am so frightened about your doing the work because Mary told me on Saturday that Mamma met Mrs Creagh at Mrs Forrester's, and she told Mamma that what caused her curvature of the spine was carrying her baby while she did her work about the house.

Oh! I do hope you will be careful of yourself dear old Emma, because if you hurt yourself like poor Mrs Creagh it will be dreadful for Gwendoline, as well as yourself. Mamma sends her love, and says that I am to tell you that she is very glad to see that I am looking better in spite of my journey. I am sure I ought to seeing the care you took of your loving sister

Blanche

P.S. I have been talking ever since my arrival, with hardly a pause. Please don't let Dick see this letter Emma.

From left: Reginald, Emma, Gwendoline, Llewellyn, Wilfred. In front: Dorothy

Epilogue

And so we come to the end of our letters. In 1887, Emma gave birth to Wilfred, my mother's father, and March of that year saw Richard back under George's purview:

AUCTIONEER'S NOTICE.

GEORGE SUMPTER begs respectfully to intimate that his business in future will include that of AUCTIONEERING, MR RICHARD DAVIES acting as Auctioneer, Auction Sales will be held in his Store, Tyne and Harbor streets. Instructions to sell will receive prompt and careful attention.

GEORGE SUMPTER,
mr17 Auctioneer.

In 1889, Emma gave birth to her fourth child, Reginald, and her grandfather, Richard Smith Newell, died at Oakleigh, at age 73.

The same year saw George embroiled in an early traffic accident, when a horse pulling a gig bolted, colliding with George's buggy. Those in the runaway gig were seriously injured; happily George's injuries were less severe, although his buggy was a write-off.

The accident made the papers across the country.

A serious accident occurred yesterday afternoon at the conclusion of the sale at Taipo, whereby Mr Gray, of Messrs Reid and Gray, had his thigh broken, and his clerk, Mr Blythe, had also his thigh broken, while Mr Sumpter sustained injuries about the head and was severely shaken. It appears that Mr Gray and Mr Blythe were riding in a gig, and had just started for Oamaru. Mr Gray's horse had been feeding, and had had the bit removed. The animal was yoked up, it appears, without the bit being replaced in its mouth. They had started, and were descending the hill leading from Taipo, when Mr Blythe discovered that the bit was not in the horse's mouth. He accordingly got out, and was in the act of putting the bridle right when the horse took fright and bolted. Mr Blythe stuck to it for 50 or 60 yards, when he was knocked down. The gig wheel passed over him and broke his thigh. The horse careered down the hill and overtook Mr Sumpter's buggy and collided with it. Mr Sumpter was thrown out on to the bank of the creek, and his buggy was overturned and smashed to pieces. Mr Gray did not escape so well. He also was thrown from his seat by the collision, and had his thigh broken as above stated, and was also somewhat bruised. Dr Garland happened to be on the spot, attended to the sufferers, and gave directions as to the best way of conveying them to town. After being brought into Oamaru Mr Blythe was attended by Drs Garland and Sylvester at the Queen's Hotel, and Dr de Lautour attended to Mr Gray at the Star and Garter. It may be mentioned that the horses escaped uninjured.

The following year was also not the happiest. George's brother-in-law, John Lemon, died in May.

OBITUARY.

DEATH OF MR JOHN LEMON.

It is with unfeigned regret that we find ourselves called upon to chronicle the death of Mr John Lemon, who, after a comparatively brief illness, passed peacefully away at his residence in Ouse street, at half-past four o'clock yesterday morning. Mr Lemon's health had not been robust for some time, but until quite recently he was in daily attendance at his office—the office of Forester and Lemon, architects and valuers—and as he invariably had his characteristically quiet yet frank and cheery greeting for his friends and acquaintances, it occurred to few if any to think of his death even as a remote contingency. However, what appeared to be a slight and merely casual illness began to trouble him noticeably a week or two ago, and as it continued he had to remain indoors; but even then it was not thought that the end was at all likely to come as it has, to the sincere and general regret of the community. Mr Lemon was a native of Kingston, Jamacia, where his father was a merchant of considerable substance, and he was born in 1828. In his early youth he went to England, and there he entered the employment of a firm of silk merchants, who carried on a large trade with China. Constitutionally enterprising, he, while yet only in his twentieth year, turned his attention to New Zealand as a field for his energies. He therefore left England in 1848 in the ship Mary, bound for Otago, and arrived here during the same year. After a three or four years' sojourn in New Zealand, Mr Lemon went to Victoria, where he went to the goldfields and did well, but could not remain, ill-health inducing him to return in a year or so to New Zealand. On his return to Otago Mr Lemon entered into partnership with Dr Robert Williams, of Dunedin, the partnership business being that of sheep-farming, or runholding, as it was then universally called in the colony. The run which he and Dr Williams owned was situated in North Otago, and comprised a large piece of country on or adjacent to the Waitaki river. Mr Lemon himself, however, seems to have resided at Goodwood in the Waikouaiti district, and his name was one of the 23 which appeared in May, 1855, on the electoral roll for the Northern District of the Province of Otago (*vide* Roberts's History of Oamaru), and in December of the same year his partner, who seems to have resided in Dunedin, was elected to represent the district in the Provincial Council. Some years subsequent to that Mr Lemon settled in Oamaru where he and his brother (now Dr Lemon, Commissioner of Telegraphs) entered business as timber merchants and builders. Latterly Mr Lemon has taken only a quiet private citizen's part in local public affairs, but in the early days he took his full share in discharging the public duties of the town of Oamaru. He was a member of the Oamaru Town Board before the establishment of the municipality, and he also took an active part in the work of bringing in municipal institutions. Mr Lemon also helped in the work of getting provision made for harbor construction at Oamaru, and was for some time a member of the Harbor Board. Other local institutions with whose initiation and development Mr Lemon's name is honorably associated are the Hospital, the Athenæum, and the Horticultural Society. Altogether, New Zealand has lost a worthy colonist, and Oamaru an excellent citizen in John Lemon, who, by his friends and acquaintances, will long be held in kindly remembrance as a singularly intelligent, upright, and thoroughly likeable man. Mr Lemon, who was married to a sister of Mr George Sumpter's, leaves behind him his widow, seven daughters, and one son, the latter being a resident of New South Wales, where he has for some time been in business.

Two months later George's long-time chief accountant committed suicide, shooting himself through the heart with a rifle in a room at George's office that was used by the Volunteers (of which the old soldier was one).

Whether his motives were in any way associated with George's financial troubles I don't know, but a year later it was announced in the paper that George owed £309 19s 9d more than he was worth. I note that among the more than 60 creditors was his oldest son, J.G.H. Sumpter, for the sum of £90 10s 6d (making him by far the largest of the unsecured creditors).

STATEMENT OF LIABILITIES AND ASSETS.

The following are the liabilities and assets in the estate of George Sumpter: Liabilities—M'Callum and Co., L23 11s 8d; N. Lane, L13 12s 5d; J. Bulleid and Co., L11; E. Grave, L3 10s; J G. Finch, L3 10s; J. Craig and Co., L12 1s; Fleming and Hedley, L28 11s 9d; National Mortgage and Agency Company, L3 13s 7d; Hodge and Jones, L10; Oamaru Mail, L40; North Otago Times, L37; A. and D Bissett, L3; Hislop and Creagh, L44; Henry Connell's Trustees, L14 15s 1d; Borough Council, L150; Oamaru Harbor Board, L66; R Davidson, L2 4s 11d; J. R. Sewell, L5; T. C. Dennison, L2 8s; Sinclair and Co., 16s; A. Fraser, L3 1s; J. Jack, L1 8s 11d; Ferguson and Mitchell, L2 17s; M. Collins, 10s; Dodds and Co', L1 5s 6d; R. W. Martin and Co., L5 10s 1d; J. Willets, 9s 6d; J. Reid, L5; J. Edmond, L38 9s 10d; W. G. Neil, L10 4s 1d; Donald Reid, L14 3s 2d; Ireland and Co., L56 3s; W. H. Reynolds, L12 10s; G. Brownlee, L10; T. Forrester, L28; Hogg, Howison and Co., L28 3s; J. Smith and Co., L35; Jas. Craig, L34 5s 4d; J. Cooney, L17 10s; H. Watson, 18s 11d; New Zealand Loan and Mercantile Agency Co. L14 4s 10d; Farmers' Agency, L6 2s 8d; Union S S. Company, L28; T. Y. Duncan, L10; Miss M. A. Hastings, L11; A. J. S. Headland, L7; Miss M. A Hastings (interest), L10 10s; Jas. Fulton (interest), L35; Arundel and French (interest) L30; Otago and Southland Investment Company (interest), L80 5s; Education Board (rent), L25; Union Bank (rent), L20; Union Bank, L32; National Bank, L100; J. J. Spence (promissory note, Churton's, endorsed), L21 11s 6d; Harrison, Jones, and Devlin, L7 10s; W. H. S. Roberts' Estate, L10; J. Annand, L10; calls on 100 shares Equitable Insurance Company, L15; T. Kennedy, L3; J. G. H. Sumpter (wages), L10 2s; C. Ferens (wages), L2 10s; W. H. S. Roberts (wages), L3 10s; J. G. H. Sumpter, L90 10s 6d; Union Bank (balance on threshing mill), L24 Total—L1405 10s 9d. Secured creditors: Miss M. A. Hastings (value of security, L350), L300; Arundel and French (value of security, L1500), L2000; Rev. P. V. M. Filleul (value of security, L250), L200; Otago and Southland Investment Company (value of security, L375), L275; National Bank (value of security, L350), L600. Estimated value of securities, L2825. Amount of debt, L3375. Assets: Interest on Education lease, section 2, block 80, Oamaru, 10-roomed house, L200; lease of sections 1 and 2, block 22, with shop and store, threequarters valuation, L50; Education lease, section 7, block 7, Oamaru, with nine roomed house, L130; Education lease, section 4, block 53, Oamaru, with four-roomed house, L50; Reynold's lease, section 5, block 6, with three stone shops, nil; do, section 7, block 93, store burnt, nil; freehold section 5, block 69 (lien on), L20; section 33, block 12, Oamaru, with four-roomed house, L75; mortgage on rural sections 3 and 5, Waimate, L10; mortgage on section 22, Ngapara, with two-roomed cottage, L15; stock-in-trade in Harbor and Tyne street stores, 50 shares Oamaru Woollen Factory, one share North Otago Building Society, estimated at L330; 200 shares Equitable Insurance Company, nil; book debts, L1471 11s 1d (estimated to produce L350); cash in hand and bank, L5 11s 6d; money expected from England in distribution of the late Miss Sumpter's estate, amount unknown; furniture, etc., at dwelling house, L250; furniture in office and store requisites, L160. Total liabilities, L1955 10s 9d. Total assets, L1645 11s 6d. Deficiency, L309 19s 9d.

That same year, Emma gave birth to a second daughter, Dorothy. Alas, this fifth child was to be her last, for in May of 1892, Richard died.

The death notice refers to a protracted illness. From the lack of auction notices bearing Richard's name after the 9th of so of January, I surmise he'd been suffering for some five months.

DEATH

On the 26th instant, at his residence, Nen Street, after a protracted illness, Richard Davies, third son of the late John Davies, Esq., of Cardigan, South Wales, aged 44 years.

The funeral will leave his late residence on Sunday, 29th instant, at 2.15 p.m. Friends are kindly invited to attend.

G. L. GRENFELL,
Undertaker,
Tees street.

After his death, Emma returned to Oakleigh with her children: Llewelyn aged 10, Gwendoline aged 8, Wilfred aged 6, Reginald age 3, and baby Dorothy. At this point, George & Susannah's youngest child (Bertie) was 13 years old.

Blanche had married George Waymouth in 1888, but otherwise, all the children were still at home, so it was a very full house!

MARRIAGE.

WAYMOUTH—SUMPTER.—On the 18th inst., at St. Luke's Church, Oamaru, by the Rev A. Gifford, George H. Waymouth, third surviving son of John Waymouth, of Auckland, to Susanna Blanche, fifth daughter of George Sumpter, Oakleigh, Oamaru.

There was a slow exodus. In 1895, Millie married John Royds, an insurance man, once of Oamaru but now living in Invercargill. In 1896, Clara married John Watson. In 1897, Mary married Mr Charles Graham. In 1898, 'young' George married Marion Keddell.

MARRIAGE.

ROYDS—SUMPTER.—On the 9th April, at St. Luke's Church, by the Rev. Canon Gould, assisted by the Rev. A Gifford, John J. Royds, son of Mr J. J. Royds, of Dunedin, late of Invercargill, to M. Millicent Sumpter, daughter of George Sumpter (Lieut.-Colonel N.Z.V.), of Oakleigh, Oamaru.

I'm not sure what we can infer from the fact that for three of these five weddings only the brief notice appeared in the paper, while accounts of the ceremony were reported for the weddings of both Millie and Mary. Neither, however, were anything like the occasion of Emma's, with flags on the ships and bunting around the town!

MARRIAGE.

GRAHAM—SUMPTER.—On the 13th January, at St Luke's Church, Oamaru, by the Rev. A. Gifford, assisted by the Ven. Archdeacon Gould, Charles Edward, eldest son of C. C. Graham, Mahinga, Dunedin, to Mary Jessica, fourth daughter of George Sumpter, Oakleigh, Oamaru.

Interestingly, George Junior served as best man at both these weddings. An odd circumstance, it seems to me — perhaps it signifies that young women of the time were most likely to marry their brothers' friends!

MARRIAGE.

WATSON—SUMPTER. — On 16th July, at Oakleigh (the residence of the bride's father), by the Rev. A. Gifford, John Watson, son of the late Henry Watson, to Clara, daughter of George Sumpter.

Of course, George, now in his sixties, was not the force in the town he had been when Emma married. His finances, too, were greatly straitened — we saw his liabilities publicly listed in 1890; in 1899 and 1900 we see George pursuing in the courts several debts owed him (he won all the cases), some of them for very small amounts. Providing for the weddings of so many daughters must have been a financial strain.

MARRIAGE

SUMPTER—KEDDELL.—On the 22nd instant, at St. Luke's Church, Oamaru, by the Venerable Archdeacon Gould, John George Howard, eldest son of George Sumpter, Esq., to Marion Harriett, third daughter of Major Keddell, Stipendiary Magistrate.

There was a good attendance at St. Luke's Church at 12.30 to-day, on the occasion of the marriage of Miss Millicent Sumpter, seventh daughter of Mr George Sumpter, of this town, with Mr John M. Royds, of Invercargill, formerly stationed at the N.M. and A. Co.'s offices here. The bride, who looked charming in a trainless white watered silk dress, covered with delicate muslin and with the usual accessories of veil and orange blossoms, was attended at the altar by Misses Royds, W. Sumpter, Lemon, and Gilchrist as bridesmaids. These ladies wore handsome cashmere dresses, two pink and two blue. They also wore dainty hats of white tulle, trimmed with white satin ribbon. Mr George Sumpter, junr., acted as best man to the bridegroom, and the bride was given away by her father. The Rev. A. Gifford officiated, assisted by the Rev. Canon Gould. After the ceremony the wedding breakfast was held at Oakleigh, where a large number of guests were entertained, and inspected the numerous handsome presents of which the young couple were the recipients. The bride and bridegroom left this afternoon for Moeraki.

WEDDING AT ST. LUKE'S.

A very pretty wedding took place in St. Luke's Church yesterday afternoon, the contracting parties being Miss Mary Sumpter and Mr C. E. Graham. The church looked very bright with the dresses of the ladies who were guests, and the grounds were dotted with others anxious to get a glimpse of the procession as it left the church. The spell of fine weather had fostered every disposition to put on light attractive drapery, and this was availed of. The church had been decorated by the lady friends of the bride, and over the spot where the bride and bridegroom stood at the ceremony a floral arch had been erected. The bride was appropriately and prettily dressed in white She was attended by Misses Lottie and Winnie Sumpter and Miss C. Graham as bridesmaids, who wore dressed in cream. The bridegroom was attended by Mr G. Sumpter jun., as best man. The bride was given away by her father, Mr George Sumpter. The officiating clergyman was the Rev. A. Gifford, assisted by the Venerable Archdeacon Gould As the happy couple left the church the organist (Mr J. G. Finch) played the wedding march The bridal party and a large number of guests then drove to the residence of Mr G. Sumpter, Oakleigh, where afternoon tea was partaken of, and the presents, which were numerous and handsome, were inspected and generally admired. Mr and Mrs Graham left by the express going south on their honeymoon trip

As, perhaps, with poor Richard, such a strain surely took a physical toll.

In March of 1899, we read that "Mr George Sumpter's numerous friends throughout this district will be pleased to learn that he is able to get about again, after his serious and protracted illness." But this news appears to have been premature. In December, we are told that "Mr George Sumpter, who has been seriously ill for a long period, has received benefit from careful nursing in Dr Colquhoun's private hospital in Dunedin, and that there is now reasonable room for hope that he will recover."

In 1900 we do indeed see him continuing a few of his activities (in August, we see him calling a meeting of the North Otago Permanent Building Society, of which he was secretary), but it's clear his health continues poor. Mostly he seems occupied in staying home writing letters and poems: in

January he is writing a lengthy poem exhorting support for the Boer War ("Our Country calls for our aid, Whilst engaged in this terrible war; Our help cannot be gainsaid – We'll conquer the treacherous Boer."); in May he is "offering, in poetical term, certain suggestions with regard to a town clock. His principal suggestion was to raise the money as a memento of Mafeking Day."; in August, at a ceremony on the presentation of a flagstaff to the Oamaru North School, "Master James McFadgen ... read well an original poem, "Salute the Flag," written by Mr George Sumpter, who also wrote regretting that his health prevented him from being present"; another poem, extolling "Lovely Dunedin" is published in the Otago Witness ("Lovely Dunedin, whose hills and whose dales Are constantly fraught with health-giving gales, How often my thoughts float back unto thee, The home of the loyal and of the free–"

On November 12 his troubles passed for ever. "Although Mr Sumpter had been laid aside from active participation in business for some two years with a severe complaint, his death was quite unexpected, even amongst the members of his own family. During the past week or so he had been able to move about the grounds at Oakleigh, and apparently in better health than for some time back. On Sunday night, however, he was taken suddenly ill, and died."

His death was reported widely across the country.

I think the North Otago Times summed up the theme of his life very well: "He was possibly the most hopeful, the most optimistic man in the community. Every cloud had a silver lining, every reverse was a victory in disguise. It was this natural buoyancy that led him into operations that the more pessimistic would have hesitated to grapple with. His watchword was "progress," but its realisation was not always consummated, and he lived to realise that optimism has its limits."

It was, by all accounts, a splendid funeral, with all military honours. Although the funeral was well attended by officers and men (Colonel Penton, Commandant of the New Zealand Forces, was expected to attend, and the North Otago Mounted Rifles, Queen's Rifles, Oamaru Rifles, Hampden Rifles, Palmerston Rifles, ½ Battalion Band, and the Waitaki High School Cadets, all paraded), nevertheless there was some grumbling about the "Defence Department's refusal to grant passes to the country volunteers of this district in order to enable them to attend Lieut.-Colonel Sumpter's funeral." This was "in accordance with a regulation which stipulates that passes can be granted only within a limit of twelve miles." It was considered by some that this regulation was ridiculous and made without any consideration in Wellington of what life was like elsewhere in New Zealand.

OBITUARY.

MR GEORGE SUMPTER.

Although Mr Sumpter had been laid aside from active participation in business for some two years with a severe complaint, his death was quite unexpected, even amongst the members of his own family. During the past week or so he had been able to move about the grounds at Oakleigh, and was apparently in better health than for some time back. On Sunday night, however, he was taken suddenly ill, and died. Mr Sumpter was one of the fast disappearing band of early settlers, who came to Oamaru when the place was a wilderness of tussock and unfenced land, and since 1862 he has made it his home. He was possibly the most hopeful, the most optimistic man in the community. Every cloud had a silver lining, every reverse was a victory in disguise. It was this natural buoyancy that led him into operations that the more pessimistic would have hesitated to grapple with. His watchword was "progress," but its realisation was not always consummated, and he lived to realise that optimism has its limits. Yet he had always prominently in his mind the idea of advancing the interests of the town he lived in. Mr Sumpter was an old colonist, for he arrived in Australia while yet quite a boy, and after serving with a firm there for some time as gold buyer, entered, we believe, into farming pursuits, but shortly after the discovery of gold in New Zealand he came to this colony, and almost immediately thereafter to Oamaru, where, after a brief sojourn, he entered into the carrying business to the goldfields, travelling via the Upper Waitaki and the Lindis to Lake Wanaka, etc. His experiences in this occupation were varied, and were full of the dangers and privations to which the rough country and rougher roads subjected all who took part in it. Many well-known settlers in the district were engaged in a similar occupation. After relinquishing the business he went into partnership with the late Mr John Lemon and carried on the largest financial business in North Otago. For years the firm of Sumpter and Lemon progressed, and with its expansion the district expanded, and at one time was the synonym for prosperity. It will be unnecessary to enter into details of the multifarious duties Mr Sumpter took upon himself as a citizen. These are closely interwoven with the history of Oamaru, and are recorded in nearly every institution in the town. A brief outline will be all that is necessary.

Lieutenant-Colonel Sumpter was born at Sunbury, Middlesex, England, on 31st March, 1839. He left England for Adelaide in 1851, remaining there for about 10 years, arriving in Oamaru on 24th January, 1862, with his wife and daughter. In 1864 he took an active part in forming the first Rifle Company. He joined the Company as a private early in 1865, and was at once elected secretary. In 1866 he was also promoted to the rank of corporal, was elected ensign in 1871, captain in January, 1873, and was gazetted major in October, 1880, to date from 1st September, 1880. The officers and men of his old Company (No. 1) presented him with a handsome field officer's sword on 9th July, 1881, bearing, in raised letters, diagonally across the upper part of the blade, the following inscription: "Presented to Major Sumpter, by the officers and members of No. 1 Company, Oamaru Rifle Volunteers, in remembrance of his long services as their captain." He was appointed to the command of the Oamaru district, comprising eight companies of adults, which formed into No. 3 Battalion. There were also three cadet companies. He became lieutenant-colonel in October, 1889, having gained a pass certificate. In 1891 Lieut.-Colonel Sumpter received a presentation of plate from the citizens of Oamaru in recognition of the interest he had taken in volunteer matters. In 1880 he won the district prize for rifle shooting at 200, 400, and 600 yards. He also obtained the medal given by the New Zealand Government for long service and efficiency, as also the Imperial long service medal. Mr Sumpter was appointed first town clerk, when Oamaru was declared a borough in July, 1866, and he retained the office till the 30th September, 1870. He was elected a member of the Provincial Council for Waitaki on 31st March, 1871, and retained his seat till the abolition of the provinces, 1st November, 1876. He was appointed a member of the Provincial Executive on 22nd May, 1875, but his ministry resigned on 3rd of June following. He for three years sat as a borough councillor. After first suffering a defeat by Mr Shrimski he was elected mayor of Oamaru, 21st July, 1875, by a majority of 84 votes over his old opponent. He had to retire from the position, although pressed to stand again, at the end of the first term, in consequence of ill-health following a severe accident while assisting to extinguish a fire. He became a member of the Oamaru Harbor Board at its initiation in 1874, and was its chairman for fifteen years, till he resigned his seat 29th August, 1891. He took an active part in the establishment of the Museum and Mechanics' Institute, being a member of committee for a number of years, and several times its president, and was made a life member in recognition of his assistance. In Church matters Mr Sumpter always took a very prominent part. He was on St. Luke's Vestry for about 30 years, eight of which he was churchwarden, and four years treasurer. He was also lay reader and superintendent of the Sunday school. The children will long remember the joyous picnics at his lovely residence, Oakleigh. He was appointed Justice of the Peace on 17th February, 1872, and held the honor till he resigned in 1891. He was one of the first promoters of the Oamaru Woollen Factory, which has turned out a veritable gold mine for Oamaru. His favorite amusements were cricket and chess, at both of which games he could well hold a good record.

MR GEORGE SUMPTER.

It is to-day our painful duty to record the death of Mr George Sumpter, who was for a great many years one of the central figures in public life in Oamaru and whose name is indelibly associated with every institution in the town and every movement having for its purpose its material and social progress. The deceased gentleman has practically been laid aside by an internal complaint of a painful and distressing character for some two years, and though he had occasional rallies, his permanent recovery was never looked for with any degree of hope. But throughout that long illness, with all its suffering, he himself never lost hope and was ever cheerful, talking freely to his friends of projects he had in view. Even when suffering bodily agony his mind was busy with some work, and during his illness he found congenal occupation in the composition of verse, some of which have been given to the public. Latterly the pain which previously completely prostrated him disappeared, and for a week or so he had been particularly cheerful and hopeful. But the easement from bodily suffering would appear to have been rather the forerunner of early dissolution than an indication of betterment of condition, for Mr Sumpter passed away about ten o'clock last night. He retained possession of his faculties up to the end, and those who saw him not long before his death say that he was still filled with hope.

As we have already mentioned, Mr Sumpter, during his long residence in Oamaru, which dates back to the beginning of 1862, was closely identified with every forward movement in the town. To record all the positions he has filled and the many movements he has been associated with would require the writing of a history of Oamaru and district in outline for a period of nearly forty years. It is, indeed, impossible to recall a public body or institution that the name of Mr Sumpter has not been associated with at some time, and for longer or shorter terms. For a long series of years he enjoyed public confidence that would have secured him a seat in Parliament had he cared to enter the list of candidates; but he never aspired to the honor, and contented himself with provincial and local fame. Mr Sumpter left home when a lad of 15 years. He had a liking for the sea, and his father gave him permission to make a trip to New Zealand and Australia, probably in the hope that it might cure him of his roving ambition. Australia proved to be his destination, and, arriving in Adelaide, he secured a clerkship, and at the age of 16 he was appointed gold buyer to the firm. The news of the discovery of gold in New Zealand caused him to turn to this colony as a fresh field for the display of his energy. He arrived at Port Chalmers on the 21st of January, 1862, and a few days later he came to Oamaru, which has ever since been his home, though he can scarcely be said to have settled down at first, for he was for some time engaged in the carrying trade with the diggings, and in that capacity saw a good deal of life and enlarged his experience in a variety of directions. Finally settling down in Oamaru, he engaged in business, and then commenced his long public career. On the establishment of the municipality he became town clerk and held that office for some time. In 1871 he was elected to the Provincial Council for the Waitaki distrcit, and held his seat until the abolition of the provinces five years later. In the Council he soon acquired a prominent position, and for a week or two had the dignity of being a member of the Provincial Executive. In 1874 he unsuccessfully contested the Mayoralty with Mr Shrimski, being beaten by [illegible] votes, but at the election of 1875 he turned the tables and defeated Mr Shrimski by 84. An accident that occurred to him while working at a fire enforced his retirement from the contest of the following year, and Mr W. J. Steward was given the position as a solace for his defeat at the Parliamentary election. Mr Sumpter was appointed a member of the Oamaru Harbor Board at the institution of that body in 1874, and in 1876 was elected vice-chairman. In the succeeding year he was chosen chairman, and held that office for an unbroken period of fifteen years. In addition to those more public positions Mr Sumpter was for years a member of the Hospital Committee, School Committee, Athenæum Committee, and quite a host of other minor bodies. He was for some years a churchwarden of St. Luke's and superintendent of the Sunday School. He took a special interest in volunteering, and was enrolled as a private in the first corps formed in Oamaru, and mounted step by step through every grade until he attained the command of the district and the rank of lieutenant-colonel, receiving a few years ago the Imperail long service medal. He was also an enthusiastic cricketer, and on very many occasions did the town good services as one of its representatives. In short, Mr Sumpter had a share in everything appertaining to the progress of the town and district and the pleasure of their inhabitants. Had he done less for the public and devoted his talents exclusively to his own business concerns the closing years of his life might have been spent in comfort, and free from the business worries and troubles which surrounded his in later years.

THE FUNERAL OF THE LATE MR GEORGE SUMPTER.

The funeral of the late Mr George Sumpter, which took place yesterday afternoon, was largely attended. Owing to the desire to allow relatives of the deceased living in Dunedin to be present, the cortege did not leave Oakleigh till after the arrival of the express train in the afternoon. The deceased having been in command of the North Otago Volunteer District for many years, the funeral was made a military one. A gun carriage and limber had been sent up from Dunedin in charge of two members of the B Battery, and on this the coffin was borne, covered with the Union Jack. Volunteers from the town companies, and several from the country corps, were present, as were also the Waitaki High School Cadets. The pall bearers were the senior officers—Lieut.-Colonel Headland, Major Murcott, and Captain Creagh and Mahan. Apologies were received from officers from a distance for non-attendance. The firing party consisted of members of the local companies. During the progress of the procession through the town, the Garrison Band played appropriate music, and at the grave the "Vital Spark," after which Bugler Smith sounded the "Last Post." Archdeacon Goold conducted the funeral service impressively.

Owing to unavoidable delays and the great distance traversed, it was after five o'clock yesterday when the funeral cortege of the late Lieut.-Colonel Sumpter reached the cemetery, and we have, therefore, a few lines to add to our notice of the event. The pall-bearers, we may mention, were Lieut.-Colonel Headland, Major Murcott, Captain Creagh, and Captain Mahan, and the horses drawing the gun carriage upon which the coffin was borne were ridden and driven by men of the B Battery stationed at Dunedin, one of the number being Gunner Seeley, lately returned from South Africa. The impressive funeral service of the Episcopalian Church was read by the Ven. Archdeacon Gould, and at its close the Battalion Band played "Vital Spark." The customary three volleys were fired over the grave by the Volunteer escort, under the command of Captain Forrester, and the "Last Post" having been sounded by Bugler Smith, of the Queen's Rifles, the obsequies were at an end. The Volunteers, of whom there was a very creditable turn-out, were marched back to town and dismissed.

George's death meant that the family could no longer afford to live at Oakleigh (it seems likely that this had been the case for some time, but that George would have resisted the sale strenuously I have no doubt). The house was put on the market in January.

WALTER SUMPTER Begs to Announce to the Public of Oamaru and District that he intends Commencing Business as AUCTIONEER, STOCK and STATION and General COMMISSION AGENT, in the premises lately occupied by Mr G. R. Hislop, Tyne street. He will be assisted by J. G. H. SUMPTER, who will act as salesman, and he hopes, by careful attention to the interests of clients, to receive a full share of their patronage.

[dated 26 February 1900]

George Junior and Walter had both followed their father into auctioneering, working together for a while at least, although Walter is far more active in the newspaper records. Walter married Eva Newton in October of 1901. Finally, in 1908, the baby of the family, Bertie, married Elizabeth Bennett. Lottie and Harriet were destined to be remembered by my mother as the two maiden aunts, their house a perfect example of Victoriana.

Emma's mother, Susanna Steed Sumpter, died in 1911, at age 73, at her house in Ouse Street. Susanna has not been a major player in our drama, but this is not because she was of such little account. Her letters are few — hardly a surprise when you consider the household she had to run! — but they give a flavour of her personality. It was with a sense of recognition rather than surprise, then, that I read in the Oamaru Mail that she was "Possessed of a generous and lovable disposition, she drew around her throughout her long residence a wide circle of friends, to whose social enjoyment she at times ministered with a lavish hand." She sounds a very apt partner for George! The North Otago Times also notes her "winning and gentle disposition [that] won for her many friends during her long sojourn in the town".

Emma was, I am sorry to say, destined to out-live all but one child, my grandfather Wilfred. Two of her sons fell in the First World War. Neither of her daughters married (victim, one assumes, to the slaughter that took their brothers). Gwendoline died in 1925, at age 41, and Dorothy in 1931, at age 39. (She was a keen reader and we still have a number of her books.)

Emma herself lived 80 years, dying in May of 1939. My mother was 14 when she died, and remembers her well as a doting grandmother.

In a curious twist of fate, Emma died on the same day as her sister Blanche. Blanche, horribly, was struck by a train as it entered Feilding railway station. It was said that she was very deaf, and her sight was failing. She apparently didn't hear the crossing bells.

Their sister Harriet, the first of George's children to be born in Oamaru, was the last of the siblings to go, in 1943. She had established a private school in Ouse street (where she lived), but her obituary tells us her "life work" was the St Paul's Senior Young Women's Bible Class, "of which she was the much-loved leader over a long period", and "many of their lives were influenced by [her] saintly example". Even after her failing eyesight made her give this up, she continued to correspond with many of her former students until her death. She also continued to make "useful articles for the orphanages". "Her quiet, unassuming and devoted services over a lifetime are appreciated by old and young alike."

In 1950, Emma's son Wilfred was awarded an MBE for his work with St John Ambulance. Charmingly, following in his father's and grandfather's footsteps, he was for many years secretary of the Athenaeum & Mechanics Institute.

Appendix

Richard & Emma's children

Richard George Llewellyn: born 1882; died 1918 in the war.

Gwendoline Susanna: born September 15 1884; died 1925.

Wilfred John: born 9 March 1887; died 1972. Married Mary Frame Doak in 1921. Two children: Wendy (my mother) and Owen.

Reginald Owen: born 1889; died 1918 in the war.

Dorothy: born 1891; died 1931.

Sumpters

Walter Sumpter (George's grandfather): Married **Mary** Sumpter (daughter of Francis Gallaway).

Children:

Mary Ann: born 5 April 1790

Joseph: born 4 December 1791

Martha: born 30 March 1797

John (George's father): born 18 October 1799, in Marylebone, Middlesex (christened at St Annes, Westminster); died 23 January 1880. Married **Emma Katharine Youngman** on September 28 1829, at Sunbury On Thames, London.

Emma Katharine Youngman (George's mother): born 28 June 1800; died 24 December 1875, at Whetstone Middlesex.

Children:

Jessica: born c 1831

Walter: born 1834; died 7 September 1903

Herbert: born 1843

Mary Emma: born 8 February, 1832; died September 1908. Emigrated to New Zealand in 1854. Married **John Lemon**.

George: christened 12 July, 1836; died 11 November 1900. Emigrated to Adelaide (Australia) in 1851. Married **Susanna Steed Newell** on 18 March 1858. Emigrated to Oamaru (New Zealand) in 1862.

Children:

Emma Katherine: born 1859 in Goolwa, Australia; died in May 1939. Married Richard Davies 19 October 1881, at Oamaru.

Harriet Eveline: born 1862; died 1943.

Charlotte ("Lottie"): born 1864; died 1938.

Mary Jessica: born 1866; died 1943. Married Charles Edward Graham on 14 January 1897.

Susanna Blanche: born 1868; died in May 1939. Married George Henry Waymouth in 1888.

Clara: born 1869; died 1938. Married John Watson in 1896.

John George Howard: Born 1871; died 1955. Married Marion Harriet Keddell in 1898.

Walter Richard: born 1873; died 1935. Married Eva Helen Newton in 1901.

Maria Millicent ("Millie"): born 1875; died 1968. Married John Ingledon Royds, of National Mortgage & Agency Company, Invercargill, on April 10 1895.

Beatrice Winifred ("Winnie"): born 1877; died 1960. Married

Humphrey George Hanmer in 1914.

Bertram ("Bertie"): born 1879; died 1965. Married Elizabeth Lander Bennett in 1908.

Newells

I had much of this information from a descendent of Albert Newell. There is, however, some uncertainty about Sarah Bailey's parents. More recent sources suggest her parents were James Bailey and Sarah Chitty; however, this account seems more consistent.

Thomas Bayley (George's great-great-grandfather): born in 1744 in Boxgrove (not far from Chichester), to **John Bayley** & **Dorothy Coote**. At 23, a farmer of Eastdean, he married **Sarah Murrell** on 2 February 1771, at the Archdeaconry, Chichester.

Sarah Murrell (George's great-great-grandfather): born in 1750, also in Boxgrove, to **Jo Murrell**, a Yeoman. She appears to have died sometime after 1795, in Oving, Sussex. She had 11 children: Thomas (1771); Susana (1773); William (1774); **Sarah** (1777/9); Ann (b. 1785); Elizabeth (1781); John (1786); Martha (1789); Mary (1789); Joseph (1791); Mary (1795).

Child:

Sarah Bailey (George's great-grandmother): was of Eastdean, Chichester. Born possibly in 1777, christened 7/1/1779. Married **Benjamin Newell** 21 September 1797 at Petworth, Sussex.

Benjamin Newell (George's great-grandfather). Died (probably) 1838/9

Children:

James (1802 -13/1/1863). Married **Ellen Unsworth** in 1837. With his wife and two younger children, emigrated to Australia in 1855, on the *Taymouth Castle*. Cabinet maker. His oldest son, Benjamin, was a pianoforte maker. He would have been around 24 when the rest of his family migrated. He had married and by 1861 had 4 sons. James died in Sydney, and is buried at old Camperdown Cemetery.

Sarah (christened January 9 1806)

Susannah (born 1809)

Benjamin (born 5 June 1814). Not included in my source's list, but included in more recent listings.

Richard Smith Newell (George's grandfather): born 30 June 1816 in Chichester; died 9 April 1889, at Oakleigh in Oamaru. Carpenter/ Master of churn maker's turners. Married **Susan Steed** on 19 October 1835 in St Peter The Great Sub-deanery of Chichester. Emigrated to Australia in 1852, on the *Gloucester*.

Lois (1819-1903)? Not included in my source's list, but found in more recent internet listings.

Susan Steed (George's grandmother): born in 1818 in Chichester; died 1877.

Children:

James (1838-1863)

Susanna Steed (George's mother)(1839-18-10/1911)

Richard (7/1/1841-3/2/1912). Married Emily Hornsby in 1861. Died 3 February 1915 in Hindmarsh, South Australia.

Albert B. (March 1844-1903)

Frederick B. (8/6/1845-1/1/1870)

Edward Ambrose (4/5/1854-9/3/1915) Married Maria Moller on 11 February 1891. Born and died in Adelaide.

Edmund Elijah (1856-1857). Born and died in Adelaide.

Davies

From an account by John Rees Davies, son of Richard's brother David.

David Davies (Richard's grandfather): born 27 November 1779; died June 1832. A builder & carpenter at Pumpsaint, Carmathenshire, in Wales. He built a row of 3 houses on the roadside a mile from Pumpsaint, called PentreDavies. In the center above the doorway, a stone is marked "Built by D. Davies".

Theodosia Saer (Richard's grandmother): from Laugharne Carmarthenshire. She was reputed to be of Flemish or Huguenot descent. She might have come to service in one of the country houses near Pumpsaint. Saer in Welsh means carpenter. My mother inherited some of her teaspoons, marked T.S.

Children:

Richard: Born July 1806; died young.

William: Born 1808; died a bachelor at around 50 or 60. Established a lucrative drapery business in Newport, Monmouthshire, and left his fortune to his brother (Richard's father) who thereupon retired with his two daughters to Quay St, Carmarthen in 1858, where he died in 1875.

John Davies (Richard's father) (1814-1875): occupied a leading position at Carmarthen in his retirement. He was buried at Caio Carmarthenshire (near Pumpsaint) — a remote Anglican graveyard where his ancestors were also buried.

Ann Price (Richard's mother)(1818-1858): died at 40, leaving 6 children. Richard would have been 13. She was the daughter of a small farm, Berriesbrook, between Caio & Llandovery. A brother was Vicar of Much Markle near Ledbury, Herefordshire.

Children:

David Price Davies (Richard's oldest brother): Born September 1841; died September 1874. Continued his father's business — general store & Post Office — after his father retired. Married Sarah Rees. They had one son, John Rees Davies, born 1869.

William (1843-1899): was in the merchant navy; became an officer in the Black Ball Line on the *Sydney Dacres* under Captain Duquid, trading with India. Owing to failing health he came home & ran a mill. Died in the train on his way home from Lady Llanover's where he was engaged in sketching a memorial to her friend Judge Johnes, Dolaucothey, Pumpsaint, who was murdered by his gamekeeper or butler. Apparently he "was very clever with his pen".

Richard (1845-1892)

Margaret: married Marcus Appelas Stephens, who with his brother Adolphus Ashben Stephens, were sons of the Governor of Carmarthen Gaol, who hailed from Devizes, Wilts & claimed connection with Dr

Arnold, Head of Rugby School. M.A.S. was Accountant at the National Provincial Bank of Cardigan, & retired to his son at Swansea where he died. Margaret had three children (George, Annie, Edith.

John: was out in the Argentine for some years on a ranch near Entre Rios, in partnership (it is thought) with others. He returned home before his father died, married, lived at Shrewsbury, travelling in Ironmongery for Burr & Sons. He had three daughters and was buried at Tenby. This is the "Jack" referred to in Richard's letters. I note that this account from Richard's nephew makes no reference to Jack's Australian adventure, referred to in one of Richard's letters.

Mary Anne (1852-1944): married A.A. Stephens as his second wife. She died in Aberystwyth, having left London on the outbreak of the war.

Lemons

John Lemon: born 1828 at Kingston, Jamaica; died 8 May 1890. Emigrated to New Zealand in 1848. Married **Mary Emma Sumpter** (George's sister) on 21 February 1855.

Children:

Mary Constance ("Connie"): born 1856; died 1913. Appointed postmistress at Newborough 1908, appointed telephonist there 1912.

John Herbert: born 1858; died 1890. Married Nellie James on 15 September 1886, in Sydney.

Grace: born 1863; Married James Finch 1883

Edith: born 1861. Married John Bambridge in 1895.

Mabel: born 1866 Married George Frank Francis in 1891.

Gertrude: born 1869. Married Herbert Thirtle in 1903 in New South Wales.

Mildred Hermione: born 1871.

Charles: born 1874; died at 10 weeks

Amy Louise: born 1875, died 1948. Married Herbert Mowbray in 1900.

References

The bulk of this material comes of course from the sources already mentioned: the letters themselves ; the National Library's historical newspaper archive "Papers Past"; W.H.S. Roberts' "The History of Oamaru and North Otago, New Zealand, From 1853 to the end of 1889" (Published by Andrew Fraser, Oamaru; 1890).

I should also mention three other books:

"White Stone Country: The story of North Otago" by K.C. McDonald. Published by the North Otago Centennial Committee, 1962.

"The Penguin History of New Zealand" by Michael King. Published by Penguin Books, 2003.

"Replenishing the Earth: The Settler Revolution and the Rise of the Anglo-World, 1783-1939" by James Belich. Published by Oxford University Press, 2009.

Notes

1. Belich
2. Roberts, p161
3. From 1871 census
4. King, p225
5. North Otago Times, 29 January 1880, p2
6. Belich, p195
7. White Stone Country, p146
8. King p230-1
9. King, p258

Name Index

Aitcheson 6, 11,
Aitken 61
Allan 87, 90, 97, 135, 137, 160, 163, 171, 172, 173
Anderson 62, 91, 102, 174
Atkins 71, 73, 91, 93, 100
Baker 111
Balmer 129
Bannerman 117
Barleycorn 36
Barnes 132
Benett 123
Bennett 185, 189
Bishop 106, 166, 167, 168, 172
Bluett 51, 54
Booth 171, 174,
Borrie 134
Borton 172
Bristed 67, 73, 76, 84, 87, 91, 92, 94, 100
Brittain 163, 164
Buchanan 55, 58
Bull 70, 71
Bulleid 121, 128
Burbury 108, 118, 119. 127
Burnett 78
Caldwell 166, 167, 172
Campbell 12
Caradices 73, 75, 84
Chambers 74, 115, 118, 130, 131, 132, 146, 147, 149, 150, 151, 161, 168
Childs 135
Christie 139
Clarke 121, 124, 126, 134, 160
Cleland / Clelland 42, 55, 77, 86
Clowes 100, 126, 169
Cole 75, 120, 122, 123, 133, 164
Collie 8, 10
Colquhoun (Dr) 181
Connell 127, 167

Cooke 121, 143-149
Cookson 149
Coster 142, 147
Cotterill 61, 83
Craig 52
Creagh 169, 175
Crompton 167
Cuttell 174
D'Oyley 103
Dannihy 54
Darroch 42, 48, 49, 50, 51, 53, 54, 60, 72, 82
Davies (Dr) 74
Davies (Jack) 76, 93, 192
Davis 8
de Lautour 166, 167
Deakin 84
Derrett 75
Downing 163
Doctors:
Dr Colquhoun *see* Colquhoun (Dr)
Dr Davies *see* Davies (Dr)
Dr Fleming *see* Fleming (Dr)
Dr Garland *see* Garland (Dr)
Dr McKenzie *see* McKenzie (Dr)
Dr Ross *see* Ross (Dr)
Dr Wait *see* Wait (Dr)
Drummond 54, 55
Duthie 137
Elder 11
Elton 69, 72, 74, 75, 76, 85, 88, 89, 91, 92, 97, 106, 109, 111
Embling 51, 54
Evans 15, 57, 62, 83
Every 5
Falconer 7, 134
Fenwick 101
Fercus 76
Ferens 68
Fergusson 117
Fidler 100
Filleul 6, 73, 92, 99, 103, 118
Finch 90, 96, 101, 111, 116, 117, 119, 120, 124, 125, 126, 128, 129, 133, 134, 135, 136, 137, 138, 147, 155, 156, 157, 168, 171, 192
Fleming (Dr) 82, 87, 89, 90
Forrest 63
Forrester 75, 128, 154, 163, 169, 175
Fox 20
French 76
Garland (Dr) 78

Gibbs 14
Gibson 100
Gifford 85, 115, 117, 118, 128, 134, 137, 149, 157, 160, 163
Gilchrist 14, 117, 120, 153, 165
Gillies 117
Gleeson 65, 99, 166
Graham 180, 188
Grant 93
Graupner 135
Gun 166
Gunion 166
Gurr 169, 172
Haggie 8
Hambleton 8
Hardy 7, 43, 44, 63, 88, 93, 99, 105, 106, 107, 137, 149, 170
Harrison 60, 62, 83, 84, 86, 87, 92, 93
Hartnell 43, 62, 85, 87, 96, 104, 108, 112, 151
Harvey 105
Hassell 7, 50, 108, 111, 127, 132
Headland 35, 167
Heaton 76
Herdman 129
Hertslet 8
Himmer 163
Hislop 128, 139, 148, 158
Holland 167
Holmes 147, 151
Houghton 61
Huxtable 117
Ingram 12, 14
Jackson 117
James 79, 80
Jeffreys 6
"Jim" 82, 89, 90, 91, 93, 94, 96, 98, 101, 102, 107
Jones 49, 50, 57, 61, 72, 79, 155, 172
Keddell 180, 188
King 39
le Cren 130
Ledez 157, 164, 173
Leech 134
Lees 80, 136, 148, 167
Lemons
John Lemon 5-9, 15, 18, 44, 173, 174, 178, 188
Dr Charles Lemon 5, 7, 142, 165
Mrs Lemon (Mary Emma Sumpter; "Aunt Mary") 5, 36, 38, 96, 120, 130, 135, 136, 139, 166, 171, 174, 188
Constance 9, 74, 86, 90, 91, 97, 116, 117, 124, 126, 134, 137, 138, 139, 155, 164, 165, 192

Herbert 5, 85, 89, 98, 117, 120, 124, 126, 134, 137, 138, 155, 157, 192
Grace 9, 135, 155, 192
Edith 9, 117, 118, 124, 136, 137, 153, 160, 166, 192
Mabel 116, 117, 160, 172, 174, 192
Gertrude 9, 134, 192
Mildred 9, 172, 192
Amy 9, 171, 172, 192
Lewis 92
Louden 149
Lowe 60, 61
Luckstone 163
Mackie 107
Maclean/McLean 41, 44, 45, 51, 60, 72, 73, 75, 78, 81, 85, 88, 92, 97, 111
Makeig 80, 135
Mann 41-7, 49-59, 65, 69, 70, 77-80, 82, 84, 85, 88-90, 93, 94, 100, 104, 105, 108, 109, 111, 112, 123, 140, 141, 146-8
Martin 74, 93
Matson 49-51, 53, 146, 150
Maude 56, 109
McAndrew 117
McCaw 96, 109, 117-8, 128, 131, 140
McCombe 49, 63
McDonald 54, 160
McFadgen 182
McKenzie (Dr) 65
McKerrow 43-5, 55, 56, 58, 63, 68, 71, 73, 76, 84, 107, 149
McLean *see* Maclean
McLeod 136
Medlicott 46
Millar 121
Miller 7, 79, 132
Millington 119
Milne 111, 120, 167
Mitchell 121, 124, 125, 136, 162, 171, 172
Moore 85, 90, 106, 119, 120, 123, 128, 129, 136, 139, 160
Morris 117
Morton 102
Muir 130
Murdoch / Murdock 133, 166
Murison 132
Murray 39, 54
Mutter 151
Newman 133
Newton 89, 129, 136, 139, 154, 185, 188
Norreys 117
Otterson 37
Parker 113
Pascoe 74

Passmore 107
Patton 42
Pearson 65, 78, 82, 89, 90, 96, 100, 101
Penton 182
Peterkin 90
Proberts 165
Pyke 94, 98, 130, 131, 135, 146, 148, 149, 150, 174
Raffaelle 160
Raine 167
Reich 103
Reid 44, 57, 70, 167, 172
Rhodes 73
Roberts 1, 5, 6, 10, 57, 82, 116, 125, 134, 139, 155, 156, 163
Robertson 8, 33, 97
Ronayne 61, 83
Ross (Dr) 145
Roxby 7, 174
Royds 180, 188
Ruddock 118
Russell 33
Rutter 124, 127, 129
Sargeant 132
Saunders (Jimmy the Needle) 6
Shalders 11
Shrimski 16, 19, 21
Sims 161
Smillie 132
Smith 82, 120, 128, 142
Stanford 92
Sutherlands 122, 137
Tate 84, 90
Taylor 43-5, 153
Tempest 88, 97, 98, 100, 106
Teschemaker 6
Thomas 11
Thompson 49, 124, 126
Todd 116-8
Trail /Traill 7, 8
Turner 54-5, 145, 147-50
Udall 16, 156
Vincent 125
Walker 121
Walkern 106
Walls 109
Walton 53
Wait (Dr) 85, 123, 160
Wait 16, 91, 92, 108
Wate 8

Waymouth 134, 163, 164, 167, 168, 174, 180, 188
Webb 96
West 71, 105, 106
Weston 167, 168, 174
Williams 6, 84, 111, 124, 125, 129, 148, 160
Wilson 97
Winter 41-5, 51-3, 56, 58-62, 66, 71, 78-84, 88, 92, 94, 105, 115
Woonton 6

www.ingramcontent.com/pod-product-compliance
Lightning Source LLC
Chambersburg PA
CBHW080726210726
48292CB00017B/2956

* 9 7 8 1 9 2 7 1 6 6 1 6 1 *